D1601227

FLAWED
LIBERATION

FLAWED LIBERATION

Socialism and Feminism

Edited by Sally M. Miller

Contributions in Women's Studies no. 19

GREENWOOD PRESS

WESTPORT, CONNECTICUT • LONDON, ENGLAND

Library of Congress Cataloging in Publication Data

Main entry under title:

Flawed Liberation.

(Contributions in women's studies ; no. 19
ISSN 0147-104X)
Bibliography: p.
Includes index.
CONTENTS: Seretan, L. G. Daniel DeLeon and
the woman question.—Miller, S. M. Women in the
party bureaucracy.—Kreuter, G. and Kreuter, K.
May Wood Simons. [etc.]
1. Women and socialism—United States—Addresses,
essays, lectures. 2. Feminism—United States—
Addresses, essays, lectures. I. Miller, Sally M.,
1937   II. Series.
HX546.F49   305.4'2'0973   80-1050
ISBN 0-313-21401-8 (lib. bdg.)

Library of Congress Catalog Card Number: 80-1050
ISBN: 0-313-21401-8
ISSN: 0147-104X

First published in 1981

Greenwood Press
A division of Congressional Information Service, Inc.
88 Post Road West, Westport, Connecticut 06881

Printed in the United States of America

10 9 8 7 6 5 4 3 2 1

To the Spirit and Memory
of these Pioneers

CONTENTS

ILLUSTRATIONS

ACKNOWLEDGMENTS

It is a pleasure as editor to extend my gratitude to the many individuals who made this collection of essays possible. I especially wish to thank several colleagues for their collaborative efforts at the various stages of the project. One contributor, L. Glen Seretan, and Sally M. Miller, the editor, read these essays in earlier versions before the Organization of American Historians in April, 1976, and a member of the audience, William C. Pratt, suggested that those papers might well form the basis for a general consideration of the subject of feminism and socialism in the American past. Neil K. Basen, who read a different paper at the session from that presented here, and Alice Kessler-Harris of Hofstra University, who served as critic, contributed additional insights. Members of the audience at this meeting included persons who themselves had been participants in the events discussed or were descendants of some of the protagonists, and their comments were most welcome and meaningful to the panelists. Among those were Maurice Wheeler of St. Louis and the late Gertrude Branstetter Stone of New York. The vice president and editorial director of Greenwood Press, James T. Sabin, was also present at the convention and was immediately enthusiastic about the idea of a collection of essays.

Special acknowledgment for the procurement of photographs is extended to Neil K. Basen, Mari Jo Buhle, and Gretchen and Kent Kreuter. The Kreuters also supplied the essay by May Wood Simons which serves as appendix to the collection. All of the contributors extend especially warm appreciation to the surviving protagonists, their siblings, or other family members for supplying extant letters, for corresponding with several of the essayists, and for submitting to interviews. This collection would be much the poorer without their cooperation.

Neil K. Basen wishes to acknowledge the critical assistance and useful suggestions of Mari Jo Buhle, James R. Green, Linda Gordon, David Montgomery, Alva Myrdal, and Lee Baxandall. Earlier versions of his essay were read to the Southwest Labor Studies Conference at Berkeley, California, in March, 1978, and to the International Conference of the Historians of the Labor Movement at Linz, Austria, in September, 1978. John D. Buenker gratefully acknowledges the helpful assistance of the staff of the State Historical Society of Wisconsin. Mari Jo Buhle extends thanks to Harvey O'Connor for his review and critique of an early draft of her essay. She also wishes to thank Neil K. Basen and Paul Buhle for their suggestions and insights, as well as Dorothy Swanson of the Tamiment Institute of New York University's Bobst Library for her generous assistance.

William C. Pratt wishes to note that an earlier version of his paper was read to the Northern Great Plains History Conference at Sioux Falls, South Dakota, in October, 1973, and subsequently published with revisions under the title, "Women and American Socialism: The Reading Experience," in *The Pennsylvania Magazine of History and Biography*, 99 (January 1975): 72-91. He extends his thanks to Nicholas B. Wainwright, editor of that journal, for permission to reprint that portion of the material which overlaps with this essay. The earlier version benefited from the constructive criticism of JoAnn Carrigan, J. Harvey Young, and Nicholas B. Wainwright. The current version, longer and incorporating additional research, was strengthened by suggestions from Linda Ray Pratt. Despite extended work on this topic, Professor Pratt warns the reader that this study remains an exploration into a subject that continues to be elusive and that the conclusions offered are tentative and subject to revision upon additional research and reflection.

My own contribution originated with a paper read to the Canadian Association of American Studies at the University of Ottawa in October, 1974. I wish to acknowledge a Faculty Research Award from the University of the Pacific which enabled me to procure archival materials and to obtain the assistance of David Brown, a graduate student at Duke University who compiled materials for me from the Socialist Party Collection there prior to their availability on microfilm. I wish also to indicate my appreciation to the staff of Stanford University's Hoover Institute for help in obtaining copies of Socialist party pamphlets in those archives and, as always, to express my gratitude for the helpful assistance of the reference librarians of the University of the Pacific. Each of the contributors and I as editor accept responsibility for his or her own interpretations and any errors of fact which may be found.

I completed most of my work as essayist and editor while in residence at the University of the Pacific in Stockton, California. However, I finished the last editorial tasks while in residence at the Centre for the Study of Social History of the University of Warwick in Coventry, England in 1978. My work was made enormously easier because of the scholarly atmosphere of the Centre, familiar to many American labor historians. It is my pleasure to underline my general appreciation to the Director of the Centre, Professor Royden Harrison, with whom it has been a privilege to be associated.

S.M.M.

INTRODUCTION

Sally M. Miller

This collection on socialism and feminism within the context of the Socialist party of America should be read with an understanding of changing interests of historians. In the 1960s fresh evidence was offered for the concept that historians respond to their own times: they ask questions and evaluate the past as prodded by their own experiences and training in the analysis of historical phenomena. In that most volatile of recent decades, American historians expanded their field of study to include the histories of various groups—black, Chicano, Puerto Rican, Native American, and women—in an effort to find the roots of the contemporary liberation movements. Studies of these groups, as well as of the antiwar and New Left movements, transformed the discipline of history. A new expanded social history based on advances in methodology, especially developments in quantification, became a major focus of the discipline.

Historians who contributed to the new social history, often with a bias toward the left of center, viewed the historical left as having established an egalitarian standard for other Americans. Among them, scholars of the Socialist party of the early twentieth century, who themselves supported the contemporary liberation movements, argued that the old left was egalitarian in theory and, sometimes, in practice. Thus, in institutional studies of the old left, a nonracist and nonsexist perspective was imposed, and, at the same time, earlier historians were chastised for having ignored or minimized these areas of crucial concern.

One of the earliest studies of the Socialist party of America was Nathan Fine's *Labor and Farmer Parties in the United States, 1828-1928.* This history, which eschews objectivity in favor of an identification with the reformist wing of the Socialist party, is a narrative rather than an analytical history. Fine traces main lines of institutional developments, such as the party's relationship to organized labor and its "americanization" of Marxism. Clinging to a narrow framework, he ignores questions of distinct groups in American society, their relationship to the party, and treatment by it. Thus, for example there is no discussion of the place of either the black American or women in the party's consciousness or program.[1]

A generation later, in the 1950s, the first objective surveys of the Socialist party were published: "The Background and Development of Marxian Socialism in the United States," a lengthy essay by Daniel Bell, and *The Socialist Party of America: A History* by David A. Shannon. Both cover the evolution of the party from its antecedents in the nineteenth century to its virtual demise in the 1930s. Neither of these books, usually considered starting points in the historiography, devotes serious attention to the party record in the areas of race and gender.[2]

The first full historical work to explore these issues was *The American Socialist Movement, 1897-1912* by Ira Kipnis, published in the same period as the works by Bell and Shannon. Kipnis, in contrast to the other two authors, casts a wide net, and includes brief sections on immigrants, blacks, and women. He argues in a few pages in this monograph that the party record on race and gender was little more than that of the stereotyping of roles and of the denigrating of inferiors by superiors. Whatever party energy was expended on equal rights was expended by those without them.[3]

The second stage of the historiography begins with the publication in 1967 of James Weinstein's *The Decline of Socialism in America, 1912-1925,* the first monograph to treat the issues of racism and sexism within the framework of the concerns of the 1960s. He devotes a chapter each to blacks and, central to our interest here, to women and the Socialist party. Weinstein argues that a growing Socialist party commitment to women's rights and a full role for women in the party evolved. His treatment of the subject is superficial, however, and he neglects to analyze fundamental party institutional responses or to get beyond the prominent women activists to the rank-and-file women members. Thus, Weinstein's assumption of leftist egalitarianism leads to an unconvincing history in this vein in which women took on a greater role until the party schism of 1919. His failure to explore systematically the extent of female integration into the party structure means that he did not advance our understanding of the issues.[4]

In the 1970s, research produced biographies of individual women activists and preliminary studies of party rank and file so that case studies and specific data moved the historiography beyond generalizations. It has become clear that the Socialist party of America, as socialist parties elsewhere, was composed of individuals whose formative experiences and traditional perspectives led to views of women characteristic of western civilization as a whole. A consensus now exists among historians that in the various leftist parties, despite their ideological pledges to the equality of men and women, "The subordination of women . . . [was] reflected in [the] revolutionary organizations. Many revolutionary men were not able to cast off a deep contempt for women, when they became socialists."[5]

The Socialist party of America fell heir to the strongest nineteenth-century ideological commitment to the full liberation of men and women. Socialists in Europe in the middle of the nineteenth century "formulated the first political theory to encompass the rights of women." Marx and Engels in their earliest years of partnership concerned themselves with the effects of industrial capitalism on women and on the family in *The Condition of the Working Class* (1844) and other writings. After the death of Marx in 1883, Engels published *The Origin of the Family, Private Property and the State* and, almost simultaneously, the German Marxist, August Bebel published *Woman Under Socialism*. They taught that the oppression of women had evolved with the institution of private property and the liberation of women would come with the socialization of property. The situation of women was far from central to Marxist theory but, rather, fit in, generally, with the ideology of the emancipation of the masses through the collectivization of the means of production and distribution. Still, Marxist writings included the Woman Question as one of the key dilemmas of modern times which socialism would resolve.[6]

In practice as well as in theory, American socialists had behind them a European tradition that provided women with a political identity. In 1891 the international socialist movement proposed that its national parties or chapters promote equality for women, and in 1907 its International Congress advocated that all member parties promote unlimited woman suffrage. In the sixteen years between those resolutions, the various socialist parties in the European countries witnessed the development of women's movements, including party recommendations of special campaigns on behalf of the class consciousness of women. In England, Denmark, Austria, and especially in Germany, women organized their own party units, published newspapers and propaganda tracts, fielded women organizers, and established propaganda networks. The German movement was the most developed and sophisticated, as was the German Social Democratic party itself. While political participation was at that time illegal for women in Germany, various subterfuges were used to promote socialist activity among women. By 1908, over 400 German women were party organizers, their newspaper, *Die Gleichheit*, enjoyed a circulation of 70,000, regular discussion groups were held in 120 different cities and towns across the

Empire, representation of women on the party executive was established, and their spokeswoman, Clara Zetkin, was an influential voice in the highest councils of the German Social Democratic party and the Second International. The activities of German women led to the founding of the International Conference of Socialist Women which drew thousands of women from parties throughout Europe and even the United States to its meetings in Stuttgart in 1907, and in Copenhagen in 1910, which coincided with the Congresses of the Second International. Thus, an exceedingly visible socialist heritage of women's rights and women's political involvement existed when the Socialist party of America was founded.[7]

The Socialist party emerged in the United States at a very special moment for the American left. With the establishment in 1901 of one unified party including nearly all American Marxists, the time seemed propitious for the development of a massive radical political party. Across Europe, socialist parties were gaining in mass support and in representation in parliaments. In the United States a mood of reform was building as the nation prepared to confront the problems of an urban-industrial milieu. Moreover, the party's ideology taught the inevitability of the triumph of socialism over capitalism. Thus, anything seemed possible. The party grew from a few thousand to a membership of 118,000 in a dozen years; it elected public officials across the nation, and its press flourished. In 1912, with its perennial presidential candidate, Eugene V. Debs, conducting his most successful race, the socialists captured almost 6 percent of the ballots cast. In 1910 and throughout the following decade except for 1912, the party elected one of its members to the United States House of Representatives in each congressional election. Pockets of strength seemed to exist everywhere from Germanic Milwaukee, where socialists dominated city government for decades, to the Plains states of the Southwest, where summer encampments attracted thousands of farmers and rural dwellers to hear socialist speakers, sing folk and labor songs, and experience a cathartic and somewhat evangelical interruption in the monotony of hard work. Cities elected socialist mayors in locales as diverse as Schenectady, New York; Berkeley, California; Kalamazoo, Michigan; and Butte, Montana. Within the party organization, a kind of cradle-to-grave environment was created so that members, unlike supporters of the major political parties, were enveloped by the party at all stages of their lives. Socialist Sunday schools were available to party members and their families as well as singing societies, discussion groups, annual picnics and bazaars, young people's groups, and foreign-language federations for the non-English speaking. In sum, the Socialist party in the first decade of the twentieth century was a vibrant political organization offering its members an ideology of hope and change encased within a life style of comraderie. Its promise to promote social reforms while working toward an eventual bloodless revolution seemed totally believable.[8]

Kate Richards O'Hare, 1897. (Courtesy of Renee Hardin.)

Women as well as men were attracted to the Socialist party. Despite the lack of any particular programming or propaganda directed to American women, they joined the party and participated in its activities, making up perhaps 10 percent of the membership in its first decade. Throughout the nineteenth century, women had increasingly become involved in social and reform organizations. Starting in the decades before the Civil War, women had banded together for various purposes. The leisure time and degree of freedom available to middle-class women, as well as the higher level of education, resulted in a pattern of institution-building and community involvement whereby women had become experienced troops in a host of movements. Charitable associations, social settlement work, and a fully developed club-women's movement were thriving, as signified by the existence of the General Federation of Women's Clubs by the end of the century. While for the most part women did not operate in a political framework, many women were seasoned veterans of the evangelical, the temperance, and finally, the woman's suffrage movement. Through these movements, they developed organizational talents and speaking skills. When some transcended these various moralistic or bourgeois movements, the Socialist party presented them with a new and challenging environment. It seemed to offer the resources and the opportunity to participate in the rebuilding of American society.[9]

A majority of the women who became prominent in the Socialist party were schooled in the middle-class morality movements. Kate Richards O'Hare (1877-1948), possibly the most renowned of the party activists, exemplifies the experiences of many of these women. Kate Richards grew up in rural Kansas until early adolescence when the loss of the family farm resulted in a relocation to Kansas City, Kansas. As an impressionable and idealistic young woman, she soon immersed herself in religious and temperance work in the inner city. At the Florence Crittenden Mission she worked with "fallen women," and she planned to enter the ministry of the Disciples of Christ. But somehow these efforts seemed insufficient. After working in her father's shop, she became involved with the local labor movement through the International Order of Machinists (which she, in fact, joined), and was converted to socialism, in part, through a speech she happened to hear by "Mother" Mary Harris Jones. In 1901, at the age of twenty-four, she attended a training school for socialist agitators at Girard, Kansas, and the pattern of her life for the next two decades was fixed.[10]

A minority of the women activists in the Socialist party had backgrounds in the labor movement, many having been immigrant working girls who became union organizers. An example of such a socialist leader was Theresa S. Malkiel (1874-1949) who had emigrated from Kiev in the Russian Empire in 1891. Her formative years were spent in a comfortable middle-class Jewish home but upon settling in New York, she experienced, as did so many young immigrant women, the environment of the sweatshop. A cloak-

maker in the disorganized garment industry, she herself organized the
Woman's Infant Cloak Makers' Union and became its president. Active in
the Russian Workingmen's Club, she became convinced that economic solidarity was insufficient; workers required political organization as well as
economic. She joined the Knights of Labor, brought her union into the
socialistic United Hebrew Trades, and then into the Socialist Labor party
(SLP). After a half dozen years in the SLP, she joined a splinter group
which helped found the Socialist party.[11]

Women party members, whether middle class and native-born or working class and immigrant, found a pledge to sexual equality in the Socialist
party platform, but neither a campaign implementing that pledge nor an understanding of any uniqueness in women's responsibilities or problems. Not
all socialist women were distressed by such omissions. But a number became determined to force the Socialist party to live up to its ideological
commitment to sexual equality and, in addition, hoped to create an awareness that the working class included women as well as men. They sought to
impose the Woman Question as a serious component of the Labor Question. Accordingly, they developed a woman's sector within the party,
which in a half-dozen short years became a significant factor in party
growth. It tapped new sources of energy and developed additional fields of
activity for the movement. However, the Achilles' heel of the woman's sector, in addition to and more serious than the party ambivalence toward the
Woman Question, was the confusion over priorities that prevailed among
the women activists. Among those who considered themselves socialist-
feminists and those who might be termed pure-and-simple socialists,
uncertainty abounded over the extent to which the movement might justifiably
focus on the plight of women under industrial capitalism. No consensus
existed as to the validity of a special campaign that might detract from the
class struggle itself. Even the feminists who argued that women's special position in the class struggle must be recognized were divided as to tactics and
emphases. The ambivalence and vast confusion led to internal weakness
and ultimately to the subordination of feminism to socialism.

The essays in this collection explore the various dimensions of the nexus
of American socialism and feminism. They demonstrate conclusively that
the Socialist party of Eugene V. Debs, Morris Hillquit, and Victor Berger
was also the party of May Wood Simons, Lena Morrow Lewis, and Kate
Richards O'Hare. The Socialist party in its "Golden Era" benefited as much
from the commitment of the latter as of the former. In exploration of this still-
neglected aspect of party history, these case studies bring the historiography
beyond the type of unsubstantiated generalization that has dominated.
The essays highlight and detail party policy and practice. The provide
biographies of some of the prominent women leaders whose lives have
been known only in outline. Further, they seek to unearth at least a glimpse
of the "Jennie Higginses," those women who formed the rank and file of the

woman's sector and who were known, at most, in their local communities. The collection begins with a short study of Daniel DeLeon, the leader of the Socialist Labor party, the forerunner of the Socialist party, and his views of the Woman Question, and it concludes with an appendix reprinting a theoretical essay on the Woman Question by one of its leading proponents, May Wood Simons.

The accumulation of data for a study of this group, neglected in its own time and later by historians and archivists, is an onerous task. Few manuscript collections contain the correspondence of these women activists. Those whose letters were collected were usually the wives of prominent party leaders. Thus, their letters, where extant, are often fragments and are sometimes scattered in collections in archives across the country. Even when letters might have been recognized as valuable and therefore preserved, accident sometimes intervened, such as in the destruction of Kate Richards O'Hare's correspondence by Frank O'Hare during their marital split in the 1920s.

The lives of few of these women activists are represented in directories, unlike many of their male colleagues of parallel prominence. The *American Labor Who's Who* in its 1925 edition, which includes those active in labor and the left in the previous decade, profiles very few women among the 1,200 names listed (only 7 percent of the entries are women compared with the nearly 15 percent of women who eventually made up the membership of the Socialist party). The same pattern of neglect occurs for these women in directories of American women. The *Woman's Who's Who of America*, issued in 1914, focuses on those women who were involved in various middle-class organizations; most of the leading socialist women, whose names were widely known beyond the confines of the party, were not deemed appropriate for inclusion in this major directory.

With sources so scarce, the scholar depends upon institutional records which may, by chance, include letters or other writings of one of these individuals. It is, thus, not surprising that it has taken until the 1980s for the lives and the contributions of these women to be reclaimed at last.

Notes

1. Nathan Fine, *Labor and Farmer Parties in the United States, 1828-1928* (New York: Rand School of Social Science, 1928).

2. Daniel Bell, "The Background and Development of Marxian Socialism in the United States," in Donald Drew Egbert and Stow Persons, eds., *Socialism and American Life* (Princeton: Princeton University Press, 1952) and David A. Shannon, *The Socialist Party of America: A History* (New York: The Macmillan Co., 1955). Shannon devotes four pages to the subject of the party and the black American.

3. Ira Kipnis, *The American Socialist Movement: 1897-1912* (New York: Columbia University Press, 1952), pp. 260-65.

4. James Weinstein, *The Decline of Socialism in America, 1912-1925* (New York: Monthly Review Press, 1967), pp. 53-74.

5. Sheila Rowbotham, *Women, Resistance and Revolution: A History of Women and Revolution in the Modern World* (New York: Vintage Books, 1974), p. 77.

6. Ibid., pp. 61-62, 72, 76; Marilyn J. Boxer and Jean J. Quataert, eds., *Socialist Women: European Socialist Feminism in the Nineteenth and Early Twentieth Centuries* (New York: Elsevier, 1978), pp. 2, 10-13.

7. Josephine Conger-Kaneko, "Socialist Woman's Movement in Germany," *Socialist Woman* 2 (June 1908): 10; Werner Thönnessen, *The Emancipation of Women: The Rise and Decline of the Women's Movement in German Social Democracy, 1863-1933* (London: Pluto Press, 1969).

8. See Shannon for a general overview of the party's history. He stresses the resemblance of the Socialist party to other American parties, which is debatable.

9. Lois W. Banner, *Women in America: A Brief History* (New York: Harcourt Brace Jovanovich, Inc., 1974), pp. 19-20; Mary P. Ryan, *Womanhood in America: From Colonial Times to the Present* (New York: New Viewpoints, 1975), pp. 224-32.

10. Kate Richards O'Hare, "How I Became a Socialist Agitator," *Socialist Woman* 2 (October 1908): 4-5; see "Introduction" in Philip S. Foner and Sally M. Miller, *Kate Richards O'Hare: Selected Writings and Speeches* (forthcoming).

11. "Theresa Malkiel," *Socialist Woman* 2 (May 1909): 2; Sally M. Miller, "From Sweatshop Worker to Labor Leader: Theresa Malkiel, A Case Study," *American Jewish History* 68 (December 1978): 189-205.

FLAWED LIBERATION

1

DANIEL DeLEON AND
THE WOMAN QUESTION

L. Glen Seretan

With the increased interest shown in recent years toward the history of
women, historians of American socialism have begun to explore the experience of women in that movement, particularly during its halcyon days
in the first quarter of this century. Generally speaking, they have found that
male socialists did not transcend the conventionally inegalitarian attitudes
and practices confronting women as much as might have been expected.
The question of why they did not is an important one for those who would
better understand the sexual dynamics of American radicalism.

The present chapter is intended as a contribution to such an inquiry. It
focuses on one prominent socialist figure of the period, Daniel DeLeon, examining his stance on the Woman Question and attempting to explain the
reasons for it. DeLeon was the preeminent personality within the Socialist
Labor party (SLP) from 1890 until his death in 1914. He edited and contributed extensively to the widely read English-language organ of the party, the
New York Daily People, and was a well-known and extremely effective
lecturer, debater, and theoretician. He also served the party as a frequent
candidate for public office, a prolific translator of European socialist literature, the leader of official delegations to congresses of the Second International,
and as its chief spokesman and strategist within labor organizations such
as the Knights of Labor, the Socialist Trade and Labor Alliance, and the
Industrial Workers of the World.

As a man of strong Marxist views who was indefatigably active in the
turbulent world of the pre-World War I American socialist and labor movements, DeLeon was often at the center of the factional controversies

endemic to that milieu. One such struggle occurred within the SLP itself
in the late 1890s, climaxing in 1899 in an ultimately unsuccessful rebellion a-
gainst his dominant role in party affairs. The anti-DeLeon faction soon after
joined forces with the Social Democratic party to form the Socialist party of
America, which quickly outstripped the rump SLP in size and influence.
Nonetheless, the ensuing rivalry between the two parties was sharp, and
DeLeon, not surprisingly, came to the fore as a persistent and unsparing
critic of the newer movement.

Certainly, then, an appreciation of DeLeon's posture on the Woman
Question can hardly be extrapolated to male socialists as a whole. Indeed,
it cannot be safely extended even to account for the attitudes of SLP adherents, for, while DeLeon's sway over the party faithful was great, it was
not absolute. Yet, his case does provide a useful starting point. Profoundly
influenced by Marxist precept, DeLeon, unlike most socialist leaders, consistently disregarded prevailing prejudices and was outspoken in expound-
ing the egalitarian imperatives of the socialist creed, strenuously opposing
racial discrimination, immigration restriction, and the elitism of organized
labor vis-a-vis the unskilled and the unemployed. He therefore offers a
standard for assessing the extent to which ideological commitment alone
was capable of transforming traditional male assumptions about women.

At first glance it would appear that DeLeon's position on women corre-
sponded to the advanced stands he assumed on other issues. "Mankind is
one," he asserted, "whatever the sex, color, or race of its component human
atoms."[1] The subjection of the female sex was, as he saw it, but an incident
of the larger historical process of class formation, not the result of any
inborn sex attributes.[2] In addition, DeLeon was the translator of August
Bebel's controversial work, *Woman under Socialism*, an effective appeal for
sexual equality which he had published in an American edition after
running it serially in the official Socialist Labor party paper he edited.
Certain aspects of his commentary on the book seemed to place him well in
the vanguard of women's rights advocates in the socialist movement. Con-
tending that "[t]here can be no emancipation of humanity without the social
independence and equality of the sexes,"[3] he maintained that monogamy
itself was a subject about which good socialists might legitimately disagree[4]
and that women constituted the most severely victimized sector of capitalist
society—sexual oppression being so pervasive as to burden even women in
the "upper ranks" of the social order.[5]

Nonetheless, a closer scrutiny reveals that DeLeon was not the champion
of female independence and equality that such statements would imply.
This is nowhere more evident than in the language he used to describe his
concept of the socialist movement—his allusions, analogies, illustrations,
and metaphors. The symbol for the movement to which DeLeon most commonly resorted was the quintessentially masculine one of the military unit,[6]
despite his deep-seated abhorrence for actual violence in the revolutionary

process. And the figurative weaponry most frequently associated in his par-
lance with the "army" of socialism was not modern ordnance but that of an
earlier day—swords, lances, and the like—requiring physical strength to
wield.[7] Taken together with the fact that DeLeon traced the source of
woman's inferior status to the appearance in history of the iron tool as the
means of production and her physical incapacity to use it,[8] the weapon
metaphors, like the martial paradigm generally, clearly suggest that he considered the work of revolution to be men's work.

This impression is strengthened when one examines the manner in which
DeLeon measured the worth of personalities and organizations in the labor
and socialist movements. The American working class was depicted in his
writings as immanently virile and manly, and class consciousness as a function of those qualities.[9] Hence, the mark of soundness for any labor organization was its virility. As DeLeon put it: "What hair on a man's face is, the
badge of virility, that is what the recognition of the class struggle is to an
organization of labor. What a beardless man is, a self-advertised creature of
impotence, that is what a labor organization without the recognition of the
class struggle is."[10] Class consciousness was, then, a concept closely related
in his mind to the ideal of manliness, and the class struggle was seen as an
arena for masculine self-assertion. Accordingly, when speaking for his own
Socialist Labor party, he stressed what he regarded as its positive male qualities, its "manly fortitude" and "manly, aggressive posture."[11] And his
praise for individual socialists he admired often took the same form: the
German Socialist, Robert Michels, for example, was extolled for "the aggressive virility with which his subjects are treated," while a kindred spirit
of the opposite sex, Margarite Faas Hardegger, was credited with "a virility
of character that many a man may envy."[12]

Moreover, since male potency was DeLeon's frame of reference for perceiving merit in people and organizations of the working class, charges of its
absence were frequently heard in his attacks on adversaries. He voiced
doubts about the manhood, for instance, of American capitalists and
scabs,[13] and he effeminized individuals, organizations, and ideas he judged
deficient by ascribing to them negative, supposedly intrinsic feminine
characteristics. Thus, as specimens of the reformist persuasion DeLeon so
heartily loathed, women's suffrage advocates were dismissed as thought-
lessness-promoting" and "excessively sentimental",[14] (features of course
alien to his eminently logical and scientific movement, whose essential
virility was the source of such pride to him). Reformers as a whole were
assailed in similar terms. Unlike true socialists, who, according to DeLeon,
were forthright and unequivocal in presenting their program, reformers
favored "the method of cajolery and seduction, . . . of charming, luring,
[and] decoying."[15] To that notion that the socialist ballot alone was sufficient to consummate the revolution in America, a claim made by DeLeon's
rivals in the Socialist party, he rejoined that without the power of support-

ive industrial organization the ballot would be "weaker than a woman's
tears" and "[l]ess valiant than the virgin in the night."[16] And in line with this
mode of criticism was his contemptuous use of the feminine pronouns,
"she" and "her," when referring to Max Hayes, the Socialist party's principal spokesman in the American Federation of Labor, in order to express his
scorn for what he deemed to be his opponent's manifest illogic.[17]

The male supremacist bent implied in these remarks became quite explicit
in the context of DeLeon's theoretical pronouncements on the proper role of
women in society. His outlook on the subject, at least as far as general values were concerned, would have elicited little argument from traditional
moralists. Controlling here was his personal commitment to the monogamic
family principle. Bristling at the oft-repeated charge that socialism would
destroy family life, DeLeon retorted that, on the contrary, it was the capitalist system that rendered the monogamic family unit untenable: low
wages discouraged marriage; the uncertainty of the labor market compelled
workers to leave their homes in search of work; women and children
were driven into the work force by the lash of necessity; and prostitution
flourished amidst the social wreckage thereby created, reflecting and at the
same time further contributing to the malaise.[18] Only socialism, he asserted,
could revive the family; the material well-being that it would afford would
eliminate the conditions causing the institution to founder.[19] Woman would
then be restored to "the dignity of her sex," which connoted to DeLeon an
exclusively domestic function at the center of the reclaimed family. Motherhood would be her defining essence, there being no comprehensible reason
for the continued practice of birth control, given the material abundance
socialism would bring.[20] Accordingly, she would be excluded from work
outside the home and no longer "unsexed" by having "to compete with men
in unseemly occupations,"[21] while the dross of capitalism's morally cor-
rosive environment—promiscuity, adultery, and divorce—would not again
degrade her.[22]

If DeLeon's vision of female emancipation would not have been likely to
generate great enthusiasm among progressive, independent-minded wom-
en, much the same could be said of several of his published comments
which betrayed an inability to abide assertiveness in members of the opposite sex. His reaction to outspoken women and militant feminism varied
from amused condescension to uneasy hostility. A revealing instance of
DeLeon's patronizing of self-confident women could be noted in one of his
press reports on the 1907 Congress of the Socialist International. It so happened that a British delegate, Mary Macarthur, had had the temerity there
to challenge, with considerable passion, a resolution on the trade union issue sponsored by his delegation. However, he did not subject her to the
ringing denunciations he customarily unleashed on alleged evildoers. He did
not take her seriously enough for that. Instead, he made light of her objec-

tions, as one might those of an unruly child, and seemed more interested in relating his impressions of her physical appeal. Macarthur, he wrote, was "a young and prepossessing maid—blonde, white and pink, with prettily curved lips, and brilliant-bright eyes. Her rage added charm to her appearance."[23] However, DeLeon looked upon the proposals and declarations of radical feminists with somewhat less insouciance. The popular notion of a sex strike as an affirmation of female solidarity struck him as "a heels-over-head concept;" for one thing, he refused to believe that there were enough women who were, as he put it, "endowed with the exceptional vigor of mind and at the same time afflicted with the exceptional physique required to carry out such a program."[24] DeLeon also scoffed at the feminist rallying cry that woman was to be the salvation of modern civilization. But he was obviously disturbed that some men had taken it up. Regarding two speeches he had heard by clergymen in which this view was endorsed, he declaimed that they "were the most absurd and undignified twaddle it ever was my misfortune . . . to listen to"—strong words from a man who closely monitored a wide range of the public discourse of his age and found precious little that pleased him. DeLeon's vehemence owed more to what the speeches represented than to their actual content. By subscribing to the idea that woman would be the determining force of social change, the "gentlemen," he said, "performed a distressing feat of self-effacement"—that is, they surrendered their manhood, their natural position of dominance, to women. That the ideology of female assertiveness had, as far as DeLeon was concerned, influenced these unfortunate men to practice and advocate a form of self-castration is indicated by a mordant observation he offered on the theme of their speeches as they pertained to the male sex. "Listening to them," he remarked, "one would imagine that male creation was a sort of 'appendix,' good only to produce social 'appendicitis,' and fit only for amputation—and that none too soon." The spread of such pernicious doctrines had, for him, perverse implications, for they portended a reversal of sex roles. "Wrong enthroned," he warned, "can wish for nothing better than for its assailants to turn freaks," and nothing, apparently, was more freakish, in his estimation, than the specter of what he called "ferocious he-females" and "grotesque 'she-males'."[25]

Worrisome as the possible consequences of unbridled feminism might have been to him, however, DeLeon would have had little cause to fear its effects on his own household. There, Victorian sanity prevailed and his patriarchal preeminence was unquestioned. Indeed, his wife, Bertha, could well have been the inspiration for his projection of blissful domesticity for women under socialism. A Kansas schoolteacher prior to their marriage, Bertha DeLeon was an intelligent woman with a keen interest in radical politics, but she cheerfully deferred to her husband and subordinated her political work to his. For a brief period after her marriage, she was a member of

a small Socialist Labor party section and dutifully performed routine
clerical and secretarial tasks for DeLeon."I was eager to make myself as useful as possible," she later recalled. But before long, she abandoned even this
minor activity to devote herself entirely to raising a large family and mini-
stering to DeLeon's needs at home. The hearth came to circumscribe her domain and the political tumult of the outside world eventually assumed a
menacing aspect. This Bertha revealed quite clearly in a reminiscence written many years after her husband's death. "DeLeon," she remembered,

wrote many of his editorials . . . at home, and I knew, day by day, all that was going on, but the matter had much the effect of a storm. The wind whistles wildly a-
round the eaves and dashes rain or snow against the windows but does not ill affect
the scene within; it does not diminish, but intensifies, the enjoyment of the comfort
and cheer of the fireside and lamplight, and the music of children's voices.[26]

Animated by such sentiments, Bertha apotheosized DeLeon's ideal of
womanhood.

Without question, DeLeon's perspective on women did not diverge much
from the conventional. To understand why that was the case, one must consider the nature of DeLeon's relationship with his parents during his earlier,
formative years. His father, Salomon, was a physician who was frequently
away from the family home in Curaçao for extended periods during his
son's childhood, and he died when Daniel was only twelve years old,[27] depriving the youth of whatever small paternal influence on his upbringing his
father's lengthy absences had allowed. Thereafter, Daniel's sole parental influence was his mother, Sarah. Having lost her two other children prior to
her husband's death, she focused her full attention on raising the only other
surviving member of the family. Even as DeLeon approached adulthood,
she remained with him, moving to Amsterdam so that he could live in her
home while pursuing university studies there and subsequently emigrating
with him to the United States. In time, however, bitter feelings developed
between DeLeon and his mother, leading to an irreparable breach. They
quarreled over the direction his life was taking in America, and their differences were fundamental. As the daughter of a prominent Curaçoan Jewish
family, and anxious that he establish himself in a reputable line of en-
deavor, Sarah was exasperated at the attenuation of her son's Jewish identity and his increasing involvement in radical politics. For him, such a course
was imperative. Experiencing an acute sense of isolation as a Jew, the result
of his exposure to the rise of modern nationalism in Europe, he wished to be
free of the stigma of his minority status and sought to identify himself as
part of a more broadly conceived community, a path that carried him ultimately to socialist universalism and self-definition as a proletarian.[28] Inas-
much as his mother presented herself as an obstacle to the exercise of this
choice, the conflict was invested with a significant sexual dimension:

DeLeon's self-realization as a man entailed overcoming the matriarchal sway she had exerted over his life. Given these circumstances, it is not surprising that he would later be inclined to see women, first and foremost, as mothers; that he would react negatively to the emasculating aggressiveness he detected in feminism;[29] or that he would perceive a commitment to socialism as an affirmation of one's manhood.

The effects of DeLeon's self-assertion in the face of matriarchal authority can be read, too, in his subsequent efforts to place himself within a countervailing family tradition of manly virtue, even going so far as to falsify details about his ancestry to this end. He freely related the pure fiction that he was descended from the swashbuckling explorer, Ponce de Leon,[30] and told his followers that he was the scion of a proud, aristocratic, Hispanic-American family—"grand old fighting stock," according to one party biographer, its male members "eternally engaged on one side or the other" in the chronic internecine warfare of Latin American nations.[31] DeLeon's memory of his father was colored by a desire to cast him in a similarly virile mold: he kept a photograph of the Civil War general, William Tecumseh Sherman, on the mantelpiece of his New York apartment and informed visitors that it was the best likeness he had of his father; and, as if to sharpen that martial image, he retained, as a treasured memento, an ornate parade sword that had belonged to the elder DeLeon.[32]

If there is anything generally instructive about Daniel DeLeon's case, it is that the broad social, economic, and cultural forces impelling him to socialism acted upon him through the medium of a personal situation which adversely affected his assimilation of the doctrine's egalitarian implications for women. Hence, the very milieu in which he came to adopt a revolutionary world-view paradoxically reinforced in him the culturally accepted norms perpetuating female inferiority at a stage when he would have otherwise been likely to reject them along with the rest of the prevailing belief-system. These conclusions suggest the power of personal and family factors to limit the impact of ideology on even the most zealous individuals, and they point to the specific contexts in which socialist ideas were received as a cause of the lack of sustained commitment to sexual equality among male socialists of DeLeon's era.

Notes

1. Daniel DeLeon, *The Ballot and the Class Struggle* (New York: New York Labor News Company, 1947), p. 9.

2. Ibid., pp. 6, 9-10, 32.

3. Quoted in Carl Reeve, *The Life and Times of Daniel DeLeon* (New York: Humanities Press for A.I.M.S., 1972), p. 170.

4. Ibid.; Daniel DeLeon, "Translator's Preface," to August Bebel, *Woman under*

Socialism (New York: Schocken Books, 1971), pp. xvii-xviii; Daniel DeLeon, "Horrible Example of 16 to 1 Mental Training," *Daily People*, November 14, 1909, in Daniel DeLeon, *Evolution of a Liberal: From Reform to Reaction* (New York: New York Labor News Company, 1965), p. 14.

5. DeLeon, "Translator's Preface," p. xv.

6. For typical instances in two of his better-known published addresses, see Daniel DeLeon, *Reform or Revolution* (Brooklyn, N.Y.: New York Labor News, 1965), pp. 22-23; Daniel DeLeon, *Two Pages from Roman History* (New York: New York Labor News Company, 1943), pp. 7-8. DeLeon also often likened the socialist movement to a ship and its members to a ship's crew—another characteristically masculine setting. For examples, see DeLeon, *Reform or Revolution*, p. 10; DeLeon, *Two Pages*, pp. 7, 84.

7. Daniel DeLeon, *What Means This Strike?* (New York: New York Labor News Company, 1947), pp. 30-31; Daniel DeLeon and Job Harriman, *The Socialist Trade and Labor Alliance versus the "Pure and Simple" Trade Union: A Debate Held at the Grand Opera House, New Haven, Conn., November 25, 1900* (New York: New York Labor News Company, 1900), p. 12; Daniel DeLeon, *The Burning Question of Trades Unionism* (New York: New York Labor News Company, 1960), pp. 26-27, 30-31, 42; Daniel DeLeon, *Flashlights of the Amsterdam Congress* (New York: New York Labor News Company, 1929), pp. 108-109, 139; Daniel DeLeon, *Socialist Reconstruction of Society: The Industrial Vote* (Brooklyn, N.Y.: New York Labor News, 1968), pp.50, 52.

8. DeLeon, *Reform or Revolution*, p. 5; DeLeon, *Ballot and Class Struggle*, pp. 6-7, 9-10, 15; Daniel DeLeon, "The Mother-Right," *Daily People*, November 26, 1909, in DeLeon, *Evolution of a Liberal*, p. 23.

9. DeLeon, *What Means This Strike?*, p. 5; Daniel DeLeon, "The Fourth of July!," *Daily People*, July 4, 1902; Daniel DeLeon, "The Barber's Second Brother," *Daily People*, September 10, 1907.

10. DeLeon, "Barber's Second Brother."

11. DeLeon, *Burning Question*, p. 37; DeLeon, *Reform or Revolution*, p. 10. For similar references, see DeLeon, *Burning Question*, p. 43; Daniel DeLeon, *Address Issued by the National Executive Committee of the Socialist Labor Party, In Semi-Annual Session Convened, New York, January 4, 1909* (New York: New York Labor News Company, 1909), p.14. Given this conception of the party, it was quite consistent for DeLeon to exhort only "the male members" of an 1890 election campaign audience "to go on the streets during the campaign and take the stump for . . . [the] party." (Quoted in "Brooklyn Nationalists: They Challenge the Plutocrats to a Public Debate—DeLeon Reviews the Work of the Boodle Parties," *Workmen's Advocate*, October 11, 1890.)

12. Daniel DeLeon, "Notes on the Stuttgart Congress, I: New Faces," *Daily People*, October 6, 1907.

13. DeLeon, *Socialist Reconstruction*, p. 54; DeLeon and Harriman, *Debate*, p. 27.

14. DeLeon, *Ballot and Class Struggle*, p. 47. Also see Daniel DeLeon, "Preface," to John H. Halls, *Woman and Her Emancipation* (New York: New York Labor News Company, 1909).

15. DeLeon, *Reform or Revolution*, p. 11.

16. DeLeon, *Socialist Reconstruction*, p. 49.

17. DeLeon, *Burning Question*, p. 42; Eric Hass, "Satire, Weapon of Truth," in Socialist Labor Party, *Golden Jubilee of DeLeonism, 1890-1940: Commemorating the Fiftieth Anniversary of the Founding of the Socialist Labor Party* (New York: Socialist Labor Party of America, 1940), p. 13.

18. "Brooklyn Nationalists"; DeLeon, *Reform or Revolution*, p. 25; Daniel DeLeon, *Anti-Semitism: Its Cause and Cure* (New York: National Executive Committee, Socialist Labor Party, 1921), p. 24; Daniel DeLeon and James Connolly, "Wages, Marriage and the Church: A Discussion Initiated by James Connolly, and Answered by the Editor of the People," *Weekly People*, April 9, 1904; Daniel DeLeon, "The Perfidy of Revolutionary Classes," *Daily People*, February 14, 1905, in Daniel DeLeon, *Russia in Revolution: Selected Editorials* (New York: N.Y. Labor News Co., 1927), p. 21; DeLeon, *Ballot and Class Struggle*, p. 23; Daniel DeLeon, *Abolition of Poverty: Socialist versus Ultramontane Economics and Politics* (New York: New York Labor News Co., 1945), pp. 60-61; Daniel DeLeon and William H. Berry, *Capitalism vs. Socialism* (Brooklyn, N.Y.: New York Labor News, 1969), pp. 60-61.

19. DeLeon, "Translator's Preface" to Bebel, pp. xvii-xviii; DeLeon and Connolly, "Wages, Marriage and the Church"; DeLeon, *Abolition of Poverty*, pp. 62-63; DeLeon and Berry, *Capitalism vs. Socialism*, p. 60.

20. DeLeon, "Translator's Preface" to Bebel, p. xviii; DeLeon, quoted in Arnold Petersen, *Daniel DeLeon: Social Architect* 2 vols. (New York: New York Labor News Company, 1941-53), II: 33; DeLeon, "Mother-Right," pp. 22-24; J. Schlossberg, "Daniel DeLeon—Fighter for Socialism in the American Labor Movement," *The Day*, December 28, 29, 31, 1952, trans. by Louis Lazarus, New York, 1960, typescript, Tamiment Collection, New York University, p. 9.

21. James Creelman, "Five Million Socialists Here, Says DeLeon; What They Stand For," *New York World*, November 9, 1902; DeLeon and Berry, *Capitalism vs. Socialism*, p. 60; DeLeon, "Perfidy of Revolutionary Classes," p. 21; DeLeon, quoted in "Brooklyn Nationalists."

22. Creelman, "Five Million Socialists"; DeLeon, "Translator's Preface" to Bebel, p. xvii; DeLeon and Connolly, "Wages, Marriage and the Church"; DeLeon, *Ballot and Class Struggle*, p. 23; DeLeon, "Mother-Right," pp. 22, 24; DeLeon, *Abolition of Poverty*, pp. 61-63.

23. Daniel DeLeon, "Notes on the Stuttgart Congress, III: The Trades Union Issue," *Daily People*, October 20, 1907.

24. DeLeon, *Ballot and Class Struggle*, p. 32.

25. Ibid., pp. 30-31.

26. Solon DeLeon to author, April 13, 1973; David Herreshoff, *American Disciples of Marx: From the Age of Jackson to the Progressive Era* (Detroit: Wayne State University Press, 1967), p. 115; Oakley C. Johnson, "Foreword," to Reeve, *Life and Times*, pp. 6, 8-9; Bertha C. DeLeon, "The 'Nineties with DeLeon," in Socialist Labor Party, *Fifty Years of American Marxism, 1891-1941: Commemorating the Fiftieth Anniversary of the Founding of the WEEKLY PEOPLE* (New York: Socialist Labor Party of America, 1941), pp. 21-25, quoted passages from pp. 21, 25.

27. Isaac S. Emmanuel and Suzanne A. Emmanuel, *History of the Jews of the Netherlands Antilles* (Cincinnati: American Jewish Archives, 1970), pp. 428-29.

28. Ibid., pp. 449-52; Director, Gemeentelijke Archiefdienst van Amsterdam, to

author, July 20, 1972, Assistant Director to author, June 4, 1973; Johnson, "Foreword," p. 4; Solon DeLeon to author, December 9, 1972, January 29, 1973; L. Glen Seretan, "Daniel DeLeon, 'Wandering Jew' of American Socialism: An Interpretive Analysis," *American Jewish Historical Quarterly* 65 (March 1976): 245-56.

29. Tending to confirm the connection between DeLeon's experience with his mother and his subsequent antifeminism was a comparison of feminism and Jewish nationalism he rendered at one point: the two were, he insisted, guilty of the same "false posture." (DeLeon, "Preface" to Halls.)

30. Charles Frederick Stansbury, "The 'Daily People' and its Staff," *Journalist*, July 7, 1900, p. 89; Benjamin Stolberg, *Tailor's Progress: The Story of a Famous Union and the Men Who Made It* (Garden City, N.Y.: Doubleday, Doran and Company, Inc., 1944), p. 31.

31. Olive M. Johnson, *Daniel DeLeon: American Socialist Pathfinder* (New York: New York Labor News Company, 1935), p. 9. The anomaly of a socialist inventing an aristocratic background for himself is explained by DeLeon's attraction to the patrician code of chivalry, especially its valorous aspects. He respected and admired the inbred fighting qualities bespeaking the virility of the feudal ruling class and reviled the bourgeoisie, the class from which he actually sprang, for its intrinsic cowardice. (Daniel DeLeon, "Tom Watson Climbs Down," *Daily People*, April 25, 1910, in DeLeon, *Evolution of a Liberal*, p. 59; DeLeon, *Two Pages*, pp. 25-26; DeLeon, *Socialist Reconstruction*, pp. 53-54.) The tale about heavy family involvement in Latin American upheavals is probably a grandiose distortion of the fact that DeLeon's father had given medical aid to the wounded in the Colombian revolution of 1860. In reality, DeLeon's relatives, Sephardic Jews who were Dutch citizens by virtue of their residence in the Netherlands Antilles, followed pacific occupations. (Emmanuel and Emmanuel, *History*, pp. 428-29, 449-50.)

32. Johnson, "Foreword," p. 3.

2

WOMEN IN THE PARTY BUREAUCRACY: SUBSERVIENT FUNCTIONARIES

Sally M. Miller

In recent years, the bibliography on women and socialism has begun to grow. Studies on the Socialist party of America have appeared focusing on the era of World War I, the party's most expansive period. Biographical articles on women organizers and intellectuals have provided additional data but have not fully illuminated basic questions about the role of women in radical politics, or that is, radical politics and woman's "place." This essay is an institutional study of the Socialist party and its women members, their role in its power structure, their views on policy, their activities, and their priorities.[1]

The Socialist party of America at its founding convention in 1901 included in its platform a commitment to "equal civil and political rights for men and women." Indeed, following the position taken in the late nineteenth century by European socialism, the party was virtually obligated to support such a position. Moreover, influential socialists abroad, such as August Bebel of the German Social Democratic party, Paul Lafargue of the French socialists and the son-in-law of Marx, and Frederich Engels himself, had acknowledged the exploitation of women in a special guise and had written on behalf of sexual equality.

Women were perhaps one-tenth of the membership of the Socialist party, and played a visible role in its internal affairs. In national conventions between 1904 and 1912, women were conspicuous, serving on subcommittees, leading floor fights, and lobbying for resolutions. Unlike the dominant political parties where women were almost never convention delegates (from 0 to under 1 percent in these years), the socialists had relatively large female contingents. In 1904, 6 percent of the delegates were women, in 1908 10 percent, and in 1912, again 10 percent.[2]

Women served the party as organizers, propagandists, pamphleteers, and candidates for public office. In 1912, the party sent sixty speakers throughout North America on a lyceum circuit, and over one-fifth of these were women. Party journalists were women almost as often as men, with copy editors and staff people tending to be women. Autonomous women's socialist study groups, organized in most of the states and also in Ontario, Manitoba, Alberta, and British Columbia, coordinated their programs and their lobbying around party initiatives. Women party members raised funds for strike benefits and campaign expenses, distributed propaganda, served as poll watchers, established and taught in socialist Sunday schools and, in general, built bridges to nonsocialist women and women's organizations. In 1908, responding to the possibility of an autonomous national organization of socialist women, the party convention established a Woman's National Committee as a clearinghouse and focus for women's party activities. A salaried woman national organizer was assigned specifically to seek out women for membership, while each state organization and every local was urged to utilize women organizers and to form a woman's committee. The Woman's National Committee raised funds, commissioned leaflets, and otherwise sought to increase party strength by appealing to women's interests and needs.[3]

However, party treatment of the so-called Woman Question and of women members often seemed perfunctory, more lip service than genuine commitment. The platform demand of 1901 for equal rights was virtually a dead letter. The platform plank of 1904 supporting equal suffrage for men and women seemed an absentminded acknowledgment. No literature was commissioned for women in these early years, no organizers assigned. It was not until the convention of 1908 when women delegates forcefully acted as a special interest group that the party pledged an active campaign for unrestricted and equal suffrage.[4]

Through those first half-dozen years prior to the appearance of a cohesive woman's bloc, the Socialist party had expended no energy in organizing women or appealing to their needs. As a leading male socialist, John Spargo complained, that not only did the party fail to seek out women, but it often held its meetings in the locker-room atmosphere of neighborhood saloons. Such locations were clearly unattractive to women who might often be circumspect about venturing into politics. When women joined the party on their own initiative, no effort was made to fit proceedings into a framework understandable to political novices. Moreover, propaganda and arguments were always expressed in terms of the male identity, concerns, and life style. No campaign was initiated to reach women in their dual capacities as wage workers by day and housewives by night, nor was any real attempt made to penetrate the ignorance in which it was believed organized religion had trapped women. Women's role in the party, some women noted, was to be no more than cake bakers and tea pourers. "Women are tired of being 'included'," one wrote, "but not really recognized." As to party politics, women could be seen, possibly, but not heard in the locals.[5]

In addition to such institutional sins of omission, male party leaders informally revealed strong reservations about women activists. When a woman was first elected in 1909 to the party executive, Victor Berger, a dominant force in the party right wing, commented to a colleague, Morris Hillquit, that having a woman on the National Executive Committee was " . . . by no means necessary for a political party at this stage of the game and under the present conditions." In 1913 when Kate Richards O'Hare was elected as a representative to the International Socialist Bureau in Brussels, the same two leaders feared that she would make the Socialist party look ridiculous abroad. Berger as a congressman fulfilled his obligation to introduce a bill for woman suffrage, only to find such efforts suspect. A woman's socialist group complained that the two socialists elected to Congress, Berger of Milwaukee and Meyer London of the lower East Side, minimized the suffrage issue, and Florence Kelley of the Henry Street Settlement House and a sometime socialist, questioned the sincerity of their commitment to protective legislation for women. To reassure doubters, male party leaders emphasized the pioneering commitment of socialists everywhere to woman suffrage, but some admitted a belief that votes for women would delay the advent of socialism since women were presumed to be dominated by reactionary priests and ministers.[6]

Patronizing of women was rampant in the party. A leading journal, the *International Socialist Review*, described women delegates as "On all questions . . . acquit[ting] themselves nobly." The socialist press was also capable of referring to one woman convention delegate as having "her feathers all ruffled", and Eugene V. Debs, the party's perennial candidate for the presidency, generously commented on the value of women speakers who always attracted a crowd.[7]

In short, women were not taken seriously by a political party theoretically committed to equality. " . . . how bitter is our disappointment," one woman wrote, "whenever we come to look upon matters as they really are." Women were not welcome in the party's power structure. They were clustered in the lower levels of the party hierarchy, far from positions of authority. Women members were relegated to precinct work and thus were effectively segregated from responsibility. At best, women played roles at conventions, although even there resentments surfaced over all-male state delegations. The National Office of the party and its National Executive

Committee (N.E.C.), the decision-making body between conventions, were masculine provinces. Even the day-to-day decisions on fiscal matters, policy determinations, and organizational campaigns were prerogatives of the professional functionaries and the most prominent party politicians. With women effectively barred from this segment of the party arena, a pattern of institutional discrimination prevailed; only upon occasion were women allowed other than marginal roles. Prejudicial attitudes and institutional arrangements meant that hers were party bazaars but not party power.[8]

The identity of the women activists was remarkably homogeneous. The background of most of these women was middle class and native American. In fact, the pattern was predominantly bourgeois WASP. Of two dozen women who served on the Woman's National Committee, three-fourths were American born, perhaps reflecting the fact that the socialist movement itself had shrugged off its nineteenth-century domination by European immigrants. Among seventeen other women featured in cover stories by the only national woman's socialist monthly, the same percentage prevailed. Among these forty-one prominent women socialists, only four could claim working-class backgrounds: Rose Pastor Stokes, Kate Richards O'Hare, Elizabeth Gurley Flynn, and Theresa Malkiel. The typical profile was of a college-educated woman, often a teacher, many with formative experiences in evangelical or suffrage movements.[9] These women were relatively youthful, in their thirties and forties, with only an occasional older activist who had participated in abolitionist struggles. A few were offspring of activist mothers. Most of these women were married, usually to men who were also socialists. In instances where couples shared a party prominence—Algie and May Wood Simons, J. G. Phelps and Rose Pastor Stokes, Victor and Meta Berger—the wife generally worked in the shadow of the husband's more important position. But whether married, divorced, or single, most appeared to live independent lives which were not male dominated.[10]

Geographically, an overwhelming proportion of these women came from the rural Middle West and the Far West, with a few hailing from the South. Illustrative of that pattern, more than 50 percent of women convention delegates from 1904 to 1912 represented areas west of the Mississippi River, and 25 percent the Great Lakes. Most of the autonomous women's socialist organizations, except for a number headquartered in New York, were established in the western half of the continent. This pattern may be explained by the fact that many western women had won the franchise a generation earlier, and therefore the political process was not alien to them. Thus, socialist women helped underline the party's own western tilt.[11]

In 1908, soon after the establishment of the Woman's National Committee (W.N.C.), a Woman's General Correspondent was appointed, and her office became the keystone of a vertical organization which extended increasingly deep and independent roots. A distinct separatism that almost no one wanted developed. While all W.N.C. decisions had to be endorsed by the party's executive and while the committee lacked budgetary authority, nevertheless its network spread throughout the country. An office of Woman's State Correspondent was also established at this time, to serve as liaison among local, state, and national woman's committees. This office, set up immediately in four midwestern and western states, was always held by women, although not so legislated, and was closely tied to a woman's state committee. In the next eighteen months ten additional states (two-thirds west of the Mississippi River) established the same offices. When other states did not follow suit, the W.N.C., after some prodding, considered submitting its own nominations for the unfilled posts, an action sure to be perceived as a threat to local autonomy. However, by 1915 such an edifice for women's activities existed in thirty-seven states.[12]

On the local level, wide discrepancies existed in practice. Party policy provided that each local organize a woman's committee, but in some locals apparently the only action was the posting of a "Ladies Invited" sign. By 1911 the woman's committees were said to have been established in 69 percent of reporting locals, but this fact was based on a questionnaire to which only 7 percent of the locals responded. Regional differences were pronounced. The Mississippi State Correspondent reported that she found that southern notions of woman's "place" and of male chivalry adversely affected party efforts toward organizing women, while the New Mexico State Correspondent reported that her state's poverty and sparse population hindered organizational drives. But the California State Correspondent wrote that 13 percent of her state's membership was female, and the New York State Correspondent estimated 10 percent. Throughout the country areas of party strength were often reflected in an expanding women's sphere, while party weaknesses were usually paralleled by a low level of such activity.[13]

However, data indicates that there was greater willingness in certain areas than others to include women in the regular party apparatus. Women still served infrequently on the National Committee, showing a small percentage growth (never more than six women, with fluctuations from 1910 to 1914 of 3.5 percent to 8.5 percent), and seldom were they elected by eastern states, despite the fact that a state like New York had many prominent women members. The all-important N.E.C., to which five to seven members were elected annually between 1901 and 1917, had only a total of three women. All three were exceedingly prominent party organizers: Lena Morrow Lewis, elected in 1909; Kate Richards O'Hare in 1911; and Anna A. Maley in 1916. Among state secretaries, women held a maximum of 16 percent of the positions. The official delegates to the International were almost entirely male in 1904 and 1907, but in 1910 three of the party's eight mandated delegates to the Congress of the Second International at Copenhagen were women, and in 1913, as mentioned above, O'Hare was elected as one of the few women ever to sit on the International Socialist Bureau in Brussels.

Ad hoc party committees tended to be exclusively male. The only type of position for which the Socialist party turned regularly to women nominees was in the field of education. In 1909 Milwaukee elected the first socialist woman to a public post in the United States when the party ran Meta Berger for the Milwaukee School Board, a position she held for over two decades. The party's National Education Committee in 1913 was chaired by May Wood Simons, and consisted of three women and four men. In 1908, the socialists named 13 women among its 271 candidates in state races (4.7 percent), and of that number, 8 were candidates for Superintendencies of Public Instruction or for Regents of State Universities. In 1910, of 255 candidates for state level public offices 16 were women (6.2 percent), half of whom ran for educational posts.[14]

Clearly, then, woman's sphere was carefully defined; in effect the party had made room for women in a hierarchy of their own. Their socialist activity was confined to their own structure, reported in their own separate newspaper columns, and it was their energy alone that would determine how widely their sector of the party might grow. The Woman's National Committee developed a "Plan for Work in Socialist Locals" which established guidelines for attracting women to membership. The plan was based on the stated assumption of "the need to make distinct efforts to reach women. . . ." Separate woman's locals were officially eschewed in favor of mixed locals, although a few women favored separatism temporarily in order to establish a relaxed environment in which to raise consciousness. But woman's committees were elected by locals from their entire membership, and each chose a correspondent to maintain contact with other woman's committees. The committees distributed party publications, promoted specific issues, sought out new members, and sponsored entertainments and social events. Increasingly, emphasis was placed upon combining serious study with social events or traditional woman's activities such as sewing bees in order to attract potential converts.[15]

After a few years, the W.N.C.'s Plan for Work became quite refined. The pioneering day of general organizing had ended, as one woman declared, and organizers had to respond to varieties of life styles among women. The woman's committees, now called Local Committees on Propaganda among Women in order to minimize implications of auxiliary functions, were to be integrated into the general work of the locals, sharing responsibilities on all issues. The members were to canvass house-to-house, in shops, and wherever women congregated. Special distributions and demonstrations occurred on the annual Woman's Day, May Day, the Fourth of July, and Labor Day. The W.N.C. published monthly programs for the guidance of local committees and routinely sent appropriate articles to the labor and socialist press.

Winnie Branstetter. (Courtesy of Theresa Branstetter Taft.)

The local committees formed strike subcommittees and suffrage campaign groups. In some large cities, a Central Woman's Committee, composed of delegates from each ward branch, was organized, and inner-city socialist locals were provided with special guidelines to transcend the suspicions of tenement women. The W.N.C. also offered suggestions for reaching women on farms and in prairie hamlets, emphasizing the ways in which the party could serve a poignant human need by alleviating the loneliness of such isolated women.[16]

The W.N.C. issued approximately two dozen leaflets of interest to women. The leaflets appealed to women in their various working capacities and dealt with issues such as suffrage, social problems, socialism and the home, the boy scout movement, and the cost of living, the most widely distributed leaflet. The party executive, bearing veto power over publications, occasionally requested revisions for stylistic reasons and sometimes for matters of substance. One leaflet was criticized for using the expression, "the sex struggle."[17]

Each year the W.N.C. focused on a few specific lines of activity. In 1913, for example, the emphasis was on promoting suffrage, winning new members, and cooperating with immigrant women's organizations. Depending on the thrust, the W.N.C. tried to route organizers on various issues and in specific regions of the country. It considered placing organizers in an area for three days instead of the party's usual practice of one-day whirlwind visits, since feeling was widespread that a more comprehensive type of barnstorming was necessary to break through the barriers surrounding women. Organizing methods were modified in favor of meetings in private homes, congenial environments where the uncommitted would feel comfortable. The Woman's National Committee established a Socialist Teachers' Placement Bureau and a Childrens' Strike Fund, and explored the idea of "family dues" instead of the humiliating lower dues for women. It encouraged using women on the party's major committees, on delegations, and as national organizers, filled requests for women speakers, and tried to arrange national tours for European socialist women. Throughout all the W.N.C.'s efforts to involve women in routine party work and to encourage the cooperation of locals, it sought to minimize any suggestion of separatism. Lena Morrow Lewis, arguing unsuccessfully against a national conference of socialist women, cautioned that their work must always illustrate the fact that the Socialist party was not a men's club: "We must never allow our woman's committees or conferences to be the means of eliminating [the] women from the regular party."[18]

The socialist women succeeded in forging an institutional structure in over three dozen states, some of which became vigorous pockets of party activity. However, despite their wide-ranging efforts, while women joined the party, they did not flock to it. Fragmentary evidence clearly indicates a rise in women members. Just prior to the founding of the Woman's National Committee, a survey of 15 percent of the locals suggested that women were 4.9 percent of the membership. In 1912, the general correspondent, Winnie E. Branstetter, estimated—based on returns from only thirty-five locals— that 10 percent of the membership was female. The next year the reports of the state correspondents suggested 15 percent, while in 1915 May Wood Simons guessed that women made up 17 percent of the party. The dimension of the struggle to increase the female contingent can be gleaned from the fact that even membership data by sex remained elusive. The W.N.C. was obviously envious when it noted that the Young People's Socialist League claimed a membership that was one-third female.[19]

The Woman's National Committee sought to develop dialogues with several peer groups external to the party proper: women in the socialist movement overseas, immigrant women, and the bourgeois suffrage movement. The American women who attended the Congress of the Second International in Copenhagen in 1910, Luella Twining, May Wood Simons, and Lena Morrow Lewis, eagerly participated in the Second International Conference of Socialist Women which preceded the Congress. German women had raised the Woman Question years before at the founding of the Second International in 1889, and by 1907 they had won an endorsement of universal suffrage and had organized an international conference of socialist women. American women, an ocean away, could not play a full role, yet the infrequent gatherings were inspirational to them. They enjoyed the collegial environment at the 1910 conference, but nevertheless did not hesitate to oppose Clara Zetkin and other leaders who eschewed reforms such as protective legislation for women. The W.N.C. studied the European women's methods of propaganda and data collection, and created a position of International Correspondent to systematize their contacts. The correspondent, Meta Stern Lilienthal of New York, monitored European publications and translated pertinent articles into English. The W.N.C. regularly sent reports of its work to Zetkin in Germany and to Annie Grundy in London, and saw its own annual Woman's Day adopted by some of the European socialists. In 1914 the W.N.C. elected its own representative to the anticipated Third International Conference of Socialist Women scheduled for August in Vienna prior to the opening of the Congress of the International, and it also prepared a report for presentation there on the woman suffrage movement in the United States.[20]

The W.N.C., whose own membership sometimes included women of European background, was somewhat slow to recognize the potential for socialism among immigrant women, but eventually the committee sought to mine that resource. At the 1912 party convention, Caroline A. Lowe, a midwesterner, pleaded for funding for translators so that W.N.C. leaflets could reach the foreign-speaking. In 1913 the W.N.C. tried to forge links with the occasional woman serving on the executives of the party's foreign-language federations and with their few woman's branches. The federations, clearly male in leadership and, among certain nationalities, in membership as well, were asked by the W.N.C. to translate its woman's publications into their own language. Translations appeared in Finnish, Slovak, Polish, Bohemian, Hungarian, German, and Yiddish, with only the South Slavic and the Italian Federations lacking leaflets. The W.N.C. debated whether perhaps a "cultural problem" existed which might preclude verbatim translations into Eastern European languages and considered preparing a "simpler" literature for immigrant working-class women. A new leaflet was issued for such women on the importance of naturalization.[21]

A subcommittee was established to formalize a link between the W.N.C. and the party's foreign-language federation women. This move made feasible a survey of ethnic women's attitudes and situations. The survey, limited to women members of the foreign-language federations, showed that the Finnish Federation led all wings of the party; with its family-based party activities, one-third of its membership was female. The Scandinavian and German Federations were 15 percent women, the Bohemian, Polish, and Jewish were 10 percent female, and the South Slav and Italian—immigrant groups in which men often came without their families—only 1 percent female. Valuable data was assembled on the occupational status of women by ethnic group, putting the W.N.C. in a position to make knowledgeable appeals to each language group.[22]

The Woman's National Committee maintained an ambivalent relationship with the woman's suffrage movement. The W.N.C. found it necessary to justify any collaboration with the National American Woman's Suffrage Association because both the Second International and the Socialist party opposed cooperation with middle-class suffrage efforts. But the W.N.C. spoke of capturing and radicalizing the suffrage movement; it maintained that its propaganda was always based on class consciousness, emphasizing that the ballot was only one means toward the goal of social transformation. Despite the fact that the Socialist party never resolved the suffrage issue, the W.N.C. always assisted suffrage campaigns in every municipality and every state, it cooperated with the non-socialist suffragists, and even joined them in testifying before the House Judiciary Committee in its hearings on several woman suffrage bills, one of which had been introduced by Socialist Congressman Berger. The W.N.C. sent observers to the conventions of the N.A.W.S.A. and shared credit with the suffragists when a state enacted woman suffrage.[23]

Most socialist women believed that the suffragists were short-sighted; they reasoned inadequately on the basis of natural, that is, political, rights, while socialist women stressed economic and social questions, and realized that the ballot was not an end in itself. Still, some socialist women considered

Caroline A. Lowe. (Courtesy of Sarah A. Kerr.)

suffrage a major goal, calling it as important as the demands of labor, while others stressed woman suffrage as a step toward socialism, and a number noted that to delay woman suffrage until the revolution would be as unreasonable as delaying the eight-hour day. To those who argued that women themselves had to energize their cause outside of the socialist movement, party feminists asked if worker propaganda should be set aside until the workers awoke.[24]

The issue crystallized at the party congress in 1910. By then, the Woman's National Committee under Simons had embarked on a sweeping educational campaign to convince women that the suffrage struggle should not be "a pure and simple feminine affair" but, rather, a class-conscious movement. Nonetheless, the debate demonstrated that a large number of women delegates favored cooperation with suffrage groups. An emotional discussion culminated in the defeat of a resolution to support the suffrage movement. Thus party doctrine still sought to restrict suffrage activity to internal efforts, and the Woman's National Committee's main thrust continued to be encouraging every local and state organization to establish a woman's committee which, in turn, would push suffrage. And yet at the next convention, when the feminist movement within the party was still at its height, a delegate questioned whether or not a belief in woman suffrage was necessary to a commitment to socialism.[25]

Aside from the Woman's National Committee and the woman's columns in the various socialist newspapers, socialist activity within the party structure was limited to the party's Information Department. In 1914 this party clearing house contacted the state secretaries of seven states with full or partial woman suffrage, and determined that, despite voiced fears, women voters were not adversely affecting the movement. The department examined the historical experiences of states with woman suffrage and also surveyed the effect of minimum wage laws for women across the country. The efforts of the Information Department, like the W.N.C. itself, were focused on social reforms rather than the theoretical impossibility of emancipation within the capitalist structure.[26]

Socialist state legislators introduced a great number of bills and resolutions which either directly related to women or were thought to appeal to them. In addition to measures on behalf of woman suffrage, legislators introduced bills for women to serve as jurors, for free school lunches and textbooks, child labor legislation and protection for the rights of illegitimate children, minimum wage laws, Mothers' and Widows' Pensions, and various other protective measures such as maximum hours and rest periods. In contrast, the national platform of the Socialist party in 1916 offered women only the equal franchise and the Mothers' Pension. Aside from those commitments, the national party apparatus was likely to turn to women only when policy required demonstrations and petitions against militarism, conscription, or war itself. Such appeals to socialist women were issued during the mobilization of American troops on the Mexican border and during the World War. Thus, women were still channeled into innocuous and undemanding areas without real responsibility. As mothers, women could always be counted on to provide antimilitary troops.[27]

But in several of the states and in various locales, the socialist woman's movement was growing into an energetic and imaginative, expansive focus for party activity. Based on their earlier socialization, many socialist women sought to tap segments of what could be termed a woman's network. Many turned to lyceums and chatauquas to interest women who might be intimidated by direct socialist approaches. In California, for example, a socialist chatauqua was held in 1909. Elsewhere in the West, women sponsored party booths at state and county fairs; they pioneered weekly or monthly party suppers in Pennsylvania, Washington, D.C., and elsewhere; and they arranged for entertainments and speakers as they caravaned out to workers in lonely mining camps in Kansas. Various approaches were used in order to transform public schools into community centers so that party activities could encompass the entire family. Plays were presented during strikes here and there to raise funds and to lift morale.

Monthly reports of the state correspondents recorded new party members, listed sympathizers, and informed the general correspondent of the names of local women organizers and speakers. Newly organized woman's committees sometimes revived an entire area. In Nevada in the summer of 1913, for example, ten new locals were 50 percent female in membership. In Utah, it was reported, women of the Mormon faith who were hesitant to join the party, nevertheless participated in party activities. Women even held statewide socialist conferences in New York, Massachusetts, and Kansas. The woman's effort, thus, was developing grassroots and a responsiveness to local conditions and emerging needs. The socialist woman's movement, in but not of the party through its separate bureaucracy, was succeeding in minimizing isolation, providing role models and opportunities for leadership, stimulating awareness and organization, and apparently spreading socialism.[28]

In regard to policy, most socialist women accepted the revisionist and gradualist direction of the party. With a few exceptions, socialist women by their votes, statements, and writings supported the reformist wing of the party which controlled the bureaucracy and policy. But while most of the women activists agreed with mainstream party thinking, their distance from party responsibilities granted them some independence in policy formulation,[29] including the paramount issues of these years which revolved around the party's relationship with organized labor. In the winter of 1909-1910 a party crisis erupted stemming from failure to attract large numbers of working people. Eventually all party leaders polled by the *International Socialist*

Review disavowed the idea of forming a separate labor party. Not one of the two dozen polled was a woman as only candidates for the National Executive Committee were interviewed, and thus women played no part in the discussion.[30]

The Wobblies, too radical a group for the tastes of most party officials, enjoyed the support of some women socialists. A woman organizer, Ida Crouch-Hazlett of Montana, argued unsuccessfully against party discouragement of any evidence of worker solidarity. When the Industrial Workers of the World (IWW) led so-called free speech fights on the west coast, using civil disobedience to publicize the closing of street corners to their soapbox speakers, Kate Sadler of Washington and Marguerite Prevey of Ohio joined a minority effort to force the party to give moral support to the Wobblies' struggle. In 1912, the party in convention amended its constitution to make an endorsement of sabotage, considered an IWW tactic, grounds for expulsion from the Socialist party. Prevey argued that such a move could only assist capitalists in the protection of private property. Women delegates divided over the amendment, fifteen supporting it and nine opposing. As a postscript, the IWW leader, Big Bill Haywood, was soon manipulated out of the party and recalled from the N.E.C. in an extraordinary procedure. Thirteen of the three-dozen activists writing to condemn the railroading tactics were women.[31]

Another issue concerned a party compromise on the subject of immigration restriction. Despite its avowed internationalism, the Socialist party did not wish to contravene the restrictionist policy of the American Federation of Labor (A.F. of L.). Socialist women, however, had little difficulty supporting internationalist principles. They tended not to be linked to the A.F. of L. as were many of their male counterparts, and thus some women freely acknowledged that exclusion was a pseudo-issue, merely a bone thrown to satisfy West Coast trade unionists. Josephine R. Cole, a California journalist, argued that labor had not reached an antiimmigrant consensus, and she maintained that the Socialist party had to assume the lead in uniting all races [sic] against capitalism. A Washington State woman, however, at the 1910 party congress, vilified Chinese workers. While such remarks were not extraordinary, one woman, a Finnish delegate from Minnesota, cited the absurdity of the pluralistic United States excluding nationality groups, and took the unusual step of forthrightly denigrating A. F. of L. restrictionism on the grounds of its minority status in the labor movement. But as in various party debates, the voices of the women members tended to be muted, at best. Since they were absent from policy-making positions, intraparty controversies lay in the male domain. Women activists were left to "woman's issues," that is, issues that fell " naturally" to their "place."[32]

Women's concerns as reflected in their writings and speeches related especially to family fragmentation and social problems under capitalism. Not only did the male-dominated party generally reserve these issues for women members, but the life experiences of these women shaped them toward such concerns which then were reinforced by the party. A consensus among socialist women appeared to exist over some issues: the importance of progressive education and the evils of child labor, the capitalist foundation of alcoholism, divorce, and white slavery. Marriage itself was likened to prostitution because some women had to sell their bodies for economic security. On many matters, however, socialist women disagreed. Most stressed the equality of the sexes while a few implied female superiority. A majority appeared to support birth control as a necessary factor in the emancipation of human beings, while a minority—perhaps influenced by Clara Zetkin— viewed increasing numbers of worker's children as assets in the class struggle. Most socialist women welcomed protective legislation for working women, but a vocal handful considered it patronizing and empty reformism. As to the future of the family, a common view held that socialism would emancipate wives from domestic drudgery; under the socialist system, readily available appliances would simplify household chores. But a few stressed the importance of women having an opportunity to be individuals, in addition to being mothers and wives, and theorized that perhaps marriage would become a relic of the capitalist past. Viewing marriage as an economic institution, some suggested that the independence inherent in the new system would drastically alter the marital relationship. Often on such basic questions a Marxist-feminist split was evident. The most radical women in terms of Marxist ideology tended to lack a feminist consciousness.[33]

On the fundamental issue, the Woman Question itself, the division among socialist women was searing. They never reached a solid consensus on the emancipation of women as a legitimate issue for the Socialist party. Those who opposed the Woman Question as an issue maintained that the socialization of property was the only means to insure economic independence for all and, therefore, overt concern for a specific group would simply waste energy. The struggle to raise class consciousness must be waged without regard to sex or color. It was argued that even a direct attack on beliefs in female inferiority would be a tactical error, resulting in a monolithic alliance of men against women. In contrast, the avowedly feminist position emphasized that the unique political and economic tyranny to which women were subject required a special campaign within the class struggle. Women, especially working women, were not only oppressed by capitalism but were also oppressed as the proletariat of the family, as Engels had noted. Many socialist feminists wrote of the double enslavement of women—bearing the burden of class and sex—and the need for double emancipation. Women's economic exploitation was more complex than that of workingmen, as a realistic appraisal of conditions would indicate.[34]

Ironically, many vigorous arguments on behalf of the Woman Question were home-centered, focusing on women's special biological nature and their greater spirituality and sensitivity, and thus were ultimately traditionalist in their thrust. American women were advised by socialist women to join the party because of their unique concerns as mothers, and they "should throw . . . [the] strength of maternal altruism into the only cause that can give equal opportunity for children of the human race." Modern women, editorialized the *Socialist Woman*, have to be taught that socialism is the only way to solve the increasing problems of the family and the home. While often socialist women objected to the view that socialism would permit women to be home full time without social responsibility, nevertheless a consistent theme placed the emancipated woman in that setting. Women party leaders were often praised as model homemakers, examples that socialism would not destroy domesticity. And, indeed, their pride as homemakers and their marital life styles, other than the not uncommon use of the hyphenated name, demonstrated little that set them apart from their bourgeois counterparts. As one woman wrote, "The genuine good old standards need never be lost in gaining the genuine goal of new freedom. . . ."[35]

The vision of socialist women was neither cohesive, incisive, nor innovative. Those who saw women's liberation as a distinct part of the class struggle often did not transcend traditional role assignments and family structure. They, like most sexist male comrades, ultimately viewed the sexes and the family according to standards which the male-dominated institutions of western society had shaped. One socialist feminist might argue that society must be organized so that women, like men, were seen as bearing potential beyond the reproductive. Another might stress that marriage must mean more for women than the termination of their personal aspirations. But no one designed a new family structure to facilitate full female liberation. A basic social transformation was never conceptualized.[36]

The Woman's National Committee, after six years of intense activity, was undercut by forces in the party that either considered the Woman Question irrelevant trimmings or a divisive threat. Thus, in 1914, work on behalf of the socialist woman's movement halted without the resolution of the internal tensions or the further development of programs then maturing. But, logically, if there were no real Woman Question, there was no need for a woman's sector. The aftermath of the national campaign of 1912 witnessed party retrenchment due to membership slippage, a type of leveling off of activity familiar to all political parties following elections. The National Executive Committee embarked on a cost-cutting crusade, involving the cancellation of meetings, publications, and any efforts thought to be unessential. Accordingly, the N.E.C. "withdrew all support from the W.N.C."

The W.N.C. could no longer publish leaflets, field organizers, effect policy decisions, or even maintain its correspondence. No money was budgeted for W.N.C. operations and its meetings were discouraged. Some of the women concluded bitterly that totally eliminating possibly flawed machinery clearly demonstrated that women's organized activities were no more than ornamental to the male hierarchy. May Wood Simons, the dominant figure in the establishment of the Woman's National Committee and the only person to have served on it since its founding, resigned in protest. In 1914 the National Committee discussed the abolition of the W.N.C., and in 1915 such a motion was passed and sustained in referendum. With that stroke of a pen, as it were, the entire structure in which the socialist woman's movement was concentrated dissolved. In the aftermath, a number of women spontaneously demonstrated against the dissolution of their party machinery, while a few women registered their approval, arguing that that mechanism had served to shunt them off to a corner of the party. Most of the protesters emphasized that women would again be invisible in the party and might once more work outside it. A few affirmative action resolutions by men and women were submitted in favor of proportional representation for women on major committees in lieu of a special hierarchy. As a probably not unconnected development, a woman did win election to the N.E.C. for the first time in four years.[37]

In the subsequent years of war and strife, culminating in the party schism of 1919, women resumed the peripheral role they had played earlier, as some had predicted. Only a few of the "exceptional" continued to be prominent, and women made up nearly 6 percent (a loss of 4 percent) of the delegates to the Emergency Convention of 1917 at the start of war intervention. Such an unimpressive figure, as well as the infrequency with which women members were nominated for public office, suggests as little visibility as before. Wartime resolutions for reestablishing a woman's sector were tabled.[38]

The unwanted party-within-a-party which had provided the movement with new sources of energy was ironically snuffed out arbitrarily in the midst of its most dynamic and vital period, just as the Socialist party itself was to be cut down in World War I by forces external to it. No evidence exists to prove a thesis that the woman's movement within the party peaked in 1912 and then declined.[39] Rather, that movement continued to sink roots and to establish an increasingly comprehensive network which, however, was handicapped by its lack of autonomy and by the constant need to fight a rearguard action to convince both men and women of the seriousness and the legitimacy of its effort. In the final analysis, the woman's movement proved a fragile structure because of the lack of a powerful base in the national bureaucracy. Tensions and ambivalence destroyed the separate and parallel movement.

Notes

1. See, for example, "Women and Socialism," in James Weinstein, *The Decline of Socialism in America, 1912-1925* (New York: Monthly Review Press, 1967), pp. 53-63. He does not systematically explore the extent of female integration into the party structure and, moreover, takes individuals' statements and party pronouncements concerning women's rights at face value. Also see Ira Kipnis, *The American Socialist Movement, 1897-1912* (New York: Monthly Review Press, 1972), pp. 260-65, for the only historical consideration of this question prior to the mid-1960s.

2. Edgard Milhaud, "Socialist Propaganda Among Women in Germany," *International Socialist Review* 1 (May 1901): 713-18; Paul Lafargue, "The Woman Question," ibid. 5 (March 1905): 547-59. See lists of delegates, Socialist Party, *Proceedings of the 1904 National Convention* (Chicago: Socialist Party, 1904), p. 16; S.P., *Proceedings* . . . 1908, pp. 16-18; S.P., *Proceedings* . . *1912*, pp. 83-85, 204-08.

3. For a general overview of women's socialist activities, see the *Socialist Woman* 1907-1913 (renamed the *Progressive Woman*, and then the *Coming Nation*; each name change was symbolic of a search for wider support). Arthur Brooks Baker, "Be a Party Builder," *International Socialist Review* 13 (September 1912): 259-62; *Socialist Woman* 2 (August 1908): 16; *Socialist Woman* 3(September 1909): 15; *Socialist Woman* 2 (April 1909): 8; Socialist Party, *Proceedings* . . . *1904*, p. 326; S.P., *Proceedings* . . . *1908*, pp. 10-11; S.P., *Proceedings* . . . *1912*, pp. 205-06; "Plan of Work for Women in Socialist Locals," Woman's National Committee, Socialist Party, 1913. For the autonomous socialist woman's clubs, see Bruce Dancis, "Socialism and Women in the United States, 1900-1917," *Socialist Revolution* 6 (January-March 1976): 109-10.

4. Socialist Party, *Proceedings* . . . *1912*, p. 204. See, for example, the instructions of Oklahoma Assistant State Secretary Winnie E. Branstetter that all speakers work for woman suffrage, in *Socialist Woman* 1 (February 1908): 5.

5. John Spargo, "Woman and the Socialist Movement," *International Socialist Review* 8 (February 1908): 449-55; Theresa Malkiel, "Where Do We Stand on the Woman Question?," ibid. 10 (August 1909): 159-62; Lida Parce, "The Relation of Socialism to the Woman Question," ibid. 10 (November 1909). 442; Josephine Conger-Kaneko, "Are the Interests of Men and Women Identical? A Suggestion to the National Convention," *Socialist Woman* 1 (May 1908): 5. Those women arguing for separate locals actually favored mixed locals but thought they were feasible only where the men were responsive to women's needs and where the women were sufficiently enlightened. Separate locals, never effected, were expected to raise women's consciousness, educate them, and give them the confidence for an active role in mixed locals. But such views led to the necessity of a public denial by the head of the Woman's National Committee that a separate women's organization was their goal. See Josephine Conger-Kaneko, "Separate Organizations," *Socialist Woman* I (April 1908): 5; "Socialist Women Hold Meetings During Convention Week," ibid. 2 (June 1908): 9-10;Theresa Malkiel, "Some Impressions of the New York State Women's Conference," ibid. 2 (August 1908): 12-13; May Wood Simons, "Origin and Purpose of the Woman's Committee," ibid. 5 (July 1911): 6; Josephine Conger-Kaneko,

"Why the Movement Has a Woman's Paper," ibid. 5 (July 1911): 15.

6. Spargo, "Woman and the Socialist Movement," p. 450; Parce, "The Relation of Socialism," p. 442. See also Victor Berger to Morris Hillquit, February 13, 1910, Morris Hillquit Collection, State Historical Society of Wisconsin; Morris Hillquit to Victor Berger, October 16, 1913, Berger to Hillquit, October 23, 1913, Berger to William James Ghent, November 13, 1911, Bronx Socialist Women's Society to Berger, March 8, 1915, Florence Kelley to Berger, May 15, 1911 and also Berger note, July 1912, Socialist Party Collection, Milwaukee County Historical Society; Josephine R. Cole, "The International and Woman Suffrage," Socialist Woman 1 (November 1907): 3. Mary White Ovington, a socialist more active in the National Association for the Advancement of Colored People than in the Socialist party, echoed these concerns, and noted that many writings by socialists featured "not a word . . . on woman and her disabilities, . . ." Mary White Ovington, "Socialism and the Feminist Movement," New Review 2 (March 1914): 114-15. John Spargo and John Work seemed to be the only male party leaders to have believed genuinely in sexual equality. John Work argued for a fuller recognition of women within the party in his "The Party Machinery," Socialist Woman 5 (July 1911): 10. One male state secretary maintained that perhaps only 10 percent of the men in the party actually believed in sexual equality, and he said that the Woman's National Committee ought to make the elevation of men's consciousness a top priority. See Party Builder, August 9, 1913, p. 5.

7. Editorial, "Sparks from the Convention," International Socialist Review 10 (June 1910): 1127-29; Henry C. Slobodin, "The National Socialist Convention of 1912," ibid. 12 (June 1912): 824; Eugene V. Debs, "Women Needed in Campaign," Socialist Woman 2 (August 1908): 4.

8. Malkiel, "Where do we stand?," p. 161. On the manifestation of oligarchic tendencies in the bureaucracy of a radical political party, see Carl Schorske, German Social Democracy, 1905-1917: the Development of the Great Schism (Cambridge: Harvard University Press, 1955), pp. 116-45.

9. See the monthly profiles in the Socialist Woman, 1907-1909. This composite is based on that important primary documentation, a crucial source since the American Labor's Who's Who (1925), the best source for biographies of radicals, lists very few women. Flynn, of course, was closely associated with the IWW rather than the Socialist party. There are few collections of the correspondence of these women; the papers of only those women whose husbands' letters have been saved tend to be extant.

10. Ages are deduced from the internal evidence in the monthly biographies. The women biographers in the Socialist Woman politely omitted the birthdates of their subjects. While Rose Pastor Stokes was more famous than her husband, he rather than she served on the National Executive Committee.

11. See list of delegates, as cited in note 2, for the geographic breakdown.

12. Socialist Party, Official Bulletin 4 (June 1908): 1; ibid. 5 (May 1909): 1; ibid. 6 (May 1910): 4; ibid. 7 (October 1910):1; ibid. 8 (August 1911): 5; Party Builder, January 23, 1914, p. 5. Two women of the Plains States, Caroline A. Lowe of Kansas and Winnie E. Branstetter of Oklahoma, served as the general correspondent.

13. Prizes were given to locals for attracting women members as part of the cam-

paign of the Woman's National Committee, but whatever its efforts or a state's conditions, an individual official could discourage women from joining the party. Socialist Party, *Official Bulletin* 5 (June 1909): 4; ibid. 7 (October 1910): 1; ibid. 7 (December 1910): 2; ibid. 9 (February 1913): 2; *Party Builder*, October 2, 1912, p. 2; October 16, 1912, p. 2; October 23, 1912, p. 2; October 30, 1912, p. 2; January 25, 1913, p. 2; July 12, 1913, p. 4; August 9, 1913, p. 5; August 23, 1913, p. 5.

14. For representative National Committee membership data, see Socialist Party, *Official Bulletin* 6 (January 1910): 4; ibid. 8 (August 1912): 8; *Party Builder*, March 7, 1914, p. 5. The Woman's Department Report in S.P. *Proceedings* of the 1912 National Convention, pp. 204-05, provides information on convention delegations. For other data, see S.P. *Official Bulletin* 5 (July 1909): 4; ibid. 5 (September 1908): 1; ibid. 7 (September 1910): 3.

15. A letter to the editor summarized these views by stating that unfortunately a special appeal to women was necessary due to their capitalist-induced conservatism. See *Socialist Woman* 1 (July 1907): 8, and also, "Grace D. Brewer," (a biographical study), ibid. 1 (January 1908): 2; Josephine Conger-Kaneko, "Separate Organizations," ibid. 1 (April 1908): 5; Ida Crouch-Hazlett, "Women's Organizations," ibid. 2 (September 1908): 11. One woman argued that any desire for separate locals was an unfortunate indication of social norms; see Mila Tupper Maynard, "Woman Suffrage as Observed by a Socialist," *International Socialist Review* 5 (January 1905). W.N.C., "Plan of Work for Women in Socialist Locals," Chicago, 1913; *Party Builder*, August 28, 1912, p. 3; May 31, 1913, p. 2; September 13, 1913, p. 5; September 20, 1913, p. 5; March 7, 1914, p. 5. Informal talks on the cost of living and on shoddy consumer goods were considered especially good openers when approaching potential women members. *Party Builder*, December 25, 1912, p. 2.

16. S.P., *Official Bulletin* 7 (October 1910): 1; ibid. 8 (June 1912): 3, 4; *Party Builder*, October 30, 1912, p.2; November 20, 1912, p. 2; December 25, 1912, p. 2; March 26, 1913, p. 2; July 19, 1913, p. 4; October 18, 1913, p. 5; February 14, 1914, p. 5; March 7, 1914, p. 5.

17. Copies of the various Woman's National Committee leaflets can be found in the files of the Socialist Party, National Office Papers, Duke University. A discussion on possible leaflet topics can be traced in the *Minutes* of the Woman's National Committee meeting of May 20, 1910, which appears in S.P., *Official Bulletin* 6 (May 1910): 4. See also ibid. 5 (November 1908): 2, and ibid. 5 (August 1909): 3, and *Party Builder*, May 10, 1914, p. 5.

18. Winnie E. Branstetter, "Woman's National Committee Enters a New Field of Activity," May 28, 1913, Socialist Party, National Office Files, Duke University; S.P., *Official Bulletin* 4 (May 1908): 2; ibid. 5 (May 1909): 2; ibid. 7 (August 1911): 5; ibid. 8 (November 1911): 2; ibid. 8 (March 1912): 2; ibid. 8 (June 1912): 4; *Party Builder*, May 31, 1913, p. 2, July 19, 1913, p. 4, July 26, 1913, p. 5, November 15, 1913, p. 5. The independent *Socialist Woman* editorialized on the need to elect a woman or several women to the party executive, arguing that women knew best their own condition. See *Socialist Woman* 1 (January 1908): 6. The *International Socialist Review* editorialized in the same vein in its issue of January 1909 (vol. 9, p. 535).

19. A 1908 survey of the membership showed that of 325 women members responding, 177 were housewives; one-third were in the 30-45 age bracket, with the

rest evenly divided between younger and older women. S.P., *Official Bulletin* 5 (April 1909): 2; ibid. 8 (June 1912): 4; Socialist Party, *Proceedings* of the 1912 National Convention, p. 205; *Party Builder*, May 31, 1913, pp. 3-4; May 16, 1914, p. 5; *American Socialist*, January 1915, p. 4.

20. S.P., *Official Bulletin* 4 (May 1908): 2; ibid. 6 (August 1910): 5; ibid. 8 (July 1912): 4; ibid. 9 (October 1912): 8; *Party Builder*, May 31, 1913, p. 2; January 10, 1914, p. 5; March 14, 1914, p. 5; June 6, 1914, p. 3; "From the International Congress," *Socialist Woman* 4 (October 1910): 2-3. See also, Second International Conference of Socialist Women, *Program*, 1910, Copenhagen (bound with *Report* of the Socialist Party Delegation to the International Socialist Congress, 1910, at International Institute of Social History, Amsterdam) and Socialist Labor Party, *Report* of the Socialist Women of Greater New York to the International Socialist Congress, 1910, Copenhagen.

21. Socialist Party, *Proceedings* . . . 1912, pp. 88,207; *Party Builder*, October 11, 1913, p. 5; S.P., *Official Bulletin* 8 (September-October 1911): 3; ibid. 6 (May 1910): 4; ibid. 8 (September 1912): 7. The issues of the *Party Builder* in 1913 and 1914 provide a good overview of the W.N.C.'s growing relationship with the foreign-language contingent. Apparently the first W.N.C. formal consideration of immigrant women occurred in 1911. See S.P., *Official Bulletin* 8 (July 1911): 1.

22. Contradictory data exist on the percentage of women in the foreign-language federations; the percentages used in the text seem the most reasonable (an unlikely listing of the Hungarian federation as 20 percent female was dismissed as suspect). Centers of activity for foreign-speaking socialist women were clearly New York City, Chicago, and some Finnish-dominated rural areas. *Party Builder*, May 31, 1913, pp. 3-4; July 5, 1913, p. 5; November 1, 1913, p. 4; February 7, 1914, p. 3; February 21, 1914, p. 5; May 23, 1914, p. 5; S.P., *Official Bulletin* 7 (August 1911): 5; ibid. 8 (June 1912): 4.

23. Corinne S. Brown, "Votes for Women," *Socialist Woman* 1 (February 1908): 4, criticizes the International's 1907 position at Stuttgart against collaboration with the suffrage movement. The Socialist party debate on this point is summarized in "Sparks from the Convention," *International Socialist Review* 9 (June 1910): 1126-27. See also Ida Crouch-Hazlett, "The Socialist Movement and Woman Suffrage," *Socialist Woman* 2 (June 1908): 5. A letter from M. J. Scanlon to Winnie E. Branstetter, Carson City, Nevada, February 22, 1915, indicates that the Nevada state suffrage movement credited local socialist help for its triumph at the polls the previous November. See letter in S.P., National Office Files, Duke University. S.P., *Official Bulletin* 6 (April 1910): 2; ibid. 8 (November 1911): 7; ibid. 8 (April 1912): 4; ibid. 8 (May 1912): 3; ibid. 9 (December 1912): 1; *Party Builder*, May 31, 1913, p. 2.

24. Cole, "The International and Woman Suffrage," pp. 1, 3; Lena Morrow Lewis, "Woman Suffragists and Woman Suffragists," *Socialist Woman* 1 (February 1908): 3; Brown, "Votes for Women," p. 4; Winnie E. Branstetter, "Socialist Party Should Make a More Active Propaganda for Female Suffrage," ibid., p. 5; Anna A. Maley, "The Suffrage and Freedom," ibid., p. 10; Crouch-Hazlett, "The Socialist Movement," p. 5; "First State Conference of Woman's Socialist Union of California," ibid. 3 (June 1909): 9; "Women at the Convention," *International Socialist Review* 7 (June 1908): 782; Parce, "The Relation of Socialism," p. 443.

25. "Open Letter to Socialists from Woman's National Committee," *Socialist*

Woman 3 (September 1909): 15-16; May Wood Simons, "Aims and Purposes of Women's [sic] Committee," ibid. 3 (October 1909): 2; E.C.U., "The Suffrage Question and the Congress," ibid. 4 (June 1910): 5; "Sparks from the Convention," pp. 1126-27; Socialist Party, *Proceedings* of the 1912 National Convention, p. 119; Ira Kipnis, *The American Socialist Movement*, p. 264. E.C.U. was no doubt the party theoretician, Ernest Untermann.

26. See the records of the Information Department of the Socialist Party in the S.P., National Office Files, 1914-1915, Duke University, for correspondence with party officials in states with woman suffrage, for a study of minimum wage laws, and for surveys of states' suffrage patterns.

27. Ethelwyn Mills, ed., *Legislative Program of the Socialist Party: Record of the Work of the Socialist Representatives in State Legislatures, 1899-1913* (Chicago: Socialist Party, 1914), pp. 13-14, 18, 20, 24, 25-26, 33, 38-39; "Massachusetts Socialist Bills," January 15, 1913, listed in Information Department Files in S.P., National Office Files, Duke University; George W. Downing to Winnie E. Branstetter, Sacramento, February 21, 1915, S.P. National Office Files, Duke University; *Official Bulletin* 8 (January 1912): 3; ibid. 8 (June 1912): 4; *Party Builder*, May 2, 1914, p. 2; *American Socialist*, September 5, 1914, p. 3; "Socialist Party Platform," in S.P., *Socialist Handbook* (Chicago: Socialist Party, 1916). As late as fall, 1914, May Wood Simons argued that it was necessary to prod socialist state legislators to introduce woman suffrage bills. See *American Socialist*, January 2, 1915, p. 4.

28. See, for example, S.P., Grand Rapids, "Suggestions for Social Center Work," S.P., National Office Files, Duke University; "News of Organizations," *Socialist Woman* 3 (September 1909): 13, 15; "Conference of Socialist Woman's Committees of Kansas," ibid. (July 1909): 9; *Party Builder*, July 12, 1913, p. 4; August 23, 1913, pp. 1, 5; September 6, 1913, p. 4; November 11, 1913, p. 4; January 7, 1914, p. 5; March 7, 1914, p. 5. S.P., *Official Bulletin* 4 (June 1908): 1; ibid. 9 (March-April 1913): 2. For examples of the extensiveness of the reports of the state correspondents, see S.P., *Official Bulletin* 9 (January 1913): 2.

29. Examples of women leaders' endorsements of reformism are Mila Tupper Maynard, "The Socialist Program," *Socialist Woman* 3 (October 1909): 12; "Hurrah for Milwaukee," ibid. 4 (May 1910): 8; S.P., *Proceedings* of the 1904 National Convention, pp. 244-63. For an overview on party policy, see Sally M. Miller, *Victor Berger and the Promise of Constructive Socialism, 1910-1920* (Westport, Conn.: Greenwood Press, 1973), pp. 6-14.

30. See *International Socialist Review* 10 (January 1910): 594-606.

31. Ida Crouch-Hazlett, "The Other Side," *International Socialist Review* 5 (March 1905): 86-91; Slobodin, "The National Socialist Convention of 1912," pp. 817, 825-27; for a list of Haywood supporters, see ibid., 13: 623; Socialist Party, *Proceedings* of the 1912 National Convention, pp. 61-62, 70-71, 135-37, 127.

32. S.P., *Proceedings* of the 1908 National Convention, pp. 114-15, 120; Josephine Conger-Kaneko, "Notes on the National Congress," *Socialist Woman* 3 (June 1910): 4-5. S.P., *Proceedings* of the 1910 National Congress, pp. 121, 140.

33. "Rose Pastor Stokes," *Socialist Woman* 1 (October 1907): 2; Robin E. Dunbar, "Girls and Bourgeois Philosophy," p. 5; May Walden, "True Home Under Socialism," ibid. 1 (January 1908): 5; "Party Politics and Prostitution," ibid. 1 (February 1908): 2; Mary S. Oppenheimer, "Is It a Handicap?" ibid. 2 (October 1908): 13-14;

Josephine Conger-Kaneko, editorial, ibid. 4 (October 1910): 12; William J. Robinson, "The Birth Strike," *International Socialist Review* 14 (January 1914): 404-06;
Caroline Nelson, "The Control of Child Bearing," ibid. 14 (March 1914): 547-48.

34. S.P., *Proceedings* of the 1908 National Convention, pp. 302-05; Charles Kerr, "Socialist National Convention," *International Socialist Review* 8 (June 1908): 736-37;
Malkiel, "Where do we stand?," pp. 159-61; "News and Views," ibid. 9 (February
1909): 630; 'Hebe,' "Message to Socialist Party Convention," *Socialist Woman* 1
(May 1908): 3; "The National Convention on the Woman Question," ibid. 2 (June
1908): 3-4; "Woman's Socialist League of Chicago Meeting," ibid. 2 (June 1908): 10.

35. Georgia Kotsch, "The Mother's Future," *International Socialist Review* 10
(June 1910): 1099; Spargo, "Woman and the Socialist Movement," p. 453; Elizabeth
H. Thomas, "Why Women Should Be Socialists," *Socialist Woman* 1 (June 1907): 2;
Mila Tupper Maynard "Our Women Delegates to the International—May Wood
Simons," ibid. 4 (August 1910): 10; "May Wood Simons," ibid. 1 (June 1907): 3;
Lena Morrow Lewis, "Letter," ibid. 4 (October 1910): 3.

36. Grace C. Brown, "Why Women Should Organize," *Socialist Woman* 1 (July
1907): 2; Lida Parce, "What is the Woman Question," ibid. 2 (March 1909): 3-5.

37. See the weekly issues of the *American Socialist* from January 1915, to September 1915, especially the letters to the editor for discussion of the dissolution of the
Woman's Department. Sophia Salkova of Cincinnati angrily wrote that the party
pattern showed that women were seen as "the rear end of the movement." Replying
to the comment by a sympathetic John Work that the loss of the Woman's Department reflected an attempt at a unifying effort, she said that by the same logic the
foreign-language federations should be abandoned. See *American Socialist*, September 25, 1915, p. 3. For the decision of the Social Democratic Party in Germany to
provide proportional representation for women members on its various executive
bodies, see Werner Thönnessen, *The Emancipation of Women: The Rise and Decline of the Women's Movement in German Social Democracy, 1863-1933* (London:
Pluto Press, 1969), p. 129.

38. Kate Richards O'Hare and Kate Sadler played possibly the most significant
roles at the Emergency Convention where the party hammered out its antiwar position, as suggested in a summary of the proceedings of the secret sessions of the Committee on War and Militarism. See S.P., *Emergency Convention, Minutes* (summary
of), Fifth Day, April 11, 1917, n.p., Second Day, April 8, 1917, p. 16; S.P., National
Executive Committee-State Secretaries, *Minutes* of the Joint Conference, August
1918, pp. 256-59. At the assembling of what turned out to be the schismatic convention, August 30, 1919, 10 of 137 (or 7.2 percent) of the uncontested delegates were
women. See list in S.P., National Office File, Duke University.

39. This position is argued in Mari Jo Buhle, "Women and the Socialist Party,"
Radical America 4 (February 1970): 51; Dancis, "Socialism and women in the United
States," pp. 126-30.

3

MAY WOOD SIMONS:
PARTY THEORIST

Gretchen and Kent Kreuter

In March of 1899, the Charles Kerr Publishing Company of Chicago issued the first pamphlet in its Pocket Library of Socialism. Entitled "Woman and the Social Problem,"[1] it was written by a young midwestern socialist, a college dropout who had once planned to be a medical missionary in heathen lands, and who had delivered a high school commencement address on "Missionary Enterprise in India."[2] The author was May Wood Simons. The pamphlet was the closest thing to a theoretical tract on feminism and its relation to socialism that the American socialist movement produced.

Over the next two decades, May Simons worked within the Socialist party to elaborate her ideas, modify them under the impetus of need and experience, and help bring about women's equality within the party itself and in the larger society. Her frustrations were considerable, but they were not unique. Like many intelligent, socially conscious women of her generation, she encountered a variety of obstacles that limited the fulfillment of her own capabilities and of the ideas in which she believed. Some of the obstacles were obvious: the man's world of politics, the male power structure of the Socialist party, the harsh realities of capitalism. Some of the obstacles were concealed from Simons herself and from most feminists of her generation. Or, at least, they were obstacles that May Simons and many women like her chose not to admit.

May Wood was born in the 1870s in Baraboo, a small community in south central Wisconsin. As a girl, she was a bright and ambitious student, and she hoped to attend college and receive the training necessary for her to become a medical missionary. Her family, however, were of modest means and could not finance their daughter's education. For that reason, May became a schoolteacher. She taught for two years in Sauk County, Wisconsin, saved her money, and in 1893 enrolled as a student at Northwestern University, where she was at least partially under the wing of relatives.

Her experience at Northwestern was not a happy one, and within two years she had left Evanston and returned to schoolteaching, her dreams of becoming a missionary gone forever, and her religious faith considerably shaken. Several experiences unsettled her in college. She was exposed to Darwinism, which was agitating the world of intellect everywhere in America, but did not fit well with the rural Presbyterianism May had brought with her to Northwestern. What Darwinism did not call into question, a petty theological dispute involving May's relatives did. It did not seem to her that much Christian love was in evidence as they quarreled over the accuracy of a translation of the Gospel of St. John.

May also felt socially out of place at Northwestern. She pledged Pi Beta Phi sorority in her sophomore year, but she was a small town girl of limited financial means, and the companionship of her sorority sisters did not change her feeling of being different.

The doubting spirit these experiences induced in May was reinforced by the personality and interests of her high school sweetheart, Algie Simons. Simons was a farm boy from North Freedom, Wisconsin. In later years he was to be remembered chiefly for his irascible temperament, his ideological somersaults, and his book, *Social Forces in American History*, the first thoroughgoing Marxist interpretation of American history. In 1891 he had gone off to the University of Wisconsin where he was exposed to some of the progressive currents of thought that would reshape America in the coming generation. He served as an assistant to Richard T. Ely when Ely was writing *Socialism and Social Reform*, a book in which Ely declared, "Nothing in the present day is so likely to awaken the conscience of ordinary man or woman . . . as a thorough course in socialism. The study of socialism has proved the turning point of thousands of lives and converted self-seeking men and women into self-sacrificing toilers for the masses."[3]

Algie sent books to May to read, and in person and by letter they discussed the meaning of what they read. In 1897 they were married and, like the men and women Richard Ely had referred to, together went down the road that was to make them "self-sacrificing toilers for the masses."[4] Both had become socialists. Working in Chicago with the Bureau of Charities and the University of Chicago Settlement in the midst of the depression of the 1890s, both grew restive at the inadequacies of settlement and social work. As soon as they were able, they planned to leave in order to do work they believed would more rapidly encourage the development of a just society. Friendly visitors and settlement workers, May wrote a few years later, "professing sincerity in their efforts to assist the laborer . . . cannot see that they form a constant hindrance in his way, as they help to perpetuate the system that binds him."[5]

Escape from settlement work came to Algie Simons in the spring of 1899, at about the same time that May published her pamphlet on "Woman and the Social Problem." He was named editor of the *Worker's Call*, a weekly newspaper sponsored by the Chicago local of the Socialist Labor party, designed both to present a socialist interpretation of the news of the day and to provide educational material that would give workers a better grasp of Marxist thought.[6]

Perhaps Algie and May, who shared so many interests and convictions, discussed between themselves the ideas that emerged in "Woman and the Social Problem." If so, no record remains, and nothing that Algie wrote during this period suggests that the Woman Question was of any particular interest to him. His main concerns were political, for it was in these years, near the turn of the twentieth century, that serious socialists worked to unify a movement that was always splintering into new and vituperative factions. Calming troubled waters, however, was not one of his talents, and before long, ideological disputes had become personal feuds, and Algie was accusing his enemies of reaching "a depth of hyena-like ghoulishness in political tactics never touched by any bourgeois politician."[7]

May Simons's pamphlet, however, reveals a considerable acquaintance with the basic texts of European socialism, nearly all of which enunciated a commitment to sexual equality. To their ideas, May added Darwinian ideas similar to those Charlotte Perkins Gilman had elaborated in *Women and Economics*, published in 1898.[8]

The pamphlet detailed the condition of women, the effects of capitalism upon that condition, the changes that socialism would bring, and the ways in which women could contribute to a socialist victory. It was, in short, both descriptive and prescriptive.

According to May Simons, women constituted a conservative force in American society only because of historical factors that worked together, through the centuries, to make women physically weak, mentally narrow, and politically powerless. If the socialist movement ignored this "large and powerful body," she wrote, "merely because it has no vote, it will lose what could be used for the most effective propaganda work for socialism." To ignore women also meant that when socialism was finally realized, there would be a vast part of the population still in a backward stage. This would, Simons continued, "hinder the realization of the best art and literature and science. The future society would find itself unable to produce the best family life; and this inferiority of woman would bring the degeneration of the race."[9]

If socialist propagandists did not soon tackle the American proletariat, female as well as male, it would be too late. The degraded proletariat would lose the power of intelligent revolt. Further, capitalism, according to May

Simons, though it exploited both men and women in the same way in the workplace, imposed particular hardships upon women and the woman's sphere—the home and family. Oftentimes the home became merely a sweat-shop, a place where all family members worked at starvation wages from dawn to dark. Frequently young, industrial workers earned so little that they could not marry and support families, and therefore indulged in what Simons called "illegal sexual relations." Never, she said, "even among sa-vages" did promiscuous relations of the sexes exist more than in our civiliza-tion of to-day."[10]

Women of the laboring class, Simons continued, suffered also from the small, overcrowded quarters that capitalism had forced on its wage earners. "Confined continuously in one or two small rooms, . . . little wonder that the mother is ill and fretful and work half done." A woman suffered too from her utter lack of educational opportunity. "If she fails to understand quickly the principles of socialism, is it not because our industrial system has well nigh crushed out the power of thought?"[11]

Socialism would change all this: "It is to socialism alone that the home life must look for its rescue and purification." In the socialist utopia, marriage would be based upon mutual affection, not economic needs. Much of the drudgery of the home would be done away with: cooking would be done by scientifically trained cooks; sewing and laundry work would be done in co-operative establishments,—but only, Simons quickly added, if that's what the individual wanted. "This in no way implies that each housewife may not if she so desire [sic] still bake, cook and scrub for herself . . . ."[12]

In the socialist society, Simons continued, women would no longer be economically dependent upon men—whether they chose to remain in the home or work "in the improved and beautiful shop or factory," or to pro-duce "works of art." Because all of these activities were socially useful, all would be rewarded—though Simons did not say exactly how, either in this pamphlet or elsewhere.[13]

Socialism would also mean the complete *political* equality of woman: voting and officeholding. Simons pointed out, however, what many advo-cates of woman suffrage failed to notice: that the vote alone would not bring the emancipation of women. One needed only to look at male suf-frage, she declared. The workingman had the vote, but he hadn't used it to vote for the interests of his class. So too a woman would be equally as op-pressed, even with the vote, unless she understood that "her vote must be used to bring about an industrial revolution that would give her economic freedom."[14] "In but one place," Simons concluded, "is there being an intel-igent effort made to secure equal rights for women and men. That is in the socialist movement."[15]

It was a brave boast. Thoughtful readers might have disagreed on both grounds—that is, that the socialist movement was truly committed to equal rights, or that if it was, it was the only social movement working for equality between the sexes. After all, there was a substantial woman suffrage movement in the United States in 1899: was this not a movement to secure equal rights for women and men? No, by 1899 it was not. It was a movement for the suffrage, pure and simple. Its leaders, unlike their predecessors in the mid-century women's rights movement, did not emphasize equality, but stressed woman's special nature, and how it would transform political activity, bringing the qualities of cleanliness and godliness into government.[16]

This point of view was not expressed in the Simon pamphlet. On the contrary, one of her aims was to show that women and men were alike in being victims of industrialization. "Machinery knows neither sex nor age," she wrote quoting John Hobson, "but chooses the labor embodied in man, woman or child, which is the cheapest in relation to the degree of its efficiency."[17]

The alleged differences between men and women in strength, intelligence, and emotional make-up were not the differences of nature but of environment. In prehistoric times, Simons declared, women were physically strong, and from women came the beginnings of all industry:

She first gathered the bark and branches and made a shelter . . . thus being the first of the architects and builders. She sewed together the skins of animals killed in the hunt . . . . With clay she shaped the first rude bowls . . . . In this stage of society, woman, strong physically, journeyed with the men on their trips, and provided food and clothing for herself and children. Children took their names from their mothers, Simons continued, and through her reckoned their descent.[18]

There was nothing of especial cleanliness of godliness about these prehistoric women, nothing that limited them from full participation with men in the life of their societies or that destined them to be relegated to a separate sphere. Only the passage of time, the institution of private property, and the nature of capitalism had eroded woman's initial equality and placed her in subjection and subordination. If she were now in a separate sphere, that was cause for lamentation, not encouragement.

Was the socialist movement, then, as she claimed, committed to securing equality between men and women? Here the case was more difficult. Friedrich Engels, the socialist founding father from whom May Simons took many of her ideas, believed that woman's inequality was rooted in the system of private property and that monogamous marriage was merely an economic arrangement to secure the descent of property from generation to generation through the family. The first division of labor, Engels had claimed, was between man and woman for child-bearing purposes. The first class opposition was in the development of antagonism between man and woman in marriage, and the first class oppression was that of the female sex by the male. Within the family, the husband was the bourgeois, the wife the proletarian. Presumably Engels, a man of compassion and justice, believed oppression in the home as reprehensible as in the workplace. Presumably. But consistency of thought and action are hard to achieve, and Engels was no more successful than most. There was a great difference between the way he wrote about women's equality and the way he related to women.[19]

The same difference was evident in the socialist movement in general and in the Socialist party of America (SP) in particular. At the founding convention of 1901, where the party attempted to weave together the varied strands of socialism into an effective political force, the party platform declared its commitment to "equal civil and political rights for men and women." Eight women served as regularly elected delegates to that convention, and in the years that followed women served on some subcommittees, led an occasional floor fight, and lobbied for resolutions. They served as organizers, propagandists, pamphleteers, journalists, and lecturers. May Simons herself participated in all such activities. In addition to her writing, she frequently set out on propaganda and lecture tours, either with Algie or accompanied only by her small daughter Miriam. Throughout the Middle West, in Chatauqua tents or second-floor meeting rooms, she brought the message of socialism to all who would listen. And though the party hierarchy was perfectly happy to have her services, neither she nor they ever supposed that this signified a commitment by the SP to female equality.

Here again Engels' ideas, which May Simons shared, reveal in microcosm the ideas and attitudes of most of the movement. Although Engels declared that monogamous marriage was an economic institution designed to safeguard a family's property, he did not believe that monogamy or the family would disappear from a society in which the socialist revolution had taken place. Although women would not be confined to the private domestic sphere, and although they would take part in socially useful production, monogamy would continue. Now, however, marriage would be based upon love, not the need for economic support, and for the first time in human history the individual attraction of a man and woman would shape the formation of families. What Engels was really saying was that the bourgeois ideal—ridiculed as a snare and a delusion when he described its prerevolution exponents—would, in the socialist society, become the reality for all.[20]

Engels seemed to be theorizing that woman's role would expand; she might leave the sequestered privacy of her home and take an active part in the productive sector of the economy, but men's roles would not change. Nor would the family change: its responsibilities would remain pretty much the same as they had been in the capitalistic society. Women would do more. Men would do the same. And the first division of labor—between man and woman for child-bearing purposes—would remain. Would no other inequalities persist under those circumstances?

Engels chose to ignore such questions, and so did May Simons. Within the Socialist party of America, however, one could see a reflection of Engels' thought. The SP was willing to have women do more even before the revolution than the two major parties were willing to permit. This was not equality: it wasn't even a very substantial move away from bourgeois notions of "woman's sphere." Fund-raising bazaars, for example, remained the most notable display of women's activity. Here, women planned the entertainment, prepared and served the refreshments, and made crafted items for sale. Women were rarely dues-paying members of the party, and if they were, their dues were substantially lower than men's—a common bit of chivalry found in many organizations: that is, women were welcomed as members but not obliged to pay dues or, they paid less than men. The concomitant disadvantage was that they should refrain from shaping organization policy. In some ways, it is analogous to protective labor legislation, which is supposed to be a concession to women's assumed limitations, but ends up creating new limitations.

In these early years, the Socialist party, despite its platform declaration on behalf of equal rights, made no effort to demonstrate any concern for equal rights. It did not try to organize women: quite the contrary, most local meetings were held in such places as neighborhood saloons, locations hardly likely to draw women who were probably hesitant about getting involved in political activity at all. When women did join the party, little effort was made to familiarize them with procedures or to educate them in the mores of political participation.[21]

Thus it seems that few men within the SP were persuaded by the logic of May Simons's pamphlet on "Woman and the Social Problem". Women made up about 10 percent of the party's membership in its first decade, and the men did not bestir themselves to increase that percentage in the interest of hastening the revolution.

Socialist women, however, began to organize, despite the official disregard by both the party hierarchy and its rank and file. Even while the national convention of 1904 was in session, a small group of women held sessions in a separate hall for the purpose of organizing a Women's National Socialist Union. In the next two years, separate women's branches of the party sprang up across the country, especially in areas where the party was growing most rapidly.[22] In June of 1907, a new magazine, the *Socialist Woman*, was founded, designed to coordinate news from various women's branches, publish articles on subjects related both to socialism and feminism, and acquaint readers with women who were leaders in the socialist movement. In all of these activities, May Simons played a central role. The very first issue of *Socialist Woman* included a brief biography of May Wood Simons.

"Those persons who are fond of nourishing the delusion that Socialism will destroy the home," the article began, "and that much learning renders womankind un-womanly, invariably find themselves undergoing a readjustment of ideas after they have met with Mrs. May Wood Simons. Slight, refined, cultured, thoroughly feminine in appearance and manner, Comrade Simons is nevertheless one of the most learned women not only in the Socialist Party but among those of the whole land."

Today's reader of these words blushes, as May Simons probably did, though for different reasons. The article concluded, "Mrs. Simons is the mother of a lovely girl, Miriam, . . . and she is the mistress of a home which reflects the culture and good taste of its inmates. She believes in the home and in the family as a social unit." In between these validations of her essential femininity were a couple of paragraphs about her writing, lecturing, and teaching.[23]

Simons wrote several articles for the *Socialist Woman*, and in them she reiterated the concerns she had first expressed in her 1899 pamphlet. She was more radical than her biographer had made her sound. She wrote of the suffrage as an economic necessity, and of the socialist movement as the instrument that could finally bring the political emancipation of woman. She wrote of the two groups of women in the working class: mothers engaged in managing the home, and women actually employed as wage earners in factories and shops. However, as the suffrage movement grew, Simons warned against making compromises with its legions of middle- and upper-class women in order to secure the right to vote. "The women of the ruling class," she wrote, "are quite as class conscious as the men, and the Socialist women must go into this struggle for the ballot with that under-standing. There can be no compromises with organizations of capitalist women."[24]

Simons also wrote about the double burden of home and work that in-creasing numbers of women had to assume, but she did not conclude—as most of her male colleagues probably would have—that the socialist utopia would "free" them from being wage earners. Women, she pointed out, "have work that is more attractive than housework. They WANT THE HOME AND THE CHILDREN AND THE WORK, [sic] but how can it be adjusted?" "Even while the children are young," she declared, "the mother will be a better mother and a better homemaker if she has at least a few hours of work outside the home. Not such as will interfere with the feeding of her child, but such as will deepen and broaden her life."

She had several suggestions: child care, restaurant/cafeteria facilities run by trained cooks, and a new variety of craftperson, the houseworker. They would be "skilled in their trade, cleaners, preferably men, for they are far more able to do this work until a race of stronger muscled women has been bred. These men can be hired by the hour; they will not "live in" as the present domestic worker does."[25] One can see that May Simons's radicalism had its limits. What she did *not* suggest is either of the alternatives that would seem most obvious to a contemporary feminist: the sharing of tasks between husband and wife, or changes in the structure of work and the work day itself.[26]

In 1907, not long after the founding of the *Socialist Woman* in the United States, the Congress of the Second International was held at Stuttgart, Germany, and before its deliberations were over, a special women's rights resolution was passed. Socialist parties throughout the world were urged to make definite provisions for women in their platforms, and to support the suffrage movement.

May Simons did not attend the Stuttgart congress, but her husband Algie did. He sent back dispatches about its deliberations to the *Chicago Daily Socialist*, the newspaper for which he was writing at the time. Although his dispatches covered a number of topics, the Woman Question was not among them.

That cudgel was taken up by another party leader, John Spargo, who scolded male socialists for their indifference, and proposed that a national committee of women be established that would be devoted to specialized propaganda among their sex. Few socialists were deeply moved by Spargo's words, or spurred to action by the recommendations of the Stuttgart Congress. Still, if women could be attracted to the party, it might be worth giving some special attention to that potential constituency. Spargo's proposal became a formal resolution before the SP National Convention in 1908.[27]

Women at the Convention were divided on the issue. A minority believed that because the socialist movement was "the political expression of the working class regardless of sex," the SP should do nothing that would discriminate between men and women or embark on any special campaign for woman suffrage, lest it be deluded into thinking that the real enemy was disenfranchisement, instead of private ownership.[28]

May Simons did not agree. "Eleven years ago," she declared on the convention floor,

when I was new in the work of the Socialist movement, . . . I might have taken the position that is taken by the minority report. Today, when I realize that the Socialist movement, if it is to amount to anything, must deal with conditions as they are today, I know that we cannot ignore the question of how to carry on the propaganda among women.

She reminded the convention of their European comrades, who had endorsed woman suffrage. She called their attention to the example of Finland, where women had received the vote and had become "more efficient workers in the Socialist party than ever before." And she declared unequivocally, in her most feminist statement, "If any one comes before this convention and says that the economic condition of men and women is identical, I must say that that person has had little experience in conditions as they actually are."[29]

Simons's position prevailed—at least officially. The majority report was passed, a Woman's National Committee was elected, and May Simons was chosen as its head. She was nominated as a vice-presidential candidate as well—described by Comrade Freeman of Alabama in his nominating speech as "one who has culture and learning, who is a graduate of one of the greatest universities in the country," and similar nonproletarian encomiums. She ran third in a field of five. Her husband Algie was nominated as a presidential candidate, and he ran last.[30]

The party did not lavishly endow the Woman's National Committee, but it did provide enough money from the SP treasury to staff a field organizer. Some women claimed, in the next year or so, that the SP was truly taking women more seriously than it had in the past. "The woman no longer sits alone at the meetings," one organizer wrote from Indiana. "Now it is a matter of comment if there be no women at the Socialist propaganda meeting; and the men agitators print on their bills, 'Women Especially Invited.'"[31]

In the pages of the *Progressive Woman*—for so the *Socialist Woman* had been renamed in the interest of securing greater circulation—May Simons explained the purposes of the Woman's Committee. It was, she said, intended to "advise and outline methods by which women may best be interested in socialism and brought into the Socialist party, and to keep the need of agitation for suffrage for women before the locals." Each SP local was supposed to appoint a committee of women who were already members. If there were no women members, the local should arrange "a lecture or entertainment which it is believed would interest women and make an effort to get as many women as possible to be present . . . ."[32] After securing the addresses of all the women at the meeting, representatives of the local should call on them in succeeding days, and invite them to future meetings. Once a woman had become an SP member, Simons advised, "Make her feel she is necessary to the local. Give her work to do . . . . Set her to work to educate and secure more members. If she makes errors in the business meetings help her to correct them." Simons was careful to emphasize that the Woman's Committee was in no way separatist: each woman, she declared, kept "in the closest touch with her local, and the local, state, and national organization, and all political issues that (might) arise . . . ." Moreover, all work being done by the Woman's Committee or its representatives was being carried on "in consultation with the party organization, and for the purpose of increasing the strength and power of that organization."[33]

When the SP met in a national congress in 1910, May Simons presented the report of the Woman's National Committee (WNC), which described what progress had been made so far and recommended steps that ought to be taken to win women to socialism and to win suffrage for women. She reminded the delegates once more why there needed to be special propaganda for women:

"The general make-up of woman's trend of thought," she observed, "of her interest and sympathies is, at least for the present, greatly different from that of a man, which does not mean that it is inferior . . . not all people can be reached by the same methods . . . . We do not attempt to apply the same means of propaganda in converting the college man as we do the laborer, the Slav as we do the Anglo-Saxon." Women were beginning to enter the labor force in large numbers, and there their experiences were similar to men's. "But though torn away from the home and her old environments," Simons continued in her reading of the WNC report, "woman still remains a slave to its traditions and superstitions."[34]

To continue the work of the Woman's National Committee, several recommendations were made: greater autonomy for the WNC was seen as essential. So, too, was financial support from the executive committee of the SP. Local committees needed to be formed where they did not yet exist, so that "we may carry on a systematic house propaganda throughout the Nation, as we have come to the conclusion that this is the only means of reaching women in the home—she [who] of all women has been the most neglected." In each industrial area, socialist women ought to elect a strike committee, "to be in readiness whenever any occasion for action appears, as the surest means of gaining the ear of the women in the trades lies in helping them during an economic struggle."[35]

Then came the thorniest issue: woman suffrage and the SP's relationship to it. The WNC recommended that the party amend its platform commitment to equal rights to read,

WHEREAS, Woman's position in industry is of a much lower status than man's as the direct result of her political disqualifications, and
WHEREAS, The Socialist Party is the direct representative of the working class, regardless of sex, therefore be it Resolved, That the Socialist Party demands equal suffrage, regardless of sex, color, or race, and pledges itself to work, advocate and agitate for it.

In order to accomplish this end, the WNC recommended that every SP local hold one meeting a month "for the purpose of agitating the suffrage to women."[36] Some delegates, however, believed that the SP ought to do

more—ought, in fact to work with non-socialist suffrage organizations—
and offered an amendment to that effect. Others, however, thought this
idea unacceptable and cited the Second International's official opposition to
cooperation with suffragist groups.

The suffrage movement in 1910 presented an even more difficult set of
choices than it had in 1908. It was larger and more bourgeois, and it was
virtually certain of victory within the next few years. Could a good Socialist
devote substantial amounts of energy to a cause that counted a Belmont and
a Morgan among its leaders? Could a socialist propagandist preach class
struggle *and* urge cooperation with all other women in the interest of
achieving the vote? The members of the WNC didn't think so. "If you tell
the working woman one moment that we must fight for Socialism," Theresa
Malkiel argued before the convention, "that that is her only salvation; and the
next minute you tell her we are all sisters together—this is a sex struggle, let
us all work together to get the vote—you mix her up and you won't get her
for anything."[37] "I want to be free to give all my strength, to give all my leisure time to the Socialist movement," Esther Laukki declared. "I have no
strength left for a bourgeois ladies organization."[38] Simons's position was
similar. In her cogent and eloquent response, she explained why she rejected
the proposed amendment. Socialists as individuals, she told the convention,
might ally themselves with middle-class women suffragists, particularly in
states where a suffrage law was before the legislature. But to socialists, the
suffrage was *not* an end in itself, but merely the means to the end that all
socialists—male and female—sought: namely, the end of private ownership
of the means of production. "You cannot wipe away the class struggle
among women and say it is just a beautiful sisterhood," she declared. "The
working woman has only a certain amount of energy to expend: if she
spends it in the suffrage movement she will not spend it in the Socialist
movement." Simons was adamant in her conviction that the SP must not
become the tail of any suffrage organization's kite: "While I want the ballot," she concluded, "I don't consider that the great thing; I am fighting for
that as a means to a greater thing. If we spend all our time in building up a
suffrage movement, then when we have obtained the ballot we shall have to
begin all over again to educate the woman to use that ballot intelligently."[39]

The amendment was defeated; the recommendations of the WNC were
adopted as proposed, and the convention went on to other business. The
debate, however, had been prolonged and heated, and it had revealed considerable conflict and ambivalence among the members—and not just about
woman suffrage. It had to do with the more fundamental question of
whether or not the SP was prepared to take women and women's issues
seriously. Algie Simons, never one to avoid a fight, brought the issue out in-

to the open, when the convention chairman had been recognizing only women to discuss the WNC proposals. "If we have reached that point that the part of woman in our movement is a joke, and a laugh, and a sneer, and only women are to take hold of it, then the membership . . . has a long way to go," he declared. "Are [women] to be here because they are pretty things to look at, or because we as men are chivalrous?" he continued, obviously trying to arouse the delegates, "I know of no chivalry in the Socialist movement; I know only equality between Socialist women and Socialist men." The debate went on; the chair kept recognizing women delegates who sought the floor. Simons continued the attack; "I say that the attitude of the chair and those who support him in that, is the very attitude that lies at the base of woman's present position."[40]

But the convention was not to be provoked into grappling with the issue Simons had so irascibly but accurately identified. Only an occasional delegate indicated that Simons's remarks had registered: Delegate Rose of Mississippi thought he'd been accused of not being sufficiently chivalrous and began to describe the blessed effects of chivalry in the South until the chair cut him off in mid-sentence. A female delegate thought women had very little voice in SP conventions and that, on this issue, the men should "keep quiet and listen." Morris Hillquit of New York called Algie Simons "the only excitable lady that we have had on the floor here . . . ."[41]

May Simons said nothing on this subject. In these years, her own way of dealing with what feminists of a later day would call male chauvinism was to operate in two different spheres. This kind of separatism was, in fact, the essence of Simons's activities, despite her official declaration about the dangers of separatism. The evidence is abundant that the SP could not think of women any differently than the stuffiest Victorian gentleman did. That is clear from the way in which Socialists—men and women alike—wrote about its women worthies. It was clear in the *Socialist Woman's* biography of May Simons—"slight, refined, cultured, thoroughly feminine in appearance and manner"—and the same characteristics continued to mark such descriptions in the years that followed. In 1910, for example, May Simons was selected as a delegate to the Copenhagen Congress of the Second International. This time her biographer observed:

It is interesting to note that the woman who seems to me to have reaped the fullest harvest from the new ideals and possibilities of our time both in public and private life happens also to be the most devoted mother of my acquaintance.

The moral was clear:

The genuine good of old standards need never be lost in gaining the genuine good of new freedom and opportunity. It is a satisfaction to have this demonstrated in the self-effaced beautiful little woman who will help to represent American Socialists in the greatest organization the world has known.[42]

Simons herself for the most part observed these same categories and kept the two spheres separate. The Copenhagen Congress again provides a case in point. As part of the Congress, an International Conference of Socialist Women was held, and she attended. "Socialist women in Europe," she wrote describing the significance of the meetings, " . . . are making public opinions on all questions that affect [sic] the welfare of women and children."[43] But when she wrote about the Copenhagen Congress as a whole, she did not mention the women's meeting or women's issues. Instead, she described the mass meetings and speeches, the male notables of the movement, and the growing international solidarity that the meeting had revealed.[44]

When the Socialist party of America was founded in 1901, one of its main concerns was that it be a truly American party, speaking in American accents and addressing American issues. Only in this way, its leaders believed, could the party become a significant political force. Often, however, it seemed that being "American" was really only a synonym for being bourgeois. Nowhere was the party more bourgeois than in its relationship to the Woman Question and in the interrelationship of women and the party. Within the SP, "woman's sphere" prevailed. The only kind of position for which the SP actively sought women candidates was in the field of education. Meta Berger, for example, was a successful socialist candidate for school board in Milwaukee, America's most socialist city, and she held that position for twenty years. May Simons herself ran unsuccessfully for superintendent of schools in Girard, Kansas, when Algie was editing *The Coming Nation* there from 1910-1913, and in 1913 she chaired the SP's National Educational Committee.[45]

In 1912, at the SP National Convention, May Simons again gave the report of the Woman's Committee. Among its recommendations this time were several that dealt with vocational education—a subject she had studied extensively. Immediately, convention members protested that this constituted meddling in matters that should not concern the WNC. Education yes, vocational education no. Comrade Goebel of New Jersey observed that the women might offer recommendations on the conduct of the socialist Sunday schools, but vocational education was quite out of their line.

The report as a whole was hardly a radical feminist document. It did not even hint that women ought to look to a larger world than hearth and home for their fulfillment. "The first duty of a housewife," it declared, "is to her husband, children and home." Still, Simons did have her supporters in the party, who were willing to accept her presence in sectors of the party other than the Women's Committee ghetto: she came close to being elected to the

National Executive Committee (NEC) in 1912, running ninth in a contest to choose seven members. If elected, she would have been the second woman on the NEC.[46]

The frustrations of the Women's Committee increased. After the 1912 election the SP retrenched because of membership slippage. It embarked on a cost-cutting crusade which included withdrawal of all support from the WNC. Even meetings of the committee were discouraged. The party's position was obvious: basically, it had never wanted to think much about feminist concerns. If attention to women's issues would bring women flocking into the Socialist party, then it was willing to give official sanction in the form of money for propaganda pamphlets and some lecturers to a Woman's National Committee. When that didn't happen—when women didn't flock in—the party lost interest in the Woman Question, and when it lost interest, it withdrew financial support as well. Did this have anything to do with SP attitudes toward women? One need only cite a parallel: the party did not lose interest in the labor question and class conflict just because working-men didn't rush to join the party.

At the end of 1914, May Simons, protesting the SP's neglect of the activities and mission of the WNC, resigned from the committee.[47] She took no further role in political activity of the Socialist party. In 1913, the Simonses had moved to Milwaukee, where Algie became the editor of yet another struggling socialist newspaper, the *Leader*, and for a while, May remained a member of the Milwaukee SP local. A highly successful party in the country's most socialist city, its membership was heavily German American.

Sometimes May regretted that she no longer went off on journeys of recruitment and exhortation for the party. When, for example, a violent strike occurred among the miners of Calumet, Michigan, she lamented in her diary, "How I wish I could go there, but these Germans do not imagine a woman can do anything." Expressions of regret like those, however, were few, and they ceased entirely after 1917: in April of that year, the SP meeting in emergency convention to determine its response if the United States should enter World War I, declared its utter opposition to the war. Algie and May Simons were shocked. This was the death-knell for the SP as they had known it. In practical terms, too, they knew that any political party that repudiated the nation in time of war was doomed.[48]

What, then, of May Simons's feminism? It, too, became a casualty of the war. Convinced, from her vantage point in Milwaukee, that America was in serious peril from disloyalty and treason, she threw herself wholeheartedly into the work of "Americanization"—the effort to nurture national loyalty in the hearts of the foreign born. In earlier days, when she had argued for woman suffrage before the conventions of the SP, she had talked of the need to naturalize immigrant working women as quickly as possible, so that they could vote the socialist ticket as soon as suffrage came. Now she argued for naturalization in the interest of national solidarity in time of war.

Two years of May Simons's work culminated in 1919, when a mighty pageant of Americanization was held in Milwaukee. Six hundred and thirteen new citizens were presented before the "altar of liberty," where, the *Milwaukee Journal* reported, "After being accepted as of the United States [they] turned and were met by the Colonial Dames and Sons of the American Revolution, who gave them . . . welcome . . . while the Battle Hymn of the Republic was sung."[49]

When the war ended, evidences of Simons's old feminism, much tranquillized, returned. After the suffrage amendment had been passed at last, she turned to the work of preparing new voters to use their right wisely. In earlier days, she had told her socialist comrades that if working women were not educated to socialist principles before the attainment of suffrage, the vote would be meaningless. Since they had not been so educated, she brushed aside the socialist principles. Since the needs of working women were more difficult to fulfill than she had once thought, she stopped talking about them. Instead, she devoted herself to voter education pure and simple. She joined the League of Women Voters in Milwaukee, and began to lecture widely to the "schools of citizenship" set up under the league's auspices. Later, after she and her family had moved to Evanston, Illinois, she became the state chairman for citizenship training in the Illinois league, and eventually became president of the state organization.[50]

She had, it seemed, become a very bourgeois feminist indeed, participating in activities of all those organizations which she and her sister socialists had deplored back in 1910. The society pages of Milwaukee and Evanston newspapers chronicled her activities under such headlines as "Restore Evanston as West's Athens," and "Women Active in Next Week's Club Affairs." When her League citizenship school was scheduled to open, the *Evanston News-Index* invited women to attend: "Store away a good reserve supply of your best powers of concentration," it reported in the patronizing and breathless style customary to ladies' journalism, "You'll be rolling along so contentedly on these main roads and byways of political wisdom that you'll never once notice the time."[51]

The message that May Simons brought to these citizenship schools was also bourgeois: she urged no particular political principles upon her audience but recommended only that they inform themselves about the issues of the day, study the platforms of each political party, and hold the party accountable once the elections were over. She did, however, believe that political parties ought to stand for efficiency in government—the same kind of efficiency that characterized American offices, factories, and assembly lines. Parties ought to work out "the best methods of doing things as they do in business plants because this United States government is the greatest business in the world."[52]

Emulate the methods of American business and industry? Was this the same woman who had once written of the cruelties of competitive capitalism and of afflictions like the "white plague" that stalked the sweatshops?[53] Her socialist past was nearly obliterated in the wake of her new career with the League of Women Voters. "The Purple Pepper," for example, a publication of Northwestern University, did a feature story on May Simons—under the column, "N.U.'s Own Authors"—in which a veil was carefully drawn over her two decades of work with the SP by describing those years as having been spent "in teaching—and home making."[54]

In other respects, too, she had become almost an archetype of the educated bourgeois clubwoman of the sort Sinclair Lewis caricatured in the 1920's. She had begun attending meetings of her old college sorority, Pi Beta Phi, even before she left the SP, and she was delighted when, in 1921, her daughter Miriam became a Pi Phi too. Mother and daughter also joined the Episcopal church.[55] She didn't seem to regret leaving the uncertainties and disappointments of her radical past. In 1923, while in New York on League of Women Voters business, May visited some of her old socialist friends. "Oh Lord," she wrote in a letter home, "I am more thankful, if I could be, than ever for our new life. Algie it was awful. While I was there the [New York] *Call* office kept calling up having spasms about a threat to stop if it could not get some money tomorrow." She was shocked by her friends' personal habits too: "Henrietta smoked most of the time. She wears bobbed hair and wants to seem very sophisticated. Oh how I did love my family when I saw it all."[56]

At the same time, however, May was not quite as uncritical of her "new life" as she sometimes sounded. "The League is becoming a rich woman's affair," she observed ruefully.[57] Although she continued her citizenship work and her lecturing for the League and other women's organizations, other activities came to occupy increasing amounts of her time and energy. For years she took graduate work in economics at the University of Chicago, and in 1930 she received a Ph.D. No professorship crowned her efforts, nor does she seem to have sought one. She was employed through the 1920s in a variety of jobs. She taught high school, graded papers for courses taught by others, and worked for a time in the personnel department of Montgomery Ward and in the advertising department of the *Evanston News-Index*. Her health, long troubled by undiagnosed but painful digestive disorders, worsened and compelled her to resign from at least one of those jobs.

Her diary, kept off and on for many years, reveals increasing preoccupation with family matters—Algie's latest job and how well he was doing at it, Miriam's progress in college and graduate school and, finally, her joy in her little granddaughter, Elizabeth Ann. May Simons never recanted her feminist beliefs, but it seems, as William James said of his own religious convictions, she put them in a drawer, and when she came back they were gone.[58]

As for the bourgeois nature of her post-socialist feminism, it hardly represented much of a departure from the ideals and behavior she had revealed before, or from the ideals and behavior sanctioned by male socialists. Neither she nor anyone else in the SP before the First World War had envisioned a new family structure that would facilitate the liberation of women. No one called into question the personal and private side of women's lives, and neither Algie nor May Simons approved of unconventional behavior between men and women. Algie frequently wrote articles explaining that the Cooperative Commonwealth, when it arrived, would in no way harm marriage and family. May felt even more strongly. She had never quite approved of Upton Sinclair after he divorced his first wife and wrote a novel describing the adulterous circumstances that led to the whole tangle.[59]

It would be simple to explain May Simons's drift away from feminism as merely the movement to the right that comes, for many, with increasing age. There were, after all, a number of ways she could have gone in the 1920s—a number of worthy goals that might have replaced the socialists' Cooperative Commonwealth as the directing vision of her social and feminist conscience.[60] Instead, she chose the least issue-oriented, the least conflict-producing route of all: citizenship education through the League of Women Voters, and then ultimately no feminist activity at all. Why?

Perhaps she had endured too much conflict. For her, as for most feminists of her generation, the failure to question the conventions of their private lives meant that they shouldered a double burden when they sought a life outside the home. May Simons understood the double burden as she revealed in her socialist writings. Sometimes, it seemed she was writing about herself: "'I am not doing the work I want to do,'" she quoted a "smooth-browed intellectual-looking woman" as saying in a 1913 article she wrote for *The Progressive Woman*:

"When I married I was a teacher and earned my living. I enjoyed my work. Now I do all my housework and care for my children and do the sewing. I love my children and try to do my best for them, but when the day is over I am too tired to read, and I am not keeping pace with the times. I shall soon be a back number. So much of my work is the same thing over and over again. It is mere drudgery." The woman who said this . . . had not been embittered by her life and was bravely trying to meet conditions with a cheerful face, but to the onlooker it was a tragedy.[61]

Although May Simons never said so directly, when one reads her letters and diaries, it becomes clear from the perspective of a contemporary feminist, that her own life was very much marked, her own struggles very much

May Wood Simons. (Permission of the State Historical Society of Wisconsin.)

heightened, by her acquiescence in accepted patterns of marriage and family life. For example, she was a trained and certified teacher, but she had a very difficult time getting teaching jobs. Ceaselessly she worked to prepare herself to "make good"—the phrase is hers—when the opportunity should present itself. Part of the reason that she had a difficult time finding teaching positions is that she moved around a great deal because her husband went wherever his job opportunities were greatest. Over the course of fifteen years they went from Chicago to Girard, Evanston, Milwaukee, and back to Evanston again. May's response, however, was to blame herself—to attribute her failure to obtain a job to her own limitations, and always to resolve to work harder and study more to prepare herself if the chance came.

She took her responsibilities as wife and mother with great seriousness. For twenty years Algie was fired from one tottering socialist publication after another, and his firings filled him with feelings of guilt and failure. Consequently May took upon herself with more than ordinary zeal the role of loyal wife, reassuring her husband that he was really a man of great ability surrounded by inferiors, and that his true greatness would one day be recognized. There is no reason to suppose she didn't believe every word.

After her daughter Miriam was born, May faced parenthood with a deep sense of anxiety. The Simonses' first-born child, Laurence, had died at eighteen months when he accidentally swallowed poison at the home of family friends. Determined that no harm should come to Miriam, May insisted that either she or a member of the family must be with the child every moment. When May went on the lecture circuit, Miriam went too, and sometimes a small voice could be heard calling out from the audience, "Come on Mama!" What one must admire is the fact that May Simons did not abandon her political and professional life in the face of her fears and anxieties, but continued to combine motherhood and activism for many years.

She, however, was unable to feel that kind of pride in herself, or much confidence in her abilities. "I am plodding on," she wrote in her diary about her teaching. "Expect it will be punk," she observed of her forthcoming Wisconsin Citizens Handbook.[62]

She took little pleasure in her public achievements. In her early years as a socialist, she worried and brooded over every public appearance for days, sometimes weeks, before it occurred. She was plagued with attacks of what she called "nervous indigestion" which always increased in intensity as the time for a speaking engagement neared. In later years, she reported her activities without comment. This too was in marked contrast to the compliments she noted about Algie, or her own frequently expressed admiration for his achievements and those of her daughter Miriam. Neither socialism nor feminism brought her the satisfaction that her family life seemed to, and so it is probably not surprising that the former were eclipsed, ultimately, by the latter. The story is a familiar one, the choice common.

Nevertheless, her achievement was considerable. None of her personal misgivings seem to have been visible in her public person. She wrote and spoke with assurance; she travelled widely; she was known and respected by socialists in Europe as well as America. She translated the works of German socialists, helped edit several socialist newspapers and periodicals, and wrote solid, informative articles on a number of subjects. Another generation passed before the issues she had touched upon in 1899 and through the early years of the twentieth century were truly engaged by American feminists. Only in the 1960s did the young women of the civil rights movement begin to question the private relationships between men and women and set forth the conviction that there must be changes in the private sphere before women can attain full equality with men. In that sense, feminists have gone far beyond May Simons. But in other ways, American feminists are still grappling with the issues that she raised in terms of socialist ideology: the relationship between an essentially middle-class feminism and the working classes of America and the world.

Notes

1. A month later Kerr published "Woman and the Social Question," also by May Simons and also listed as No. 1 in the Pocket Library of Socialism. The two works are almost identical in content, although the order and arrangement of material are different, and the later publication devotes somewhat more attention to woman's emotional nature and her interest in the personal rather than the ideological.

2. *Sauk County Democrat*, June 18, 1891; *Baraboo Republic*, June 4, 1891.

3. Richard T. Ely, *Socialism and Social Reform* (New York: Crowell, 1894), p. 145.

4. This account of May Simons's early life is taken from Kent Kreuter and Gretchen Kreuter, *An American Dissenter: the Life of A.M. Simons* (Lexington: University of Kentucky Press, 1969), pp. 36-38.

5. May Wood Simons, "How I Became a Socialist," *Comrade* 2 (November 1902): 32.

6. Kreuter and Kreuter, *American Dissenter*, p. 41.

7. *Worker's Call*, September 9, 1899.

8. There is no evidence that May Simons had read *Women and Economics*. She speaks of Gilman in 1911 in a letter to Algie, "Thursday Charlotte Gilman and I are the guests at a dinner," but without further comment. May Simons to Algie Simons, February 13, 1911, in A. M. and May Simons Papers, State Historical Society of Wisconsin, Madison, Wisconsin. Hereafter cited as Simons Papers.

9. May Wood Simons, *Woman and the Social Problem* (Chicago: Charles Kerr Publishing Co., 1899), pp. 5-6.

10. Ibid., pp. 20-21. This is, of course, an erroneous but, in 1899, still commonly accepted view of the evolution of marriage and family—from the promiscuity of the savages to the monogamy of Victorian gentlepersons—which saw any deviation from that pattern as "anti-evolutionary," a reversion to "primitive practice."

11. Ibid., pp. 21-22.

12. Ibid., pp. 22-23.

13. Ibid., p. 23. Perhaps May Simons was just as stumped as everybody else in determining how to achieve "economic justice" for the homemaker. In 1978, the Bernays Foundation offered a $3,000 prize for the best essay on this very question of rewarding, financially, the woman who chose not to work outside the home.

14. Ibid., p. 24.

15. Ibid., p. 29.

16. This view of the latter years of the suffrage movement, now a commonplace of historical interpretation, was first emphasized in William O'Neill's *Everyone Was Brave: The Rise and Fall of Feminism in America* (Chicago: Quadrangle Books, 1969).

17. Simons, *Woman and the Social Problem*, p. 15.

18. Ibid., pp. 7-8.

19. For example, when Engels heard that Florence Kelley was offended because he had not met with her while he was in the United States—she had translated his *The Condition of the Working Class in England* and had long been active in radical causes—he wrote to a friend, "[Florence Kelley] seems to be hurt by a breach of etiquette and lack of gallantry . . . . But I do not allow the little women's rights ladies to demand gallantry from us; if they want men's rights they should also let themselves be treated as men." (Quoted in Alice Rossi, ed, *The Feminist Papers* [New York: Bantam Books, 1973], p. 475.)

20. Friedrich Engels, *The Origin of the Family, Private Property and the State* (New York: International Publishers, 1942). Excerpts from this essay are easily accessible in various paperback editions. See, for example, Rossi, *Feminist Papers*, pp. 480-95.

21. This was pointed out by Socialist John Spargo, as noted in Sally Miller, "Women in the Party Bureaucracy: Subservient Functionaries," supra, pp. 14-16.

22. Sally Miller, "Women in the Bureaucracy," ibid.

23. "May Wood Simons," *Socialist Woman* 1 (June 1907): 3.

24. May Simons, "Economic Reasons for Woman Suffrage," *Socialist Woman* 1 (February 1908): 6.

25. May Wood-Simons, "Revolution in Housework," *Progressive Woman* 7 (June-July 1913): 9.

26. On the sharing of household work see, for example, Pat Mainardi, "The Politics of Housework," reprinted in June Sochen, ed., *The New Feminism* (Lexington, Mass.: D.C. Heath Co., 1971), pp.113-19. On restructuring work, see, for example, Rosemary Ruether, "Working Women and the Male Workday," *Christianity and Crisis* 37, no. 1 (February 7, 1977): 3-8.

27. Mari Jo Buhle, "Women and the Socialist Party," *Radical America* 4 (1970): 42.

28. Socialist Party, *Proceedings of the 1908 National Convention* (Chicago: Socialist Party, 1908), p. 302.

29. Ibid., pp. 303-04.

30. Ibid.

31. Quoted in Buhle, "Women and the Socialist Party", *Radical America* 4 (1970): 44.

32. May Wood Simons, "Aims and Purposes of Women Committee," *The Progressive Woman* 3 (October 1909): 2.

33. Ibid. See also, for example, May Wood Simons, "Origin and Purpose of the Woman's Committee," *Progressive Woman* 5 (July 1911): 6.

34. Socialist Party, *Proceedings of the 1910 National Congress* (Chicago: Socialist Party, 1910), p. 178.

35. Ibid., p. 180.

36. Ibid.

37. Ibid., p. 185.

38. Ibid., p. 188.

39. Ibid., pp. 210-11. Simons had articulated these ideas in almost the same way two weeks before the convention opened, in an article for the *Milwaukee Journal*. See May Wood Simons, "Should Women Want to Vote?", *Milwaukee Journal*, April 29, 1910. Clipping in box 5, Simons Papers.

40. Socialist Party, *Proceedings of the 1910 National Congress*, pp. 188-89, 190.

41. Ibid., pp. 193, 198, 199.

42. Mila Tupper Maynard, "Our Women Delegates to the International: May Wood Simons," *Progressive Woman* 4 (August 1910): 10.

43. May Wood-Simons, "Especially for Women: High Cost of Living," *Coming Nation*, November 26, 1910, p. 4.

44. See, for example, May Wood Simons, "Welding International Bonds," *Coming Nation*, October 1, 1910, p. 3.

45. Miller, "Women in the Party Bureaucracy," p. 18, and Kreuter and Kreuter, *American Dissenter*, p. 137.

46. Kreuter and Kreuter, *American Dissenter*, p. 137. Lena Morrow Lewis was elected to the N.E.C. in 1909.

47. Ibid., p. 150. In 1915, the W.N.C. was officially abolished.

48. Ibid., p. 149 and p. 163.

49. Quoted in ibid., pp. 168-69. She resigned from the Americanization committee not long after, complaining that it was being taken over by a group of "extreme reactionaries."

50. Ibid.

51. Miscellaneous clippings, undated, box 5, Simons Papers.

52. "Big Question Referendum on Wet and Dry at Election League, Speaker Says," *Moline Daily Dispatch*, September 30, 1926.

53. See, for example, her short story, "Ground in the Mill," *The Coming Nation*, September 10, 1910, p. 5.

54. "N.U.'s Own Authors: May Wood Simons Honored in Several Fields," *The Purple Pepper*, June 7, 1923, clipping in Simons Papers.

55. Diary of May Wood Simons, entry of December 6, 1921, typescript p. 24, Simons Papers.

56. May Simons to Family, July 23, 1923, and May Simons to Family, undated, 1923. The second letter is clearly from the same trip. Simons Papers.

57. Ibid., undated.

58. Diary of May Wood Simons, typescript, pp. 22-25, Simons Papers, covers these years.

59. On A.M.'s views of family see, for example, "After-Election Work," *International Socialist Review* 5 (December 1904): 304. On May's views of Sinclair, see typescript comments of Miriam Simons Leuck, Simons Papers.

60. J. Stanley Lemons describes many of them in *The Woman Citizen: Social Feminism in the 1920s* (Urbana: University of Illinois Press, 1973).

61. May Woods-Simon [sic], "Household Work: the Belated Industry," *Progressive Woman* 7 (May 1913): 4.

62. Diary of May Wood Simons, entry of April 29, 1919, typescript pp. 22-23, Simons Papers.

4

LENA MORROW LEWIS: HER RISE AND FALL

Mari Jo Buhle

> There may also be those who will see in her a soft and gentle heart for which her intelligence finally taught her to construct a shield—more or less effective—against buffetings which would have destroyed or, worse still, maimed her.
>
> David Graham Phillips
>
> *Susan Lenox: Her Fall and Rise*

Lena Morrow Lewis was one of the most prominent and influential women in the Socialist party during its prime. While women represented at most only 10-15 percent of the party's national membership, Lewis managed to carve a niche for herself within the leadership. In 1909 she became the first woman to be elected to the National Executive Committee, and in the following year served as the party's delegate to the prestigious International Socialist Congress in Copenhagen. Forty years old, Lena Morrow Lewis had reached the peak of her political career. Although her commitment to social reform was life-long, from her first efforts as a temperance agitator in the 1890s to her last stand as an uncompromising socialist during World War II, it was during the first decades of the twentieth century that she gained both the recognition and satisfaction only a flourishing movement can provide.

Lewis excelled because she was an unusually talented organizer and popular lecturer. In a period when most socialist strategists believed that the road to the Cooperative Commonwealth was paved with electoral victories,

Lewis's activities on behalf of the party consisted of touring the country, setting up party locals, and preaching a neatly conceptualized sermon on "scientific" socialism. She saw her task as educating the citizenry, for like others in her milieu she assumed that only an intelligent, well-organized working class, through a political party, could capture the reins of government. She never strayed from this mission.

Lena Morrow Lewis had more resources, however, than merely an aptitude for political agitation: she enjoyed the loyal support of a small but highly visible socialist women's movement. During her years of prominence, women in the Socialist party had secured a place of importance for the Woman Question, had established a national committee structure for their own political work, and had virtually assured the ascendancy of at least a few capable women to leadership positions. Socialist women took pride in those among them who made a mark on the larger movement. They felt, rightfully, that through their own struggles they had paved the way, and they were eager to publicize the accomplishments of their comrades, thus throwing light on their own movement. Socialist women frequently prepared short sketches of prominent women like Kate Richards O'Hare, May Wood Simons, and Rose Pastor Stokes and offered these eulogistic essays to the press. Lena Morrow Lewis received a full share of this publicity, and indeed graciously supplied a host of colorful anecdotes about her own adventures. She was regularly spotlighted as an exemplary figure, and always touted as a "first" among women. Wherever she traveled, Lewis could reap the benefits of this attention and find a ready-made constituency eager to extend hospitality and assist her work.

Lewis nevertheless felt ambivalent about the woman's sector of the socialist movement. She supported women's struggle for equality, steadfastly clung to her own woman's rights principles, and attacked the ever-present elements of sex discrimination within the party. At the same time, she refused to endorse any programs that might guarantee women an autonomous, collective role in organizational affairs. As the party, in her mind, demanded absolute loyalty from all comrades, feminists who inclined to profess their socialism independently could not but appear as detractors or alien critics. Lewis insisted that, regardless of the difficulties, women should put aside their discomfiture at the organization's masculine character. In a strangely individualistic way, she asserted that female self-emancipation was essentially a matter of will and persistence, and through the development of these character traits rather than any special pleading for their sex, women would emerge from their age-old servitude.

Although inappropriate for most women—and inadequate ultimately for herself—the norms of a "strong-minded woman" gave Lewis a star by which she steered her own course. Perhaps better than any other individual of her generation, Lewis exemplified the grass-roots woman reformer transformed into hardened socialist agitator and leader. She possessed the necessary stamina. Simply to become a pioneer organizer required a toughness and inner light, a resilience against the many obstacles facing political women in those presuffrage days. To be a socialist required a great deal more. In grafting on to her reformer's vision a roughly Marxian conception of historical materialism and a faith in working-class education, Lewis created a role for herself that few women were willing to undertake, that of a woman organizer in a "male" culture. This role would require her to stay on the road for years on end, to form easy relationships with hundreds if not thousands of comrades, and to devote energies selflessly without thought to home and family life. Lewis's images of herself on the open trail, in the backwoods of California, the Pacific Northwest, and Alaska, riding the service locomotive to lumber camps, dog-sledding in subzero weather—images she liked to paint vividly for her admirers—show how she relished this role. In fact, for more than a score of years, Lewis continued a series of exploits slightly larger-than-life for most women, extraordinary for any socialist.

As a youth, Lena Morrow Lewis developed a political style that would mellow over the years but always retain a characteristic vitality. At the center was a strong belief in woman's potential as a social mover, a faith that would deepen as she spent a decade training in the woman's movement. Like hundreds of small-town, midwestern Protestant women at the turn of the century, Lena traversed a seemingly unlikely path from Christian philanthropy to temperance and woman suffrage and finally to socialism. In her mind, the climb was upward. At each ideological plateau she renewed her commitment to humanity, and her sense of dedication never wavered. By the time she joined the Socialist party in 1902, Lena Morrow Lewis had already cultivated the self-discipline and determination that would carry her through decades of difficult political work.

Born in 1868 in the small town of Gerlaw near Monmouth, Illinois, Lena grew up at a time when thousands of American women were preparing for a life of Protestant social service. Before the Civil War, many women had been active in Bible, tract, and cent societies and various volunteer agencies, and a few had joined their husbands as foreign or domestic missionaries. But in the late 1860s and 1870s women entered church welfare work on a genuinely large scale. Following the Social Gospel then in fashion, many denominations encouraged women to form auxiliary societies to help the poor, sick, and destitute, and the most far-sighted ministers went so far as to deem women's participation critical if the church were to survive the secular and materialistic temptations of the Gilded Age. By the 1880s, the German-American Protestant churches and Methodists led the field in organizing female communicants, with their sisterhoods and deaconess movements establishing women in the vanguard of missionary and charitable work. Other churches also sponsored a wide range of activities, from lend-a-hand clubs, friendly societies, women's employment and sewing circles to day nurseries. Most were managed by boards of female governances, and therefore required programs to train women for administrative leadership as well as for prescribed charitable work.[1]

Lena, christened Martha Lena Morrow, was nurtured in this new religious environment. Her father, Rev. Thomas G. Morrow, had been ordained a minister in the United Presbyterian Church shortly before her birth and served as pastor of the oldest church in Warren County, Illinois, from 1869 to 1873. Her mother, Mary Story Morrow, was active in the local Woman's Missionary Association and undoubtedly reared her daughter to acknowledge her duty as a Christian woman.[2] As in the New Testament verse extremely popular among these groups, wherein Jesus suggests that Mary and Martha put aside their kitchen duties and listen to His teachings, the Morrow women certainly felt the call. From a very early age, Lena taught Sunday school.[3] Later, the editor of the campus paper at Monmouth College, a small Presbyterian denominational school, cited Lena Morrow at her graduation as best suited for the pulpit.[4] Lena chose instead a related mission, the social ministry embodied in that great catalyst of late nineteenth-century women's organizations: the Woman's Christian Temperance Union (W.C.T.U.).

Lena joined the W.C.T.U. just as Frances Willard was reaching the peak of her popularity and influence within the organization. Willard had taken over the leadership in 1883 and had transformed the W.C.T.U. from a holy crusade against drink into a grand political movement with far-reaching goals. She had introduced the "do-everything policy," that within ten years of her presidency had spawned thirty-nine departments to address the great issues of the day, and "that blessed trinity of movements," temperance, woman's liberation, and labor. While Willard continued to stress the Social Gospel side of temperance work, she gave it an increasingly secular and so-cialistic tinge. By the 1890s, she was openly preaching the harmony of Christianity and socialism and urging women to forge themselves into a grand army to meet the Republic's impending crisis of class warfare. In her last address before a national convention at Buffalo in 1897, Willard listed the reasons behind her conversion to socialism and told the delegates that she wished she were young again so she could join the great socialist strug-gle against Mammon.[5]

Many women soon to join the socialist movement, especially in the Mid-west and Plains states, heard Willard's pleas, and later they would typically trace their political origins to the W.C.T.U. Like the young Lena Morrow, they considered Frances Willard the greatest woman of the century. But Lena learned something far more practical from her mentor than the beauty of Christian socialism; she acquired a lasting appreciation for organiza-tional skill.

Far more than her socialistic teachings, Willard's genius for organization left its mark on the W.C.T.U., and on many women who would redirect their energies into the socialist movement. Willard had reorganized the W.C.T.U., self-consciously cultivating an esprit de corps, or, as she called it, a "comradeship among women," and had by the 1890s created the largest movement of women the country had yet seen. She was extremely proud of her "army, drilled and disciplined," trained in a method of organization proven successful. Committees had been abolished, except for the executive, replaced by superintendencies that made each woman individually responsible for her assigned line of work. "This puts a premium upon personality," Willard explained, "develops a negative into a positive with the least loss of time, and increases beyond all computations the aggregate work accomplished." Willard insisted that a secret of the W.C.T.U.'s success lay in its "quick and cordial recognition of talent," the utilization of women, "young and old, who can speak, write, conduct meetings, organize, help keep accounts."[6]

Frances Willard might easily have been describing her new recruit. Within months of graduating from Monmouth College, Lena Morrow became superintendent of the sixth district of the Illinois W.C.T.U. In this capacity she was, as Willard had specified, personally responsible for its success or failure. For the next six years Lena devoted herself wholeheartedly to the welfare of her district centered in Freeport. She canvassed the area regularly, and during a typical year appeared before all varieties of women's assemblies, delivering more than a hundred addresses, and setting up local branches. In this setting, Lena developed precisely the "personality" Willard expected of her star organizers.[7]

Along with acquiring basic organizational skills from the W.C.T.U., Lena came to share Willard's primary political ambition: the shaping of the W.C.T.U. into a massive woman suffrage army. Willard had been patiently wooing members and the old leadership to her suffrage position for the past fifteen years. At the 1892 national W.C.T.U. convention held in Denver, Willard proudly introduced Anna Howard Shaw, who had only recently resigned as national superintendent of the W.C.T.U.'s suffrage department to climb the leadership rungs of the National American Woman Suffrage Association. Following the thunderous applause and shouting that met Shaw's speech, Willard remarked: "Shoo, ladies; this is different from what it was in Washington in 1881 when you refused to let me have Miss Anthony on my platform. Things are coming around, girls."[8]

Indeed, they already had. The W.C.T.U. then claimed over 200,000 suffrage workers among its ranks, including the newly matriculated Lena Morrow, who attended the convention and described for the Monmouth College newspaper her unreserved enthusiasm for this decisive endorsement of woman's ballot. Noting the presence of other Monmouth alumnae in the audience, Lena evidently felt at home and basked in the glory of the indomitable Willard. Outside the church, Lena wrote, no organization had "done so much for humanity" as the Woman's Christian Temperance Union.[9]

Lena's progress toward leadership of the Illinois W.C.T.U. also strengthened her Willard-inspired interpretation of temperance philosophy. Of the state organizations, the Illinois union proved to be the strongest advocate of woman suffrage. Willard's home ground and site of her first interorganizational triumph in 1878, when the Union endorsed the temperance ballot, the Illinois W.C.T.U. by the mid-1880s, had inaugurated a campaign for full enfranchisement and was cooperating with local woman suffrage societies. Illinois women, it was commonly reported, actually placed suffrage before prohibition. Lena Morrow was unquestionably part of this mainstream. Gaining the superintendency of the Freeport district suffrage department at age twenty-three, she upheld her commitment to woman suffrage until the passage of the Nineteenth Amendment.[10]

In 1898, the year of Willard's death, Lena Morrow left the W.C.T.U. to take up full-time suffrage agitation. With the zeal she had shown for temperance organizing, Lena served as secretary of the Illinois Equal Suffrage League. During the winter of 1899, she campaigned in Chicago among the city's trade unions. Appearing primarily before male audiences, she secured resolutions endorsing woman suffrage from twenty-two local unions.[11] Lena continued this line of work for the next several years, speaking to both men's and women's groups as she worked west from the towns of southern Iowa finally to join the 1898 and 1900 state referendum campaigns in South Dakota and Oregon. Now under the auspices of the National American Woman Suffrage Association, she agitated principally among Portland's trade unions and fraternal orders.[12]

In a remarkably short period, Lena had abandoned both temperance and a woman-centered milieu for wider political vistas. She had, as a suffragist, already gained many friends in western socialist ranks; Ida Crouch-Hazlett, for example, who later would become an important functionary in the Socialist party, had worked closely with Lena on the Oregon suffrage referendum.[13] Among trade unionists she discovered many allies, and found a great deal of support for her suffrage work within the California socialist movement.

The California Socialist party provided the perfect climate for Lena's further political development. It had already attracted an unusually high percentage of women, estimated at 20 percent of the state membership, many of whom had shared Lena's path toward socialism. The women's leadership, still steeped in Christian socialism, had acquired training and discipline in the temperance and suffrage movements, and displayed a love for agitation that Lena could appreciate. These women formed an all-women's league with its center in Southern California, unaffiliated with the party, and self-consciously continuing the W.C.T.U.'s tradition of female political autonomy. Building on a few branches in the north, they founded the first state-wide league in the country, the California Woman's Socialist Union established in San Francisco in 1902.[14]

Although new to the area and the movement, Lena quickly became a favorite guest among the various socialist women's clubs. She often appeared at their meetings, reading poetry, delivering short, educational sermons, or merely offering public endorsements of their efforts.[15] But with a decade of organizational work behind her, she could not settle down to club life. She chose to work instead in her accustomed manner, alone on the agitational trail.

Within months of joining the Socialist party in 1902, Lena Morrow resumed her journeys, visiting state party locals, speaking on various issues at meeting halls, or in her inimitable style, on street corners. The comrades quickly recognized her talents and encouraged her to organize full time. The Karl Marx Club of Oakland took up a collection to send her north into the "wood country." For six nights she spoke on a cracker box on the streets of Eureka, California, and from there began a tour of lumber camps. She later recalled with pride her experiences in places accessible "only by riding in the engine of a work train." She rejoiced in her triumphs there. "Several hundred workingmen were addressed," she remembered, "and the literature sold in those camps has undoubtedly opened the eyes of many a wage-slave."[16] From there, she traveled up and down the West Coast, from the Oregon line throughout the small towns of California to the Mexican border, relying on all types of transportation from railroad to steamers and stage coaches.

Beginning in mid-year 1903, she curtailed her agitational tours somewhat. Lena had married the renowned socialist lecturer Arthur Lewis in July, and for the next two years limited her engagements to the Bay Area, except for a dozen or so trips out of state.[17] Domestic life, however, did not slow the pace of her work. She took up nightly soap box oratory on Grant Street in San Francisco and arranged with the party local to sample some "untried" areas of the city during the Socialist congressional campaign of that summer. A few weeks after her marriage, she was arrested for the first time, when the chief of police decided to crack down on street-corner speaking. Bailed out of jail after a few hours, she later won in court an important round in the free-speech battles which were to consume California socialist energies for the next several years.[18]

Lena eventually could not be restricted to the Bay Area. For a time, she practiced her talents as a journalist for the *California Socialist*, published in San Francisco, but by 1905 she returned to the trail, carrying the socialist message into British Columbia and back through the northern mountain states. Arthur, who now shared her name as she did his, accompanied her on many of these trips, aiding the further development of her oratorical style.[19]

Together the two constituted a remarkable team. Arthur Morrow Lewis, one of the leading pedagogues in the socialist ranks, believed that propaganda was necessary to attract workers to the movement but was merely the first step in a thorough "scientific" education. His own special forte lay in a popular explanation of the natural sciences, using their evolution with the increase of knowledge as a kind of metaphor of expanding human self-consciousness about the universe and social life. Able to speak lucidly on dozens of subjects, Arthur also became master of the "book talk," the selling of literature at lectures. Lena Morrow Lewis's lectures during these years of her marriage reflected her husband's strong influence. She now spoke on a wider assortment of subjects, addressing crowds in the mining town of Butte, Montana, for example, on "International Socialism," "Education," "Science and Socialism," and the "Historical Revolutions." Local socialist papers could rightly take pride in her delivery, entertaining as well as educational, scholarly, and witty. Arthur and Lena lived off the sales of literature and collections taken at speaking engagements, a common practice at the time. In 1906, party officials listed the accomplishments of one short tour as follows: "In 20 days in Arizona she sold $133.30 worth of books; in 11 days in Colorado and Utah $77.65 worth; in 13 days at three points in Montana, $140.85 worth."[20] At the contemporary prices of fifty cents for Socialist books and nickels or even pennies for pamphlets, this sum represented a vast quantity of literature.

While Lena thrived on this circuit-rider's regimen, Arthur seemed to prefer a more stable environment for his deliveries. He settled in Chicago and began an enormously popular lecture series at the old Garrick Theater. Lena, meanwhile, toured the Midwest and southern states, narrowly averting a second arrest in one of the mining camps of West Virginia.[21]

In general, her travels were easier during these years. Now permanently separated from Arthur and on the party's payroll as a national organizer, she could plan her itinerary in advance and depend on party locals to bring out crowds and guarantee her lodgings. She had won recognition as one of the party's most talented lecturers and successful organizers.

Lena Morrow Lewis was entering her prime as a Socialist agitator. Her admirers marveled at her skills and energy and attached an almost mystical significance to her rapid rise in the movement, although in fact she had merely used to the fullest the opportunities around her. The Protestant zeal of her youth, harnessed to the agitational methods pioneered by the Woman's Christian Temperance Union, led her down a well-trod path toward the woman suffrage movement, and finally to the Socialist party. Her talent and determination allowed her to stand out so prominently that many observers, and sometimes Lena herself, forgot how much she owed to the collective sisterhood of her political past.

At the turn of the century, thousands of women gravitated toward the socialist movement. Most were native-born Protestants, many with years of

Lena Morrow Lewis, c. 1910. (Permission of the Tamiment Library, New York University.)

experience in temperance and woman suffrage campaigns. They had great regard for the party's advocacy of women's equality but nevertheless hesitated to join an organization chaired exclusively by men. Older than Lewis by a generation, the women's leaders remembered vividly the antifeminist attitudes of the nineteenth-century socialist and labor movements and consequently avoided quickly-formed alliances. Moreover, many of these women were wedded ideologically to the principle of all-women associations, believing that women shared a special relationship with one another, a relationship invested with powerful political and moral connotations. Thus while a few women joined Socialist locals in their home towns, occasionally to rise within the various state organizations, most socialist women continued to believe that only a political sisterhood free from male domination could agitate successfully among their sex. In areas where women's organizations grew most rapidly, the Midwest, Plains states, and California, the leadership insisted on preserving an autonomous structure parallel to the party. When Morrow Lewis joined the party, it was these women, with their seemingly old-fashioned notions, who provided the strongest support for feminist issues and by their growing presence, unquestionably, contributed to her rise as a national figure.

Although recurrent plans to unite in a grand, national federation had repeatedly failed, loose networks of socialist women's clubs dotted the political landscape of several states, California and Kansas in particular. Socialist editors frequently saved a column or two in their newspapers for a "woman's department," announcing meetings and supplying short propaganda pieces on the Woman Question. In 1907, another midwesterner, Josephine Conger-Kaneko, launched a special national monthly, the *Socialist Woman*, which would prosper for the next six years. Conger-Kaneko, who believed unreservedly in the principle of female autonomy, sought to promote separate women's organizations, and she found an avid readership among the independent clubs.

Not all Socialists, however, approved the spirit of these heterodox endeavors. Large numbers of metropolitan women, principally from the German and Jewish sectors, were concurrently advancing from their nineteenth- and early twentieth-century status as auxiliaries to full standing in Socialist locals. Like many middle-class young women drawn from the urban settlement houses and colleges, they professed absolute loyalty to the party and regarded the separate women's organizations at best as an expedient rather than necessary or permanent fixtures. Thus, by 1907, the independent socialist women, now a significant force in American radicalism, began to face growing opposition from women in the party who disliked their style of organization.

After several months of heated contention, the various factions struck a balance on this question. In 1907, a resolution from the Stuttgart Congress of the Socialist International had buoyed the position of party loyalists by calling for a new, unified program for woman suffrage agitation. The party used this occasion to institute a Woman's National Committee to co-ordinate propaganda and organization, and to encourage local branches to form woman's committees in their areas. Almost at once, in 1908, women's place in the party apparatus gained at least nominal importance. Independent socialist women, a bit suspicious but mostly heartened by the expectant mood, fell into line with the urban women's sectors, especially once the newly formed Woman's National Committee proved itself an active publicist of woman suffrage. The committee, however, composed entirely of hard-line party loyalists, discouraged signs of blatant feminism among its ranks and sought, even as it escalated suffrage agitation, to subordinate woman's emancipation to the overall demands of the class struggle.

The solution suited Lewis's political inclinations perfectly. But although she viewed enfranchisement as essentially only a means to integrate women into the larger political society, she nevertheless remained a tireless supporter of woman suffrage and helped to ensure its support by the party's hierarchy.[22] Her support was especially needed around 1910, when wealthy women were flaunting their organizational prowess, and a powerful faction within the Socialist party called for a moratorium on all cooperative ventures with so-called bourgeois suffragists. Lewis remained loyal to her former coworkers and voiced a strong opposition to such a policy, calling it unwarranted because it sorely misrepresented the situation. Only if suffragists had asked for a property restriction on voting, Lewis argued, could they be construed as enemies of the working class. She carefully explained that the National American Woman Suffrage Association asked only for the enfranchisement of all women by virtue of their natural rights as citizens, fighting therefore not at all along class lines but only for the advancement of women as a sex. She added that wealthy suffragists gained a lot of publicity for their acts but in reality represented only a small minority of women demanding their rights. Lewis concluded that the party therefore had no political principle to lose by supporting the suffrage campaign.[23] And against those socialists who promised that men would "take care" of women after the revolution, suggesting that the entire issue be postponed until that glorious day, Lewis argued eloquently that her sex had to "enter the front door of the Temple of Liberty" or not at all.[24]

Lewis nevertheless rejected any feminist interpretation of this commitment. As the struggle for socialism was, in her mind, taking place at the ballot box, she inferred that women required political rights to participate on equal terms with men. Once enfranchised, women would unite with men and enlarge and enrich party affairs by their presence, for politically emancipated women would be able to see their class interests more clearly. Under current conditions, Lewis explained, women tended to identify with their own sex; as full citizens they would be less concerned with their sex interests and naturally incline toward their respective classes. Socialism would then advance more quickly because the minor contradiction of sex antagonism would be lessened, class conflict thereby gaining a purer expression. In a strange but not atypical twist of logic, Lewis suggested that women ultimately required the ballot not for sex but for class reasons.[25]

Such a view closely paralleled Lewis's understanding of her own political evolution. For a time, she recalled, she had believed that "political bondage was the cause of many of the ills endured by those of my own sex." Experiencing a second awakening, she discovered that a "man without a job was about as badly off as a woman without a ballot. In fact a little worse, for we can live without voting, but we cannot live without eating." Once she had learned that the economic organization of society determined its basic quality, she rejected reformist plans which could only meliorate conditions. She realized finally that the "real" antagonism in society was not between the sexes but rather between capitalists and workers, and concluded that women suffered more from class oppression than from the injustices meted out to them as a subordinate sex. Although she still respected and sought to aid the woman suffrage movement, she admitted that for herself "whatever revolutionary spirit there is in me finds expression today in the Socialist movement."[26]

Thus, Lewis did not disavow her past in the woman's movement; indeed, she commended the temperance and suffrage agitations for serving, in her own case, as steppingstones to a higher cause. But precisely because she had made the transition from feminist to socialist activities so smoothly, she carelessly disregarded the problems of other women, who were less independent, experienced, or mobile than herself. For those women with lingering reservations about the propriety of working unguardedly with men, she proposed a philosophical mixture of Marxist materialism and sheer voluntarism.

Lewis began her popular explanation in a commonplace fashion, asserting that differences in sex roles could be traced to economic causes. Drawing upon the anthropological-historical explanation used by socialists, she recounted the familiar story of woman's fall with the overthrow of the matriarchy, the birth of private property, and the simultaneous dawn of sex and class oppression. The old equality of economic roles had been destroyed, as men became the breadwinners and women the caretakers of men's homes and nurturers of their children. Like other forms of slavery, woman's subordination resulted from her subsequent economic dependency. Not that women had actually contributed less to sustaining the human race; indeed, they had been constant participants in the struggle for survival. But as men's property, women had nevertheless been considered

tangential to the economy because they labored for their families and in
their homes. In Lewis's view, it was modern capitalism that had begun to
change drastically the age-old character of these social relations. The removal of food and clothing production from the home to the factory meant
work once designated "feminine" lost its gender quality. And women, by
following their traditional occupations into the labor market, had set about
establishing the bases for their own emancipation through their increasing
economic independence. The *idea* of women's inferiority still persisted, but
this hoary remnant of a bygone era would, Lewis concluded, be ultimately
banished.[27]

Lewis implied in her analysis, rather uniquely for her generation, that
women had never in their darkest historical hours actually become inferior,
and today stood within range of grasping full equality for themselves. She
warned, however, that equality would not come automatically. Although
economic conditions had changed, the psychological effects of male domination persisted and "to a degree became primary in themselves." Lewis
even hinted in a neo-Lamarckian fashion that men, in centuries of oppressing
women, had "as a class developed brain cells that respond to or harmonize
with their past economic development." Against the weight of tradition and
biology, Socialists had to aid the struggle to "stamp out the last vestige of
male egotism and [men's] desire to dominate over women."[28] In no arena was
this struggle more important than among Socialists themselves. "As the pa-
lid heroine has passed into oblivion and the physically and mentally healthy
modern woman has taken her place," she explained, Socialists along with
others had to concede sex equality.[29] Some male comrades still thought that
"all a woman is good for in any organization is to raise money for them to
spend," an attitude understandable in the church but unconscionable in a
political organization that upheld woman's equality as a basic tenet.[30] Although Socialists, more than other men, could be brought to understand because their theories evoked a natural sympathy, the primary responsibility
fell upon women themselves. By taking up tasks usually reserved for the
presumably more effective male workers, women could prove their pro-
ficiency, win men's respect, and thereby assert their rights.

Lewis gave personal testimony to this faith by relating her own experience in overcoming feminine reticence. She recounted with relish an engagement in Butte, Montana, where a crowd fleeing from a runaway horse
knocked over her lecture stand. Thrown to the cobblestones below, she was
badly bruised. A "vigorous treatment of witch hazel and massaging," however, enabled her to go back on the stump the following day. In this mishap,
she had lost only that symbol of modesty, her dress, the main one she used
for traveling "torn to smithereens." Like the recurring throat ailments she
suffered from too frequent speaking engagements, such minor problems

could not be allowed to interrupt her schedule.[31] On the contrary, she seemed to derive an ever greater strength from such acts of abnegation. "The
price I personally have paid," she boasted, "has been to relinquish any and
all ideas of a home. Not that it matters . . . to be truthful I have quite
forgotten the sensation of having personal belongings about me other than
my clothing." She could report by 1911 that she had been touring for
seventeen years, "and in all that time I have never slept for fourteen consecutive nights in the same place."[32] She had sensibly refused to be
frightened by the stigma of "masculine" sometimes used to characterize her
behavior and instead warned that men often utilized that capitalist
"bugaboo" of calling unwomanly those spirited enough to assert their
independence. She pleaded with other women to join her and cast aside
their reservations or inhibitions and thus "escape the system of exploitation."[33]

Stripped of theoretical pretensions and inconsistencies, Lewis's strategy
demanded that women free themselves by acts of will. She even conjectured
that women's capacity to survive many centuries of oppression proved a
natural *superiority* that had only been wanting a modern environment and
sufficient stimulation to show itself. Women should, in her perspective,
simply refuse to accept men's designation of their character and stand up for
themselves. Particularly in the socialist movement, strong-minded women
were needed for the crucial work of organizing for the revolution.

"Comrades," she implored, "the overthrow of the capitalist system, the deposing of
the capitalist class and placing the working class in power is no prayer-meeting job,
and the woman who is afraid of a few men who are trying to secure the same thing
she is working for . . . had better go back to her sheltered nook and give place to the
woman of courage."[34]

Not surprisingly, then, Lewis did not identify with the feminist currents in
the party at any level. She did write a few short articles on the Woman
Question, included appropriate addresses in her repertoire, and worked hard
to ensure the party's support for woman suffrage. But she remained un-
sympathetic to the plea that many women preferred to work among their
own sex and needed separate organizational space to develop their political
interests independently of men. Most members of the Woman's National
Committee, agreeing with Lewis, strongly opposed this tendency and believed that, as women in general now took an interest in public affairs and
the world of labor, socialist women should be able to work comfortably in
the one organization formally pledged to female equality. Lewis herself interpreted the party's creation of the special committee structure as evidence
of its sincere commitment, proof that women could participate without risk
alongside their male comrades. Any other position, she hinted, constituted
a concession to old-fashioned chivalry and provoked an unnecessary exaggeration of gender distinction within the movement.

As a prominent organizer, a member of the National Committee since 1905 and the National Executive Committee since 1909, Lewis had considerable influence in the socialist movement. A female representative, she could speak authoritatively on women's issues and play no small part in formulating the party's official position on the Woman Question. Grateful to have a strong supporter of woman suffrage in these higher ranks, socialist women in turn admired Lewis for her determination and perseverance. But on matters that most gravely affected women's status in the party, those of feminist leanings would not find a political friend in her. They still preferred to heed Frances Willard's advice to consider the timidity of most women, and they continued to nurture strong reservations about political involvements with men. However committed to the goals of the Socialist party, many women remained provincial in outlook, were encumbered with domestic responsibilities, and lacked the opportunity to attend college, for example, or to become public personalities. They could no more adopt Lewis's style than she could remain one of them. But when Lewis spoke against women's organizational autonomy and insisted upon the primacy of the class struggle over women's emancipation, many of these women felt that Lewis had deprecated her own political heritage: she had failed to appreciate how much of her own success was due to the very tendency she wished to see superseded by the socialist advance.

In a fateful, symbolic manner, party women exchanged views on the very question of Lewis's rise to prominence. When she became the first woman to join the National Executive Committee, many interpreted her victory as a sign that the party had finally been compelled to live up to its claim as an organization free of sex discrimination. Because women had become an influential sector of the movement, the party had rewarded them by recognizing Lewis's admirable record of service to the cause. Mary Marcy, leading staff writer for the *International Socialist Review*, objected to this reading and admonished women to rejoice that Lewis had been elected *not* because of her sex but merely because she had demonstrated her ability as a worker for socialism. Lewis's integration into party leadership constituted proof, for Marcy, that women were eschewing special privileges and were finally acknowledging efficiency as the only test of a good agitator.[35] Lewis no doubt agreed. She, too, had insisted that the woman who could serve the party well must maintain her place in the movement solely on "grounds of her merit and fitness to do things"; she must ask herself not what the party could do for her but what she could do for the party.[36]

Anita Block, editor of the *New York Call*'s "Woman's Sphere,' responded to Marcy by addressing the limitations of such a perspective; inadvertently, she also refuted the core of Lewis's beliefs on the Woman Question. Block agreed that Lewis had been rewarded for her hard work in the field, and that male chivalry had no part in her elevation. But in concluding as Marcy had done, that all women should be expected to follow Lewis's lead, she too, made a serious error. Lewis needed no roses strewn in her path to make work easier. Neither had Susan Anthony, Emmeline Pankhurst—nor Mary Marcy, by all appearances. But for every similarly undaunted woman agitator there existed "thousands of women, so saturated with tradition, so atrophied by sex-slavery that they actually barricade themselves within their own prison, the home," until some sympathetic woman came on the scene to aid them. Precisely because so many socialists had determined to become effective workers for the cause, they had to understand the problems of women too hesitant to become involved in public affairs, let alone join a radical movement. The most efficient feminist agitators had, in fact, taken upon themselves the responsibility of discovering what special methods were needed for the task of women's organization. "This does not mean drawing up the Comrades along sex lines, or bringing the party a new brand of sex differentiation," Block explained. It merely meant creating a milieu wherein women would be able to participate in the movement as freely and as effectively as men did. Indeed, socialist women could do little else. Most party men remained "still regrettably male," satisfied to express their support of women's freedom in theoretical abstractions. Women sensitive to the "degraded position of their sex" had to create their own programs of uplift if their sisters were to take a higher place in party affairs.[37]

Perhaps Lena Morrow Lewis needed such support, although she would have been the last person to admit it. At the peak of her fame and influence, scandal drove her from the centers of power to a self-imposed exile. She returned to find the socialist movement in the midst of an insoluble political crisis, and her claims to orthodoxy placing her in a shrinking old guard. Lewis spent decades more as a relentless political propagandist, organizer, and functionary. But she never regained the special role of a leading woman within the American Left.

Her fall from political grace had the quality of bitter irony. Lewis, who had done so much to separate herself from the women's sector of the Socialist party, suddenly found her "femininity" held in question by erstwhile comrades. Her style as fearless organizer was never fully accepted, and she had often had to defend herself against recurring charges that her boldness actually damaged the cause. Now her factional opponents located a weak spot in her political armor: the ostensibly private life of a divorced woman.

The assaults on Lewis's character had a petty nature, but given the times proved sufficiently damaging. During 1911, when shifts in the party leadership foretold the major blow-up at the 1912 convention, several people in the National Office became targets for scandal-mongering politicos. One of the targets was J. Mahlon Barnes, national secretary of the party, who was linked publicly with an incident long-known in inner party circles, involving an illicit relationship and the fathering of an illegitimate child some eleven years before. Lewis, a secretary alleged, had recently been seen with Barnes during working hours at the National Office, going off to bars with him or sitting around holding a whiskey bottle, her feet up on the desk. Although no specific accusation was ever made, by inference Lewis had become immorally involved with the notorious free-lover, Barnes.[38] A few months after these innuendoes had surfaced, an organizer in upstate New York complained that Lewis had conducted herself improperly during a speaking engagement. She had, he reported, insulted her hosts by filling the dresser drawers with trash, throwing her blankets under the bed, and emptying a washbowl on the floor. Lewis refused to dignify this complaint with a denial. She astutely noted, however, that she was being cited not for political misconduct but for failing to act in a "ladylike" manner. "Perhaps," she wrote acidly to the National Office, "it is only a woman's sin to leave a room in disorder." Men had done worse and their transgressions had been readily overlooked.[39]

The irony in her situation became stronger as her defenders rose to clear her name. Perceiving Lewis's womanhood attacked, friends countered by describing her as the quintessence of femininity. "She is a very little woman to be a secretary of a very large association," one writer offered, "a slight woman with ridiculously small hands and feet."[40] Many persons had called her masculine, but as another writer noted, Lewis absolutely confounded the image of the radical woman as "short-haired, loud-voiced and unprepossessing female," and was in reality "tall, slender, low-voiced, with an admitted love of pretty finery and possessor of dainty gowns."[41]

One can only imagine Lewis's reaction to such defensive affirmations of genteel femininity being raised in her behalf, for all her adult life she had fought against attempts to limit women's participation on grounds of traditional propriety. Nevertheless, having rejected the female world, she could not fully enjoy the moral latitude of male society. Despite reassurances from her friends, Lewis no doubt felt betrayed. Shortly after the factional controversy peaked, she once more won nomination to the National Executive Committee. She thanked her supporters but this time declined, preferring to return to her former post as national organizer.[42] Although her motives remain a matter of speculation, Lewis very likely chose to work farther away from the spotlight and its accompanying political glare.

Lewis found refuge in Alaska. Departing for the north country, she returned, in a sense, to her earlier leanings, finding in America's last frontier the comradeship demanded by rugged conditions and geographical isolation. She worked again in an environment where the rare woman was

valued highly and the talented organizer enjoyed respect for the ability to
shape a coherent political movement out of social chaos and untrammeled
exploitation. What began as a seasonal visit turned into one of the more
lengthy and productive phases of Lewis's career.

Alaska, hardly more in the popular mind than an image of the gold rush,
of wide open towns, uncivilized prospectors, and dance hall girls, actually had
by 1913, the aspect of a primitive romance drawing to an end. As Lewis
noted, the prospector was being displaced by the employed miner, the dog-
team trails by railroad tracks, and the Indian hunting grounds by commercial byways of extractive industry and fishing. With the last escape from
wage-labor rapidly closing, "the nightmare of capitalism already haunts the
workers of Alaska," Lewis wrote.[43] Largely emigrés from Britain or its pro-
tectorates, the territory's laborers had brought with them a union tradition
that readily turned radical. A few years before Lewis's first tour in 1912,
socialists had argued over the value of hiring a paid organizer for Alaska; in
1912, the small Alaska Socialist party won a disproportionate number of
votes, almost carrying the territory. Where miners and fishermen faced
capitalists without any substantial commercial class in the middle, where
workers had practically no cultural institutions but the tavern, and few
amusements but drinking and gambling, socialist organizers, in their own
minds, could serve as class-conscious civilizing agents. Lewis was in her element.

The able functionary, editor-propagandist Lewis readily, almost gleefully,
adapted to the climate. Touring in the summer months, she traversed the
major cities including Nome, Fairbanks, and Dawson, visited the mining
creek villages, ventured to outposts like the military encampment at St.
Michaels, stayed overnight in igloos, and moved by ship, rail, and dogsled
to reach her proletarian constituency. By all reports, including her own, she
received an appreciative response.[44] In 1916, Lewis was named the Socialist
party's congressional candidate.[45] The same year she delivered the major
address dedicating the new hall for the Alaska Labor Union, which she
served as vice-president and editor of its newspaper.[46] Writing for a half-
dozen other socialist and mainstream newspapers, Lewis meanwhile had set
up winter quarters in Juneau, where she proceeded to draw a circle of activists and local residents around her.

The success she enjoyed stemmed from the freedom she had to integrate
various aspects of her work. Adhering to her old faith, she continued to
provide the basic lessons in evolutionary socialism, seeking to raise the
audience's educational level in general while offering political guidance.
While she delivered her time-tested orations on the promise of the socialist
electoral victory, she lectured in addition on subjects ranging from language
to modern drama, the writings of August Bebel to current sociology, and
provided courses on English and naturalization procedures.[47] In Juneau, she
turned her small home into a political center:

I keep house in a two-room cabin, with a large woodshed adjoining, and have room enough to seat about twenty or twenty-five, so I have the children under 10 come for one class, another evening of the week I have the women come for a study class, and then I have a course of lectures for the general public. Keeping house as I do I have lots of company, and my place is a sort of headquarters for the Comrades to come to when they come in from the country roundabout.[48]

Comfortable in this environment, Lewis worked more closely with women than at any time since the beginning of her career in the 1890s. In Juneau, she participated in a local program designed to encourage women to use their right of franchise and helped to organize a mass meeting to discuss women's role in the upcoming municipal elections. She regularly made a point of defending women's place in the labor market, chastizing those union men who wished to "protect" their trades by keeping women out. She also widened her range of activities. She conducted a special women's socialist study group but also joined the Juneau Woman's Club and took part in various social and civic affairs of interest to women.[49] In light of her former preferences, Lewis seemed unusually at ease in women's society during these years. Perhaps she believed her female peers possessed a toughness matching her ideal of modern womanhood. She did write that she found the atmosphere conducive to sexual equality. The Alaskan frontier quickly smashed the pernicious stereotypes of masculinity and femininity, she reported. Men had become "as fine housekeepers as a woman," did their own cooking, cleaning, and laundry, and perhaps from this, Lewis conjectured, understood the plight of the household drudge better.[50]

For the first time in years, Lewis experienced relatively little of the internecine socialist wrangling that had caused her to leave mainland political life. The Industrial Workers of the World (I.W.W.), strong among the miners, attacked her when she first arrived, and at least one socialist sheet demanded her removal from the organizer's post.[51] But for one accustomed to bitter in-fighting, Lewis happily found the balance of forces such that no faction could dictate to others. An unquestionable "right" socialist and a bitter opponent of the I.W.W. in the past, Lewis seemed to shift her stance after working with the miners. She could probably better understand the limitations of an electoral strategy and the appeal of "One Big Union" to an isolated miner or fisherman than she could the propaganda offered by urban I.W.W. agitators. As world war approached, she found herself fighting hand in hand with the trade union left against the encroachments of nationalism.

In Alaska, if only for a few years, Lewis had found a social atmosphere conducive to her training and talents. But in the United States proper, long-time socialist constituencies drifted farther from the reach of her old-style educational methods. The thirst for learning which brought an Alaskan miner into town for a socialist lecture had far less meaning for a modern city dweller tempted by the theaters and films; the "American" worker most receptive to the party's educational message tended to be displaced industrially by the foreign-born laborer with little inclination toward the didactic side of the English-language socialist agitation; and the bridge that Lewis hoped to build between the sexes could not withstand the pressures of the new sexual and social morality of the 'teens. The socialist movement had entered its final phase. The political self-confidence underlying the movement's messianic character had been all but demolished, exposing raw nerves among the survivors and provoking another, far worse bout of internecine strife. Leaving Alaska in 1917, Lewis had departed from her last socialist frontier.

By the time she returned, the socialist women's movement had virtually disappeared. In 1915, in the midst of political hard times, the party had voted to disband the Woman's National Committee, the *Progressive Woman* (renamed from the *Socialist Woman*) had collapsed a year earlier, and veteran organizers reported a steady decline in women's membership in areas once known as feminist strongholds. Native-born women like Lewis drifted with their male counterparts to the fringes of the movement, their places taken by the women of the "new immigrant" groups which numerically dominated the party by war's end. Contrary to Lewis's predictions, the attainment of suffrage had eclipsed the only burning agitational issue native-born socialist women would ever possess. The electoral socialism which emphasized the importance of woman's ballot now paled before the wartime strike wave and the Russian Revolution.

Lewis reentered the mainland socialist movement in Seattle, Washington, then booming as a shipyard city and bastion of "red" trade union fervor. Still self-confident in her interpretation of socialist doctrine, she became an editor of the party's *Seattle Daily Call*. But events outstripped doctrine, as the socialists willingly folded their operation after six months in favor of a daily "progressive" union paper endorsed by the city's central labor federation. Two years later the same federation spearheaded the city's General Strike, the high point of labor activism in contemporary America.[52] Lewis lacked the temperament for these extrapolitical excursions. She drifted south, toward remaining pockets of old-time constituencies and "orthodox" electoral socialist politics. In California she found another home, probably less exciting than in earlier days but nevertheless sustaining in this difficult period.

The great 1919 split in the socialist movement left Lewis with no doubt as to her loyalties. Many younger radicals who had never experienced the earlier optimism about electoral prospects instinctively abandoned the well-worn socialist ship for the uncharted seas of American Communism. Lewis, like nearly all of her old friends and cronies, denounced this impetuosity. The splintering of forces and the wave of fear accompanying the Red Scare decimated the entire left movement. By the early 1920s, only a scattering of veterans remained true to Debs's party. Of these loyalists, still fewer were confident enough to proceed energetically, but Lewis, the dedicated campaigner, held fast to her life's commitment.

Lena Morrow Lewis now became one of the last, great shining stars in the fading socialist firmament. In 1920 she directed northwest operations for the last significant national Socialist party political campaign. She almost single-handedly sought to put the West Coast organization back on its feet. By steady touring, she revived old locals and founded new ones, and soon assumed the state secretaryship of the California party. An attractive figure in the new era of women's full political equality, she repeatedly ran for state and local office, more than once finishing well ahead of the national ticket. In 1924, she played an important role in the short-lived but intense socialist support of the farmer-labor political insurgency. Having written for the new publications springing up here and there, like *New Justice* of Los Angeles, in 1925 she assumed the position of managing editorship of the *Oakland Labor World*, one of the most powerful and progressive labor dailies of the period.

Now and again Lewis probably experienced a familiar sense of gratification from the work she knew best. The socialist press of the early 1920s recorded the receptions she enjoyed as she traveled across the country, from Massachusetts to upstate New York, Missouri to the West, conducting study classes for youth on American history and contemporary affairs, reminding socialists to draw women into the movement, and occasionally testifying at government hearings on the condition of labor.[53] But if the inner fire remained, the combustible social situation had dissipated. The Socialist party, increasingly frail, was becoming an appendage to the garment unions and the aging Jewish socialist movement in New York. The depression killed the *Labor World* and weakened other elder institutions. Lewis found herself drawn toward the East, where a small group of functionaries could still secure financial support.

Now in her mid-sixties, Lewis headed for disillusionment. In the 1930s she wrote with evident sadness that her forte, the street meeting, had been checked by the popularity of automobiles and radio, and the socialist stump speaker was a figure of the past. In the summer months, Lewis could nevertheless occasionally be seen taking the open air to preach the old doctrines, now adapted to defend the socialist faith against Franklin Roosevelt's popular appeal.[54] But in 1936, Lena Morrow Lewis severed her last relations with the Socialist party. Younger radicals in the organization had advanced a program opening the door to cooperation with Communists and had wrested control of the political movement from the old guard. Lewis followed her friends in seceding from what she called a "party of dictators."[55] She immediately became a leading spokesperson for the new entity, the Social Democratic Federation (really an aging group of New York garment trade unionists who threw their support to Roosevelt via the American Labor party). The old ways had been lost in all but sentiment, and Lewis's milieu dwelt heavily upon the past; she herself, was determined to salvage at least the proper memory of American socialism in its prime.

Lewis did not lose her faith in socialism, but she never again found an arena for agitation and thus lost the one calling that gave her life a distinctive and irrefutable purpose. To many old friends and acquaintances she was judged a tragic case: isolated from contemporary currents, she had planned no retirement and was virtually penniless. In her last years, she worked at the Tamiment Institute, the repository of the defunct Rand School archives. Indexing the records of a movement now passed into history, she must have appeared strange to those who knew of her exploits a half-century earlier. But determinedly maintaining her health through the rigors she had learned so long before, Lena Morrow Lewis remained to the end an emotionally self-sufficient and independent woman—a free spirit.[56]

Between 1900 and 1920 the socialist women's movement supplied thousands of radical women with the basic necessities of political survival. The strong networks of local women's societies reinforced a genuine feeling of sisterhood and allowed activists to struggle collectively against discrimination within socialist ranks and society at large.

Drawn from this milieu, Lena Morrow Lewis nevertheless maintained an ambiguous relationship with the women's sector of the socialist movement. Like so many of her peers, she had been trained within the most significant political institution created by women in the late nineteenth century, the Woman's Christian Temperance Union. Transferring allegiance to the Socialist party, she continued to speak for equal rights at the polls and in labor market. Yet, unlike the majority of socialist women, Lewis soon shed all traces of her origins within female-centered institutions. Indeed, during her prime, her departure from circles of grass-roots women enhanced her status among the party bureaucrats. She acted always as an individual and renounced sex solidarity as a sign of weakness, an obstacle to women's achievement. Through the best and worst of times, she never relented on her unique position.

For this reason a story of otherwise heroic proportions assumes a tragic air. By insisting that any woman could through sheer will power struggle successfully against male prerogatives, Lewis failed to anticipate her own vulnerability as an individual amidst the male-dominated leadership of the Socialist party. In 1911, when aspersions against her moral character clearly derived from narrow notions of "feminine" behavior, Lewis might protest, but she could not in good conscience rally women as a group to her defense.

During times of political retreat, Lewis could neither find solace nor companionship.

We do not know whether Lewis, stranded by the tides of political fortune, lived to regret her tenacious individualism. But surely one can say about her what David Graham Phillips concluded about his own larger-than-life heroine, the resolute Susan Lenox: "Yes, she has learned to live. But—she has paid the price."

Notes

1. Aaron I. Abell, *The Urban Impact on American Protestantism, 1865-1900* (Cambridge: Harvard University Press, 1943), pp. 194-207, 218-23. Annie Wittenmyer, later to become the first president of the Woman's Christian Temperance Union, wrote a tract on the value of Christian women's voluntary labors. Her *Woman's Work for Jesus* (New York: privately published, 1871) captures the spirit of these endeavors.

2. U.S. Census, Hale Township, Warren County, Illinois, 1870. For background on Lewis's paternal ancestors, *Past and Present of Warren County, Illinois* (Chicago: H. F. Kett and Co., 1877) is a handy reference. The church register of the First Presbyterian Church of Monmouth for October 12, 1867 lists among its communicants the Rev. T. G. Morrow and Mary Morrow, Lena's parents. Mary Story Morrow's activities are recorded in the minutes of the Monmouth Presbyterian Missionary Society, Woman's Missionary Association; she was a regular participant as late as the 1890s. These records are located at the Faith United Presbyterian Church in Monmouth, and I am indebted to Neil Basen for supplying these as well as other materials related to Lena's background. For additional information, see also Hugh Moffet and Thomas Rogers, *History of Warren County, Illinois* (Chicago: Munsell Publishing Co., 1903).

3. I would like to thank Mrs. Herman Stanley, president of the National Woman's Christian Temperance Union, for supplying this information from her files. Mrs. Esta Crear, Illinois Woman's Christian Temperance Union president, was also very generous with materials related to the Freeport Union.

4. "Diagnosis of the Class of '92," *The Annex* 3 (May 20, 1892), 11.

5. Excerpts of this address were later published by the Socialist party as a leaflet entitled "Frances Willard on Socialism." For an assessment of Willard's impact on the W.C.T.U., see Mary Earhart, *Frances Willard, From Prayers to Politics* (Chicago: University of Chicago Press, 1944).

6. Frances Willard, *Glimpses of Fifty Years* (Chicago: Woman's Temperance Publishing Association, 1889), pp. 472-73, 476-77. See also, Frances Willard, *Woman and Temperance* (Hartford, Conn.: Park Publishing Co., 1883).

7. *Minutes*, State President's Address and Reports of Work of the Woman's Christian Temperance Union of the State of Illinois and the Twenty-Fifth Annual Convention, Elgin, 1898 (Chicago: Woman's Temperance Publishing Co., 1898), pp. 49, 122-23. According to records of the Illinois W.C.T.U., housed in Springfield, Il-

linois, Lena Morrow was president of District 6 from 1892 through 1895, and president of District 9 from 1896 through 1897: Mrs. Esta Crear kindly confirmed this fact. For Lena's work, see also "News from the Field—Illinois" *Union Signal* (Chicago), January 10, 1895.

8. Quoted in Earhart, *Frances Willard*, pp. 196-97.

9. "Alumni et Alumnae," *The Annex* 3 (November 11, 1892): 11-12.

10. *Monmouth Ravelings* (1892), p. 32, lists Martha Lena Morrow as superintendent of the Suffrage Department of the State W.C.T.U. and "editress" of this volume. Morrow also attended national conventions of the W.C.T.U. during these years; the published minutes list Morrow as a delegate from Freeport, Illinois, District 9 of the Illinois W.C.T.U.

11. "Labor's Views of Woman Suffrage," clipping from a Chicago morning newspaper, dated February, 1899, in Scrapbook no. 1, Box 3, Lena Morrow Lewis Papers, Tamiment Library, New York University.

12. Clipping from *Iowa State Register*, dated March, 1899; clipping "Woman's Suffrage in Wyoming," *Omaha World Herald*, March 11, 1900, in Scrapbook no. 1, Lena Morrow Lewis Papers. John William Leonard, ed., *Woman's Who's Who of America: A Biographical Dictionary of Contemporary Women of the United States and Canada, 1914-1915* (New York: American Commonwealth Co., 1914), p. 489, lists these activities.

13. Abigail Scott Duniway, *Path Breaking*, 2nd ed. (New York: Schocken Books, 1971) p. 118; John Work, "X-Rays," *Iowa Socialist* (Dubuque), March 28, 1903.

14. Reports of California organization among women may be found in the *Los Angeles Socialist*, beginning with the November 23, 1901 issue and running frequently throughout 1902 and 1903.

15. "Labor's Cause," *Vallejo Evening Chronicle*, June 3, 1902, clipping in Scrapbook no. 1, Lena Morrow Lewis Papers; "Women's Column," *Los Angeles Socialist*, April 11, 1903.

16. Lena Morrow Lewis, "Experiences as a Socialist Propagandist," *Common Sense* (Los Angeles), April 1, 1904; reprinted in the *Chicago Daily Socialist*, July 3, 1907, and more recently in Gerda Lerner, ed., *The Female Experience: An American Documentary* (Indianapolis: The Bobbs-Merrill Co., Inc., 1977), pp. 373-76. "Experiences in the Lumber Camps of California," *Seattle Socialist*, March 13, 1904; and "California Department," *Seattle Socialist*, April 3, 1904.

17. "Rice at the Local," *California Socialist* (San Francisco), July 25, 1903.

18. Lewis, "Experiences as a Socialist Propagandist."

19. The *Western Clarion* (Vancouver, Canada) reports Lewis's trips in these areas. See issues for 1905.

20. Reports of tours in *Montana News* (Butte), undated clippings in Scrapbook no. 1, Lena Morrow Lewis Papers. Lewis's exploits are summarized in a short biographical sketch, "Lena Morrow Lewis," *Socialist Woman* 1 (September 1907): 2.

21. "Refused to be Arrested," *Chicago Daily Socialist*, December 7, 1907. May Wood Simons, "Story of a Woman Agitator," undated clipping from the *Chicago Daily Socialist* in Scrapbook no. 1, Lena Morrow Lewis Papers; also reprinted in *St. Louis Labor*, December 14, 1907.

22. Lena Morrow Lewis, "Woman Suffragists and Woman Suffragists," *Socialist Woman* 1 (February 1908): 3.

23. Lena Morrow Lewis, "The Woman Suffrage Movement," *Progressive Woman* 4 (March 1911): 4, 7.

24. Lena Morrow Lewis, "Woman's Day," *New York Call*, February 27, 1910.

25. Lewis stated her position clearly at the 1910 party congress, saying, "you can't draw the class line effectively until you have obliterated the sex line politically," Socialist Party, *Proceedings of the 1910 National Congress* (Chicago: Socialist Party, 1910), pp. 15, 16.

26. Lewis, "Experiences as a Socialist Propagandist."

27. Lewis, "Woman's Day;" Lena Morrow Lewis, "The Woman Question and Socialism," *Oakland World*, February 13, 1913, clipping in Scrapbook no. 1, Lena Morrow Lewis Papers.

28. Lewis, "Woman's Day."

29. "Mrs. Lewis' Views," *Emporia Convincer*, February 17, 1912.

30. Lena Morrow Lewis, "Women and the Socialist Party," *Chicago Daily Socialist*, May 10, 1907.

31. Undated clipping from *Montana News*, c. 1906, Scrapbook no. 1, Lena Morrow Lewis Papers.

32. Ethel Lloyd Patterson, "Lena Morrow Lewis: Agitator," *The Masses* 1 (July 1911): 13; reprinted in part in the *Emporia Convincer*, February 24, 1912.

33. Lena Morrow Lewis, "Women and Social Problems," *Dallas Laborer*, April 25, 1914.

34. Lewis, "Women and the Socialist Party."

35. Mary E. Marcy, "Efficiency the Test," *New York Call*, May 8, 1910.

36. Lewis, "Women and the Socialist Party."

37. Anita Block, "A Reply to Mary E. Marcy," *New York Call*, May 15, 1910.

38. The Barnes scandal was one of a series of free-love exposés in the party. For details, see "Barnes Forced to Resign," *Christian Socialist* (Chicago), August 17, 1911; "National Executive Committee's Great Contortion Act," *Christian Socialist*, August 31, 1911. Reports of the party's investigative committee are published in the *Official Bulletin* (Chicago), February, 1911. Moral in form, the charges were ostensibly political in effect; John Spargo (oral history interview, Columbia University Oral History Collection, pp. 205-07) remembered the controversy as a struggle between the right and left wings of the party. Several documents, including testimony by Mary (Mother) Jones against Barnes and Lewis, are located among Thomas J. Morgan's papers, Illinois Historical Survey Library.

39. Lena Morrow Lewis to John Work, October 11, 1911, in response to a letter from John E. Parson, organizer for the Niagara Falls local, September 27, 1911. Correspondence, Box 4, Lena Morrow Lewis Papers.

40. Patterson, "Lena Morrow Lewis."

41. Clipping from *Omaha Daily News*, June 29, 1909, Scrapbook no. 1, Lena Morrow Lewis Papers.

42. Lena Morrow Lewis to John Work, letter published in *Progressive Woman* 5 (December 1911): 16.

43. *Alaska Labor News* (Anchorage), December 1916, untitled clipping in Scrapbook no. 2, Lena Morrow Lewis Papers.

44. For samples of her exploits, see "Mrs. Lena M. Lewis Gave Entertaining Lecture," clipping from a Nome paper, August 31, 1912; "Noted Socialist Lecturer Ar-

rives from Interior," *Daily Nome Industrial Worker*, August 31, 1912; "Experiences in Alaska," *Alaska Citizen* (Fairbanks), November 11, 1912; all clippings in Scrapbook no. 2, Lena Morrow Lewis Papers. See also "Lena Morrow Lewis Campaigns in Alaska," *Party Builder* (Chicago), October 16, 1912; "Experiences at the Military Post, St. Michaels, Alaska," *Shawnee County Socialist*, September 20, 1913; Lena Morrow Lewis, "Experiences and Observations in Alaska," *Progressive Woman* 6 (March 1913): 12, 14.

45. "Socialist Campaign Is Now Opened," *Daily Alaska Dispatch*, October 1916; "Crowd Cheers for Candidate Lena Morrow Lewis at Big Rally," *Alaska Labor News*, November 14, 1916. Clippings in Scrapbook no. 2, Lena Morrow Lewis Papers.

46. "Dedication Alaska Labor Union Temple," *Alaska Labor News*, clipping dated December, 1916, in Scrapbook no. 2, Lena Morrow Lewis Papers.

47. "She Lectured on Language," *News-Miner* (Fairbanks), April 20, 1914, clipping in Scrapbook no. 2. Lena Morrow Lewis Papers. "Socialism Asks Only a Hearing and Opportunity," *Ballot Box* (Fallon, Nevada), March 15, 1913.

48. "From Lena Morrow Lewis in Alaska," *New York Call*, March 1, 1914.

49. "Women in City Politics," clipping from Fairbanks paper dated 1914; "What Happened to Woman's Meeting," *Sunday Morning Post* (Juneau), November 1, 1914; "Editorial," *Alaska Labor News*, undated clipping; all in Scrapbook no. 2, Lena Morrow Lewis Papers. See also, Solon DeLeon, ed., *American Labor Who's Who* (New York: Hanford Press), p. 138.

50. Lewis, "From Lena Morrow Lewis in Alaska."

51. *Alaska Socialist* (Fairbanks) repeatedly criticized Lewis; for sample editorials see issues for October 17, 1913, and April 19, 1914, July 13, 1914.

52. Harvey O'Connor, *Revolution in Seattle, A Memoir* (New York: Monthly Review Press, 1964).

53. Lewis's activities in California are catalogued by numerous newspaper clippings in Scrapbook no. 5 and Scrapbook no. 7. Lewis summarized these activities in a letter to Morris Novik, August 3, 1938, Box 2. Scrapbook no. 1 and Scrapbook no. 3 are filled with clippings from the *Seattle Daily Call, New York Call, New Justice*, and the *New Leader*. Scrapbook no. 4 and Scrapbook no. 6 contain clippings from the *Labor World*. Lena Morrow Lewis Papers.

54. "Summer's Work in the Bay State," *New Leader* (New York), October 5, 1935, clipping in Scrapbook no. 1, Lena Morrow Lewis Papers.

55. Lewis to Novik, August 3, 1938.

56. Lena Morrow Lewis died in 1950. The Monmouth College *Bulletin*'s Alumni directory for 1951 gives Lewis's last address as Jamaica, Long Island.

5

THE "JENNIE HIGGINSES" OF THE "NEW SOUTH IN THE WEST": A REGIONAL SURVEY OF SOCIALIST ACTIVISTS, AGITATORS, AND ORGANIZERS, 1901-1917

Neil K. Basen

Some of the most creative work in American historical writing has centered on the people and institutions, both black and white, of the states of the Old Confederacy during the post-reconstruction era. Despite the recent renaissance in southern history, only a slender body of published studies has focused on southern and southwestern women, particularly women dissenters and their working-class sisters.[1] For decades prior to the turbulent 1960s, radical women had been ignored by southern and southwestern specialists. In its largest compass, the traditional historical treatments of women below the Mason-Dixon line have been inadequately researched, conceptually flawed, regionally biased, and demographically constrained. Such studies, by and large, have portrayed the image of the submissive and virtuous "southern lady."[2] Below the strata of upper-class southern ladies, however, existed radical enclaves of women, rural and urban, engaged in an array of political undertakings at the state and local levels. The newer, innovative works surveying southern and southwestern radicalism have done little to rectify this traditional image of southern womanhood. In spite of thier "history from the bottom up" methodology and foci, the "movement culture" monographs of southern Populism and the "new social" histories of southwestern socialism have either underestimated or omitted the contributions of women activists.[3]

In recent years, a spate of women's studies volumes has documented the pervasive forms and manifestations of sexist discrimination practiced in virtually all sectors of late nineteenth- and twentieth-century American society, including socialist communities. Yet in the mining fields, lumber regions, railroad maintenance centers, and tenant farm belts sprawled throughout the Southwest, many women affiliated with the Socialist party of America (SP) assumed positions of political leverage in the course of the progressive era. Within this section of the country, as elsewhere, socialist women christened themselves the "Jennie Higginses" of the movement.[4] Unlike their eastern sisters, however, these Jennie Higginses were not assigned exclusively to auxiliary activities, or totally excluded from important, day-to-day party affairs and policy decisions. After 1910, women were integrated into the SP and functioned as equals with men in the organization at the local and county levels. Across the southwestern states, they served with distinction as agitators, organizers, journalists, and local secretaries.

Like nearly all of their male counterparts, few, if any, of these sunbonnet militants were ivory tower theoreticians, original thinkers, or ardent feminists. With some exceptions, they were more likely to be class-conscious autodidacts who were "converted" to the socialist gospel by reading Marxist popularizations and directly experiencing painful dislocations generated by American corporate capitalism. Fusing Second International Marxist doctrines with regional traditions, they sought to build a socialist Cooperative Commonwealth. Most socialists believed this goal could be achieved gradually, at the ballot box through agitation, education, and organization, without resorting to violence. Assisted by a colorful cadre of "outside," professional agitators and organizers, the Jennie Higginses made manifold contributions in establishing the strongest American grass-roots socialist movement, in the Southwest during the "Golden Age of American Socialism."[5]

The present essay will explore the activities of Socialist women, the leaders and the rank and file, and assess their contributions to the southwestern movement. A regional investigation of these indigenous radicals also provides an opportunity to test a number of generalizations that have been advanced by historians, social scientists, and women's studies practitioners: Who were these Jennie Higginses? What were their class backgrounds? What types of sexist barriers did they encounter in party ranks? What types of roles did they play in the SP? Did these roles conform to the southern lady model? How should these regional female participation and leadership patterns be interpreted from a broader comparative perspective? What happened to these Jennie Higginses after the demise of the southwestern movement during World War I?

Students of southwestern radicalism have done their work so meticulously that further research probing the social context of socialist discontent in the progressive era would be superfluous. Back in the Gilded Age, American corporate capitalists began tapping the Southwest's rich extractive resources, notably cement, coal, zinc, lead, timber, oil, and natural gas. From the outset, great fortunes were earned and lost by industrialists, railroad promoters, oil developers, coal operators, and land speculators in this frontier region. Industrial entrepreneurs, often headquartered in Kansas City and St. Louis, heralded the region as a "new empire" for minerals, markets, and cheap sources of labor. The reckless development of these resources within the "New South in the West" created a severe maldistribution of wealth.[6] In the scattered population of the region's vast hinterlands, unstable economic conditions and technological innovations generated waves of radical unrest. In the rural areas, moreover, low farm values, high rates of farm tenancy and mortgaged property, recurrent droughts, boll weevil plagues, and the dependency upon wheat and cotton as staple crops, created acute pockets of poverty. After the turn of the century and the decline of Populism, an identifiable, embattled lower class emerged throughout the New South in the West. With the formation of the SP in 1901, thousands of indebted yeomen and tenant farmers, miners, and other workers, including some veterans of the People's party, Knights of Labor, and American Railway Union, flocked into the movement to redress their grievances. One militant southeastern "Kansas Balkans" coal digger summed it up succinctly: "The 'system' drove me here [into the SP]."[7]

Although women were conspicuously absent from the founding southwestern state conventions and in pioneer SP organizing drives, they began to make their presence felt at the end of the decade preceding World War I. Following the crucial 1908 SP National Convention, women's committees were belatedly organized across the country, including all of the southwestern states. According to the extant evidence, we know that hundreds of southwestern women became "red card" rank-and-filers after these women's committees were set up by SP local and state organizations and national organizers. No data exists, however, revealing the percentage of women members in the ranks of the southwestern SP during the progressive period. Hence, a prosopography, complementing James R. Green's illuminating study of the "Salesmen-Soldiers" of the *Appeal* "Army", cannot be undertaken here. Still, the small amount of data available yields useful information.[8]

A SP survey conducted nationally in 1912 estimated that women constituted 15 percent of the party's membership roster. Despite the limitations of these data, it is still plausible to suggest that this figure was somewhat higher in the southwestern states, perhaps as high as the twenty-five to thirty-five percentile range. For example, shreds of regional evidence disclose that women composed about 40 percent of the Arkansas SP in 1912. But these figures were probably inflated for propaganda purposes. According to the more reliable data published in the socialist press, however, we know that between 1910 and 1914, approximately 6 to 9 percent of the SP's local secretaries in Arkansas and Oklahoma were female. At the same time, we also know that these women were not elected by all-male locals. They were not token female leaders. The regional socialist press, particularly in Arkansas, Oklahoma, and the southeast Kansas Balkans, abounded with reports of women's activities at the grass-roots level. Although no refined conclusions can be drawn from these rough estimates, some qualified generalizations are possible.[9]

No other southwestern political institution and few, if any, social organizations offered women similar avenues of opportunity. The Democratic party and the various Protestant denominations relegated women to the spheres of auxiliary organizations and missionary societies, respectively. The women's clubs, suffrage groups, and temperance of societies of the progressive era were all-female organizations and thus failed to provide women with opportunities to establish pragmatic, day-to-day working relationships with men. Yet it would be misleading to suggest that these Jennie Higginses were not assigned to a hodgepodge of "kitchen parliament," culinary, clerical, fund-raising, and other tedious, back-breaking tasks. In the trans-Mississippi South, as elsewhere, both the locals and women's committees sponsored bazaars, cake sales, "pie socials," picnics, and "box suppers." Nevertheless, within the SP locals and women's committees, women also had a rare chance to debate and vote on pressing political, social, and economic issues, to learn new ways of communicating in mixed groups, and to gain confidence in newly acquired skills, including leadership.[10]

Furthermore, women who served as local secretaries clearly made countless personal sacrifices, but they were also vested with several major responsibilities, particularly in the Southwest, where decentralization and local autonomy sentiments were deeply rooted in the ranks. Unpaid and overworked, they presided over local meetings, collected dues, sat as poll watchers on election day, routed itinerant speakers on the socialist lyceum circuit, and circulated petitions on public issues in their precincts and wards. These Jennie Higginses also kept their comrades fully informed about state and national SP affairs and relayed reports on local conditions to the state and national offices. "Socialists want to do a lot of propaganda for the cause," one Sooner State organizer observed, "if some brave comrade will do all the work." Much of this educational and recruitment work fell into the laps of the local secretaries. To perfect and build their organizations, several of the more industrious secretaries canvassed their neighborhoods and kept a poll book of the wage earners and tenant farmers in their precincts. Beyond these routine duties, women secretaries represented their locals on the county committees and drew up the agendas for the annual county conventions. As community educators and leaders, they planted and nurtured the seeds of socialism at the grass-roots level throughout the New South in the West and "were the foundation of the organized Socialist party." Without them, the southwestern socialist movement would have stagnated into an empty bureaucratic shell.[11]

Correspondingly, a diverse group of rank-and-file women also contributed to the southwestern movement in various other callings and ventures. After the harvest season, rural Oklahoma insurgents such as Emma
Norman of Antlers and Anna Sample of Farry "dropped the [ir] hoe-
handle[s]' to speak at socialist encampments and to write regular columns
for local socialist weeklies. Professional women, like Grace Arnold of Ardmore, Oklahoma, and Belle Williams of Texarkana, Texas, held positions
as Socialist newspaper editors. Other Jennie Higginses, including Hattie
Watkins of Okemah, Oklahoma, Ruth Williamson of Shattuck, Oklahoma,
and Winnie Fouraker-Hardy (1889-1969) of Dallas, Texas, published
articles and poems that made direct appeals to women and promoted equal
suffrage. Although one woman acknowledged that she felt uncomfortable
discussing and debating politics with men, Lulu Middleton of Indianola,
Oklahoma, barnstormed the Oklahoma-Arkansas border region, preaching
the gospel of socialism and organizing new SP locals. "I am here to support
the principles that I love best," Middleton exclaimed, "and I would be
a traitor to my conscience if I failed to do my part when the occasion
demands it." In southeastern Missouri, too, housewife evangelists, like
Marguerite Loyd and Carrie Scott, left their kitchen drudgery and children
in the care of others and blitzed the Bootheel lowlands, carrying the torch of
socialism to cotton-farm tenants. And in the southeastern Kansas Balkans,
Laura A. Lasater of Pittsburg, a blue-collar widow, served as district clerk
of Crawford County.[12]

Although scores of southwestern rural and mining communities were
bustling with Jennie Higgins agitators and organizers, the range of opportunities for women within the male-dominated SP was limited. A
multitude of activities and positions was informally considered off-limits
for most SP women members. According to James R. Green's findings, for
example, only 2 percent of the *Appeal* "Army's Salesmen-Soldiers" brigade
were female. As a rule, women were not recruited to hawk the *Appeal to
Reason* on urban street corners or at factory gates and mine sites. Furthermore, when women were nominated for public office, they generally
contested for local school board and state school superintendent positions.
With few exceptions, the rest of the SP ticket was dominated by male candidates. These sexist patterns occurred in equal and restricted suffrage states
alike. Even after 1910, only a handful of women left their communities to
serve in high-level SP positions at the state, regional, and national levels.
To cite only one graphic example, more than 98 percent of the delegates to
the 1914 and 1915 Oklahoma State SP Conventions were male.[13]

Notwithstanding these sexist barriers, a coterie of talented and versatile
Jennie Higginses was conspicuous at the state and national levels. In fact,
most of the outstanding national SP women leaders were natives or residents of the southwestern region. Although a preponderance came from
working-class backgrounds and were sensitive to the plight of poor workers

and farmers, more than a few of these leaders were professional and club women with college degrees and normal school educations. In some cases, the career profiles of this elite cadre of Jennie Higginses were cast in the same mold as their prominent, progressive era female contemporaries. Compositely, these middle-class Jennie Higginses, despite their radical perspectives, had more in common with non-socialist female elites than they did with their rank-and-file brothers and sisters.[14]

On the northern rim of the New South in the West, Luella Roberts Krehbiel (1866-1933) (also spelled Kraybill in the socialist press) of Coffeyville, Kansas, was, in the words of one male Sunflower State Socialist, "a jewel in our ranks." An unwavering suffragist and spellbinding speaker, she served as a delegate to the 1904 National Convention and was also elected by her Kansas comrades to the post of state organizer. In 1905 alone, this former Univeristy of Kansas student, former Socialist Labor party member, and middle-class divorcée filled 104 speaking engagements in the southwestern states. On her tours, she held "parlor propaganda meetings" for women and distributed socialist literature "to the sisters in bondage" she met in this region. "If all of our men were willing to work as hard to keep up locals as I am to organize," Krehbiel asserted in 1904, "we should soon have Socialism." A prolific author, Krehbiel also published articles and short stories in the socialist press condemning capitalist institutions and advancing women's political and economic rights.[15]

In the heart of the coal fields of the Kansas Balkans, Grace D. Brewer (1881-1975) of Girard served as editor of the *Pittsburg Workers' Chronicle* and associate editor of the *Appeal to Reason*. From her Girard office, she also coordinated and commanded the *Appeal* "Army's" grass-roots operations. According to her fellow journalists, Brewer was instrumental in mobilizing the "Grand Army of the Revolution" and building it into a popular working-class "institution."[16] Flanking Krehbiel and Brewer's efforts, Caroline A. Lowe (1874-1933) of Pittsburg held several high-ranking positions in the party and was a popular stump-orator from coast to coast on the socialist lyceum bureau. A teacher, trade union official, attorney, and erstwhile Methodist lay leader, "Carrie" Lowe testified before a congressional committee in 1912 on behalf of woman suffrage for wage earners; two years later, she garnered 35 percent of the vote in her 1914 race for the Kansas State Legislature. During that same year, she also helped to launch the People's College of Fort Scott, Kansas, an innovational working-class educational institution, that offered a law school curriculum. Later in the war and postwar periods, Lowe served on the legal teams defending a legion of Wobblies at the Everett Massacre and Wichita trials.[17]

Similar leadership patterns surfaced in Arkansas, most visibly in the coal fields nestled in the Ozark foothills. Under the SP auspices, Bessie Bartholomew journeyed thousands of miles each year on her agitational sorties

Grace D. Brewer. (Courtesy of Neil K. Basen)

Freda Hogan Ameringer. (Courtesy
of Freda Hogan Ameringer.)

Ida Hayman Callery. (Permission of the Tamiment Library, New York University.)

Mary H. Jackson and Robert S. Jackson, 1905. The white ribbon is a WCTU ribbon. (Courtesy Ruth F. Jackson.)

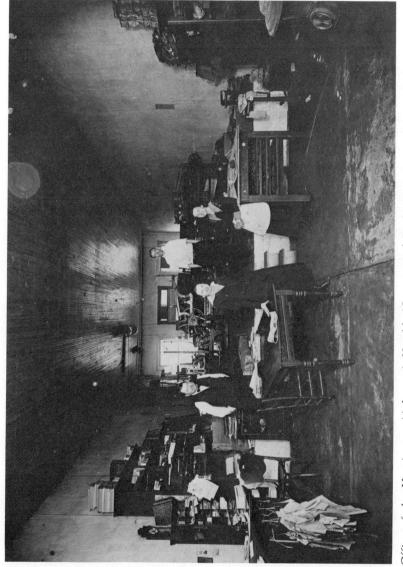

Office of the Huntington (Arkansas) *Herald*. (Courtesy of Freda Hogan Ameringer.)

among famers and workers in Arkansas and other southwestern states. Rose Justice of Booneville supervised all party activities in the Fourth Congressional District and Carrie Hallowell Turnidge (1865-?) of Rogers occupied the same post in the Third Congressional District. A former Missouri state organizer and the spouse of a red-card nursery proprietor, Turnridge was an indomitable suffragist and a big "drawing card" on the socialist chautauqua circuit.[18] Both Edna Snow and Freda Hogan (1892-   ) of Huntington sat in the party's state secretarial chair. Daughter of the perennial leader of the Arkansas SP, Hogan wrote a regular column for several socialist newspapers, participated in the statewide woman suffrage crusades, and agitated shoulder to shoulder with the United Mine Workers of America (UMW) - District 21 rank and file during the violent 1914 Arkansas mine wars. Outside the coal-rich Ozark foothills, Mary Hilburn Jackson (1879-1966) of Malvern, a working-class autodidact, militant suffragist, and former Woman's Christian Temperance Union member, was recognized as the "intellectual" of the Razorback State movement.[19]

Much of the success of the Arkansas SP, which mustered 8 percent of the popular vote in 1914, rested on the organizational skills of Ida Hayman Callery (1885-1917). As one rank-and-filer intoned: "She's a humdinger of an organizer." Reared in a moderately prosperous, rural Kansas and Oklahoma Territory milieu, Ida Hayman had been groomed for political leadership by her radical father. In 1909, this former "red diaper baby" and Indian schoolteacher was elected state secretary of the Oklahoma SP. Less than a year after her marriage to "Country Boy" Phil Callery in 1910, she brought her Sooner State organizing techniques over to Arkansas, where she transformed the movement. Between 1911 and 1914 as state secretary, Ida Callery, often working alone in her Huntington and Fort Smith offices, broadened the party's membership base by 600 percent. During this period, she also represented her state on the SP's National Committee. After resigning from both offices in 1914, she attended law school at the University of Oklahoma and subsequently became a member of the Kansas State Bar. Until her untimely death in 1917, Callery served as the official counsel for the UMW-District 14 in Pittsburg, where she handled compensation cases and endeavored to "stick the [coal] compan[ies] under F.E.L.A. [Federal Employers Liability Act]."[20]

To the west, four Jennie Higginses stood out in the Oklahoma SP ranks. A former machinist, teacher, and church missionary worker, Kate Richards O'Hare (1876-1948) first received regional recognition by taking part in the pioneer organizing drives in the Indian and Oklahoma Territories. By 1910, this native of rural Kansas had earned a national reputation as a spellbinding orator and popular leader. During the Golden Age of American Socialism, O'Hare sat on the National Executive Committee, served as editor of the *National Rip-Saw*, ran for the House of Representatives and Senate, and presided as chairwoman of the War and Militarism Committee at the St. Louis Emergency Convention in April 1917. To add to her impressive credentials, she was elected international secretary of the SP—the only American woman to have held that position in the Second International.[21]

The less flamboyant Winnie Shirley Branstetter (1879-1960) of Norman and Oklahoma City likewise left her mark on the southwestern movement. A child orphan, homesteader, one-time department store clerk, and spouse of a resourceful SP leader, Branstetter took out a red card in Norman in 1904 and immediately became engrossed in organizing work. Between 1908 and 1909, she served with distinction as territorial organizer in New Mexico, where she worked tirelessly to recruit women into the SP. After resettling in Oklahoma, she sat on the State Executive Committee, acted as a party liaison to the Oklahoma City trade union movement, and contributed innumerable articles to the national socialist press. With somewhat less distinction, she subsequently administered the day-to-day business of the Woman's National Committee at the SP National Office in Chicago until the former was dismantled in 1915.[22]

Together with O'Hare and Branstetter, Carrie C. Block (1890-1926) of Lookeba and Dora Merts of Oklahoma City were also instrumental in forging the strongest American state organization. The former, a homesteader and wife of a SP county organizer, represented her state on the National Committee from 1909 to 1912; while the latter, a former farm laborer, schoolteacher, and UMW-District 21 organizer, exercised her influence as associate editor of the *Oklahoma City Social Democrat*. A gifted debater and "Christian lady of ability," Merts was also renowned for delivering "rapid fire bombardments against the citadel of greed and plunder" on the southwestern socialist hustings.[23]

Elsewhere in the Southwest, a few unheralded Jennie Higginses made valiant attempts to spearhead mass socialist movements in Texas and Louisiana. In the Lone Star State, Laura B. Payne (1865-1936) of Fort Worth became the first southern woman to run for the House of Representatives. During her 1906 campaign, she made over thirty-five speeches in the Fifth Congressional District, championing woman suffrage and espousing public ownership and democratic control of all consumer goods industries. A former teacher and labor organizer, Payne also served on the SP's National Committee and led the Texas delegation to the 1908 National Convention. After 1908, she gradually lost faith in political action, including equal suffrage agitation, and subsequently embraced the doctrines of syndicalism and direct action. About this time, she mc ed to southern California, where she married her second husband and joined the Industrial Workers of the World (IWW). Employing "McKees Rocks tactics," Laura Payne Emerson agitated among Chicano gas utility and construction workers during their 1910-1911 labor disputes and helped to launch an IWW branch of Hispanic wage earners in San Diego. As a member of the One Big Union's Local 13, she played a leading role in the 1912 San Diego free-speech fight. Harassed by vigilantes, and clubbed, firehosed, and arrested by local police, Emerson courageously carried on her street-corner exhortations throughout the duration of this protracted battle. Two years later, she published and edited a syndicalist fortnightly, the *International*, that featured her Wobbly polemics and poetry.[24]

East of the Sabine River, two working-class Jennie Higginses advanced the class struggle in Louisiana. A former one-room schoolteacher, Viola Locke Dietz (1882-1971) of Lake Charles sat on the Woman's National Committee and also participated in the violent struggles in the piney wood parishes that led to the founding of the Brotherhood of Timber Workers in 1912. Across the Bayou State, May Beals-Hoffpauir (1879-1956) of Abbeville and Jennings, an erstwhile Quaker, schoolteacher, and United Mine Workers activist in the eastern Tennessee coal fields, published the only southern working-class culture magazine of the period, the *Red Flag*. Though often billed as a "Dixie Girl" on the Socialist soapbox circuit, she was one of the few southwestern Jennie Higginses to develop a rudimentary socialist-feminist analysis. In this heyday of Debsian socialism, Beals-Hoffpauir's witty speeches, essays, and poems, embellished with local color, feminist, and class-struggle themes, were extremely popular in the New South in the West.[25]

Why did these restrictive yet impressive patterns of participation and leadership emerge in the southwestern states? There are no simple explanations to this question, but a few tentative observations can be made. Southwestern radicalism was, in part, a postfrontier phenomenon, not because the frontier was a seedbed for democracy, but because unstable economic conditions sparked new forms of social organization. Throughout this section of the country, the SP, like the church and public schools, was a principal agent of social organization. Under these circumstances, the roles of women were less sharply defined than they were in the East and upper-Midwest. Additionally, in contrast to many of the municipal socialist strongholds, the southwestern movement was not dominated by male immigrants. The native white Protestant male leadership tended to be less skeptical of opening up the ranks to women. And for good reason. They had little choice. During the first decade of the progressive era, the southwestern SP organizations operated tenuously on the brink of financial collapse. Hard-pressed for new members, these locals probably recruited women as silent and inactive dues-paying members, in order to keep the movement afloat. Once they were ensconced in the SP fold, however, some of these Jennie Higginses impressed their brothers with their talents and skills and were awarded the opportunity to hold the reins of leadership.

Yet to indict all male southwestern socialists for this petty opportunism would not be fair. The surviving wisps of evidence point in a different direction. Many SP leaders and articulate rank-and-filers were committed to full franchise and equal political and economic rights for women. In some localities, where only a few women had enlisted in the movement, SP spokesmen embarrassingly acknowledged this fact and worked to fill the void. For many of these male socialists, women were "true comrades and equals."[26]

Equally significant, these class-conscious Jennie Higginses were not steadfast feminists. Under the guise of an orthodox Marxist perspective, they failed to consider the cross-class-lines character of sexist exploitation. Despite their militancy on equal suffrage and other related issues, moreover, nearly all of these women extolled the cult of domesticity—marriage, family, and home. Most of the cultural norms of the New South in the West were not seriously questioned. Alternative life styles were never even vaguely articulated. Even the socialist-feminist May Beals-Hoffpauir echoed her sisters' sentiments when she stated that marriage and family were the "noblest vocation[s]." In sum, the southwestern humorist Oscar Ameringer was probably correct when he boasted that "we have no long-haired men and short-haired women in the Oklahoma Socialist Party."[27]

Not surprisingly, controversial issues like birth control were considered taboo and a detriment to the movement's growth. Only Winnie Branstetter had the courage to raise the subjects of family planning and contraception in her speeches. For her efforts, she received a series of stiff reprimands from male leaders. In addition, the vast majority of these activists, with the exception of Branstetter, Freda Hogan, Laura Payne Emerson, and other anonymous rank-and-filers, abided by the southern code of race relations. While Branstetter's daughters were harassed in school for being "Socialist nigger-lovers," most SP women, particularly outside Oklahoma, either ignored or calumniated blacks and Chicanos and rarely tried to recruit them. Like some of their male comrades, a few white-supremacist women dubbed themselves the "Rebels of the New South." And even the more advanced Jennie Higginses refused to endorse "social equality" (the code-word for integration and miscegenation) for Afro-Americans. In short, these socialist women held traditional values that were not foreign to the southwestern cultural landscape. They were both southerners and socialists. This merger of regional customs and international doctrines laid bare both the strengths and weaknesses of southwestern socialism. Since most Jennie Higginses were inactive during the disputes over the question of women's autonomy in the years before 1908, they were not viewed as threatening feminists and were more easily integrated into the mainstream of the movement. In the end, they won strong support from male leaders in their agitational, educational, and organizational missions. Under these circumstances, many Jennie Higginses remained loyal activists until the destruction of the southwestern Socialist movement during World War I.[28]

Across the Southwest, the party was over by the eve of the November 1918 Armistice. What happened to the Jennie Higginses after the disintegration of the southwestern movement in the post-World War I era? Following the important 1919 Socialist-Communist (CP) split, these activists, despite their initial enthusiasm for the Russian Revolution, found it difficult to function in the new climate. Given the CP's obsession with Soviet models and its complete subordination of women's issues, nearly all of them were marooned without a viable democratic socialist movement. Some veteran activists, fearful of being branded as "red-baiters," responded diplomatically or silently to the rise of the CP. Others, however, became militantly anti-Communist and anti-Soviet and refused to participate in coalitions with CP cadres in the thirties. While remaining independent radicals, only Luella R. Krehbiel and Caroline A. Lowe harbored sympathies for Soviet Russia and the international Communist movement during the mid-1920s and early 1930s.[29]

Without an outlet for their energies and abilities, several women socialists entered related reform work and gave Franklin D. Roosevelt and the New Deal programs critical support during the depression decade. Winnie Fouraker-Hardy practiced law in San Antonio and unsuccessfully campaigned as a reform Democrat for the Texas State House of Representatives in 1929. Mary Hilburn Jackson served as a probation officer and librarian in Hot Spring County, Arkansas, and later channeled her energies into various Unitarian Church, women's club, and food cooperative undertakings in Eugene, Oregon. In Minnesota, Washington, and California, Grace D. Brewer managed the Non-Partisan League speakers' bureau, worked for a labor bank in Seattle, and served as a volunteer for numerous Democratic party election campaigns before her death in 1975. Across the country, Freda Hogan of Oklahoma City remained active in sundry radical and reform causes, most notably the progressive labor press. During her long career, Hogan has yearned for the revival of the American socialist movement and has kept the faith. Since the 1930s, this last-known surviving Jennie Higgins has pulled an oar in the CIO, civil rights, and women's liberation movements.[30]

In a similar vein, Kate Richards O'Hare always reflected proudly on the accomplishments of the old southwestern movement. After her release from prison by Woodrow Wilson in 1920, "Red Kate" demonstrated her considerable talents in myriad prison reform, labor education, and civil rights crusades. She also played an active part in Upton Sinclair's EPIC campaign in 1934. Discouraged by factional splits and isolated from the mainstream of American radicalism, she grew increasingly cynical and anti-Communist during this period. Though she remained sporadically active in the political arena until her death in 1948, she felt "restless" and frustrated because "I can see no organization or movement that seems to offer a satisfactory field for my services . . . So I cook my husband's meals and darn his socks and pamper him shamefully. I putter around the flowers . . . and wonder if fate has decided that it[']s time for me to call it a day's work and sit down to rest. . . ." By the 1940s, this "first lady" of American socialism had painfully discovered the "end of ideology" and she conceded that workers "can make their way in fair comfort in the capitalist economy." In her last years, she often advised old friends and comrades that she "was more interested in making jellies than in Socialism!"[31]

Other Jennie Higginses drifted into obscurity and would never again return to the southwestern hustings. The militant Laura Payne Emerson moved to the right politically and found salvation in Christian fundamentalism. Winnie Branstetter retreated from political concerns after her husband's death in 1923 and worked as a seamstress in Washington and Providence; Dora Merts pounded a typewriter as a secretary in Norman, Oklahoma. Viola Locke Dietz devoted most of her later years to household and farm chores in Lake Charles, Louisiana. Perhaps the greatest tragedy of the southwestern movement was May Beals-Hoffpauir. Diagnosed as a paranoid schizophrenic in 1920, she spent her last thirty-six years confined to the East Louisiana State Hospital in Jackson. True to the traditions of American radicalism, a generation of talented activists would disappear with their movement.[32]

In retrospect, the SP fell short of offering women equality in all spheres. Like their Second International comrades, primary socialist goals and the nature of the leadership limited the meaning of equal rights for women. Existing regional working-class norms filtered through socialist views. Sexism and misogyny were never absent in the ranks, and some male socialists continued to address the Woman Question only with platitudinous phrases based on principles embalmed in party platforms. To the extent that feminism penetrated the southwestern movement, it remained an accouterment grafted onto a socialist program concerned chiefly with economic issues. The class struggle remained paramount in this volatile region, and the Jennie Higginses shared a tenacious loyalty to working-class priorities.

Although they failed to formulate a socialist-feminist synthesis, women made notable contributions to the SP throughout the New South in the West. Without the risk of romanticization, the Jennie Higginses set the tone and formed the backbone of the strongest grass-roots American socialist movement during the progressive era. In contrast to their eastern sisters, these sunbonnet rebels assumed wider, yet restricted participation and leadership roles. In fact, most of the nationally distinguished SP women leaders launched their careers in the southwestern movement. While they may be unimpressive by contemporary standards, the "recruited from below" participation and leadership rates for women in the Southwest were higher than those of analogous Second International sections and other American radical organizations before the revival of the women's movement in the 1960s. Only in Finland, Denmark, and Norway were these participation and performance rates surpassed or equalled before World War I. Viewed from this comparative perspective, the evangelical activities and formidable achievements of these Jennie Higginses should not be shunted off to the wings on the southern historical stage. In view of the current social and political climate of the Southwest—a region that has been designated as the Bible and Sun belts—we can more fully appreciate the significance of this lost generation of radical activists, agitators, and organizers who propagated the gospel of the socialist Cooperative Commonwealth during the early twentieth century.[33]

Finally, despite their conservative social mores, the limited diversity of their activities demonstrates that the Jennie Higginses were not submissive and demure southern ladies. Though the SP never attempted to dislodge many traditional notions regarding women's sphere, its spirited attempt to expand their roles in theory and practice shows greater complexity in progressive era attitudes and behavior than has heretofore been recognized and suggests that there may have been other attempts to create wider roles for women throughout the Southland. At present, further historical investigations are needed in this field. Until we examine in more detail the activities and value systems of southern working-class women, historians are in no position to assume *ipso facto* that the traditional image of the southern lady enjoyed widespread acceptance in blue-collar communities or had far-reaching social consequences below the Ohio and Potomac.

Notes

1. See for example, Claudia Goldin, "Female Labor Force Participation: The Origin of Black and White Differences, 1870 and 1880," *Journal of Economic History* 38 (March 1977): 87-108; Julia Kirk Blackwelder, "Women in the Work Force: Atlanta, New Orleans, and San Antonio, 1930 to 1940," *Journal of Urban History* 4 (May 1978): 331-58; Julie Roy Jeffrey, "Women in the Southern Farmers' Alliance: A Reconsideration of the Role and Status of Women in the late Nineteenth-Century South," *Feminist Studies* 3 (Fall 1975): 72-91; Jacquelyn Dowd Hall, *Revolt Against Chivalry: Jesse Daniel Ames and the Women's Campaign Against Lynching* (New York : Columbia University Press, 1979); Ruth Allen, *The Labor of Women in the Production of Cotton*, Univeristy of Texas Bulletin no. 3134 (Austin, 1931).

2. See for example, Anne Firor Scott, *The Southern Lady: From Pedestal to Politics, 1830-1930* (Chicago: University of Chicago Press, 1970), esp. pp. x-xi, 4-5.

3. Lawrence Goodwyn, *Democratic Promise: The Populist Moment in America* (New York: Oxford University Press, 1976); Robert C. McMath, *Populist Vanguard:*

A History of the Southern Farmers' Alliance (Chapel Hill: University of North Carolina Press, 1975); Garin Burbank, When Farmers Voted Red: The Gospel of Socialism
in the Oklahoma Countryside (Westport, Conn.: Greenwood Press, 1976); James R.
Green, Grass-Roots Socialism: Radical Movements in the Southwest, 1895-1943
(Baton Rouge: Louisiana State University Press, 1978).

4. See for example, Mari Jo Buhle, "Women and the Socialist Party, 1900-1914,"
Radical America 4 (February 1970): 36-55. Unless indicated otherwise, the terms
"Southwest" and "New South in the West" encompass the states of Arkansas,
Oklahoma, Texas, Louisiana, Missouri, and Kansas, where the popular Socialist
weekly, Appeal to Reason, had its headquarters and strongest influence. The sections of Missouri and Kansas under consideration were also economically linked to
the Southwest. The entire region was the heartland of American socialism during the
progressive era. "Jennie Higgins" was the female counterpart of "Jimmie Higgins," a
mythical, exemplary rank-and-filer created by socialist Ben Hanford. For the definition of "New South in the West" used in this study, see Green, Grass-Roots Socialism, pp. 1-11.

5. James R. Green, "The 'Salesmen-Soldiers' of the Appeal 'Army': A Profile of
Rank-and-File Socialist Agitators," in Bruce M. Stave, ed., Socialism and the Cities
(Port Washington: Kennikat Press, 1975), pp. 32-35; Green, Grass-Roots Socialism,
p. xviii. In this discussion, I have also adopted Gerda Lerner's distinction between
the women's rights movement and the broader women's emancipation movement.
She defines the former as a quest for political and legal equality and the latter as a
search for "freedom from oppressive restrictions imposed by sex; self-determination
and autonomy . . . financial and cultural independence, freedom to choose one's
own life-style regardless of sex." Gerda Lerner, "Women's Rights and American
Feminism," American Scholar 40 (Spring 1971): 237.

6. Quoted in Kansas City New Empire 1 (February 1903): 1. On the social origins
of southwestern socialist insurgency, see James R. Green, "Tenant Farmer Discontent and Socialist Protest in Texas, 1901-1917," Southwestern Historical Quarterly
81 (October 1977): 133-54; Burbank, When Farmers Voted Red, pp. 1-11; Grady
McWhiney, "Louisiana Socialists in the Early Twentieth Century," Journal of Southern History 20 (August 1954): 315-36; Ellen I. Rosen, "Peasant Socialism in America:
The Socialist Party in Oklahoma Before the First World War" (Ph.D. diss., City
University of New York, 1976).

7. Quoted in D. P. Ballard to Victor Berger, November 9, 1910, Social Democratic Party Papers, Milwaukee County Historical Society, Milwaukee. For the
definition of "class" used in this discussion, see E. P. Thompson, The Making of the
English Working Class (New York: Pantheon Books, 1963), pp. 9, 11.

8. See for example, Dallas Southern Mercury, October 17, 1901; Little Rock
Union Label Bulletin, January 16, 1904; Pawhuska (Oklahoma) People's Tribune,
November 9, 1906; Cestos (Oklahoma) Reporter, January 19, 1906. Prior to the
launching of the woman's committees in 1908, branches of the autonomous
Woman's National Socialist Union were organized in a few Oklahoma Territory
communities. See Stillwater Common People, November 12, 1903.

9. Mari Jo Buhle, "Feminism and Socialism in the United States, 1820-1920"
(Ph.D. diss., University of Wisconsin, 1974), p. 184. These estimates are based on a

poll conducted by the SP's Woman's National Committee in 1912. During that year, Buhle has found that 158 women were known to have served as local secretaries across the country. Since there were approximately 4,000 locals in the SP, less than 4 percent of the secretaries were female. The Arkansas and Oklahoma figures were derived from the 1910-1914 issues of the Oklahoma City Socialist weeklies: *Social Democrat, Industrial Democrat,* and *Oklahoma Pioneer;* and Freda Hogan, "Women Socialists in Arkansas," unidentified clipping, April 14, 1912, Freda Hogan Ameringer Papers, Oklahoma City (privately held). My rough estimates were obtained from over seventy-five southwestern SP newspapers and other regional sources.

10. See for example, "Rural Education Plan," *Rogers County* (Oklahoma) *Voice,* August 16, 1913; J. L. Stark, "The Local as a School for Socialists," *International Socialist Review* 14 (November 1913): 310; H. M. Sinclair, "The Real Democracy of the Socialist Party," *Harlow's Weekly,* April 25, 1914, pp. 62-63; *Socialist Woman* 2 (January 1909): 6; *Joplin Free Press,* February 28, 1914. Although women were integrated into the southwestern SP locals, the woman's committees were not disbanded in many localities until the demise of the movement in 1917.

11. Quoted in *Stillwater Common People,* July 14, 1904; *Oklahoma City Oklahoma Pioneer,* September 3, 1910, May 20, 1911, January 20, 1912; *Kingfisher* (Oklahoma) *Tenant Farmer,* May and October 1915; *New York Call,* January 3, August 27, 1916; *Cornish* (Oklahoma) *New-State Socialist,* April 17, 1908; *Snyder* (Oklahoma) *Otter Valley Socialist,* March 28, 1918; *Texarkana* (Arkansas) *Socialist,* January 9, 1913; Nat L. Hardy, "The Texas Program," *International Socialist Review* 11 (April 1911): 622-23; Grace D. Brewer, "A Few Words to Local Secretaries," *Party Builder,* October 16, 1912; Ida Crouch-Hazlett, "Party Organization," *Chicago American Socialist,* March 11, 1916; *National Rip-Saw,* October 1911, pp. 8-9.

12. Quoted in *Okemah* (Oklahoma) *Sledge Hammer,* July 10, 1913, March 5, 19, 1914; *Goltry* (Oklahoma) *News,* September 19, 1913; *Hot Springs* (Arkansas) *Clarion,* May 17, 1913; *Shattuck* (Oklahoma) *Ellis County Socialist,* August 19, September 2, 1915; *Dallas Laborer,* July 5, October 11, 1913, June 6, 1914; *Hallettsville* (Texas) *Rebel,* March 7, April 18, July 11, 1914; *San Antonio Light,* January 1, 1970; telephone interview with Harvey Hardy, April 14, 1979; *Alva* (Oklahoma) *Constructive Socialist,* May 1, October 23, 1912, April 23, 1913; *Ardmore* (Oklahoma) *X-Ray,* July 4, 1914; *Gibson* (Missouri) *Justice,* May 8, June 26, 1914; *Pittsburg* (Kansas) *Labor Herald,* October 25, 1912; Kansas State Census, Population, 1905, 1915, Crawford County, Kansas State Historical Society, Topeka; *Pittsburgh* (Kansas) *Workers' Chronicle,* June 26, July 31, October 9, 23, November 13, 1914. Winnie Fouraker-Hardy also served as president of the Working Woman's Equal Suffrage League of Dallas. Due to migration patterns, name changes, incomplete records, and the unavailability of the 1910 Federal Manuscript Census, it has been difficult to develop complete biographical profiles on every woman activist, particularly those in the rank and file. To make matters worse, scores of socialist newspapers published in the Southwest during this period have not been preserved. Whenever possible, I have indicated the years of birth and death, along with other biographical data, in the text.

13. Green, "The 'Salesmen-Soldiers' of the *Appeal* 'Army'," pp. 16-17. For the Oklahoma delegate figures, see *Proceedings of the 1914 Oklahoma Socialist State Convention, 1914,* (Oklahoma City, 1915), pp. 2-5; *Proceedings . . . 1915,* (Oklahoma City, 1916), pp. 2-7. South of the Red River, the woman delegate figure was somewhat higher. According to the available data, women constituted approximately 6.8 percent of the delegates at the 1913, 1915, and 1916 Texas State SP Conventions. *Hallettsville* (Texas) *Rebel,* November 22, 1913, November 20, 1915, November 25, 1916.

14. Barbara Kuhn Campbell, "Prominent Women in the Progressive Era: A study of Life Histories" (Ph.D. diss., University of Illinois-Chicago Circle, 1976). Campbell's sample was drawn from *Woman's Who's Who of America, 1914-1915,* edited by John William Leonard. Several Jennie Higginses like Grace D. Brewer and Winnie Branstetter were included in this volume.

15. Quoted in *Wichita Social Ethics,* June 10, September 16, October 21, 1904, January 13, 27, 1905; *Cestos* (Oklahoma) *Reporter,* December 20, 1907; *Winfield* (Kansas) *Southwestern Advocate,* December 9, 1901, June 19, 26, 1902; *Chicago Daily Socialist,* May 10, June 7, 1907; *Larned* (Kansas) *Tiller and Toiler,* December 16, 1904; Pauline S. Stidham to author, July 3, 1978; Kay Roberts Light to author, July 9, 1978; *Chanute* (Kansas) *Daily Tribune,* April 27, 1905; *Hinton* (Oklahoma) *Record,* July 14, September 1, 1905; Transcripts Records of the University of Kansas, 1886-1887, University Archives, Spencer Research Library, University of Kansas, Lawrence; *Socialist Woman* 1 (June 1907): 1; ibid. 1 (July 1907): 3; ibid. 1 (May 1908): 2, 4; *New York Socialist,* August 8, 15, 1908; William R. Mailly to Luella R. Kraybill, April 3, 1903, Socialist Party Papers, National Office Files, Duke University.

16. Quoted in George Allan England, *The Story of the Appeal* (Revised ed., Girard, Kansas: Appeal Co., 1917), pp. 71, 301; E. Haldeman-Julius, *My Second 25 Years* (Girard, Kansas: Haldeman-Julius Publications, 1949), p. 60; undated clippings, Grace D. Brewer Papers, Box 1, Labor History Archives, Wayne State University, Detroit; *Socialist Woman* 1 (January 1908): 2; *Progressive Woman* 5 (May 1912): 6; *Appeal to Reason,* September 2, 1911; *Woman's National Weekly,* February 13, 1915; interview with Walter Wayland, May 24, 1975, Girard, Kansas; *Pittsburg* (Kansas) *Worker's Chronicle,* January 8, 1915; Death Certificate, October 2, 1975, State of California, Department of Health, Sacramento.

17. On Lowe, see *Nineteenth Biennial Report of the Secretary of State of the State of Kansas* (Topeka, 1914), p. 70; *Pittsburg* (Kansas) *Workers' Chronicle,* August 24, October 2, 9, 1914; *Socialist Woman* 2 (November 1908): 2-3; *Progressive Woman* 3 (June 1909): 4; ibid. 3 (July 1909): 9; *Oakland World,,* October 6, 1916; *Chicago Daily Socialist,* May 18, 1910; *Gutherie* (Oklahoma) *Daily Leader,* December 4, 1912; Lowe Family Bible, (in custody of Lucy Lowe, Kansas City); Sarah Kerr to author, September 19, November 17, 1976; *Hoye's City Directory of Kansas City, Missouri, 1898* (Kansas City, 1898), p. 467; People's College News (Fort Scott, Kansas), 1 (August 1914), p. 10; Kansas State Bar Records, Supreme Court of the State of Kansas, Topeka; interview with Henry Allai, July 31, 1976, Pittsburg, Kansas; Lowe to Eugene V. Debs, January 19, February 4, 1916, Debs Papers, Indiana State University, Terre Haute; Louisa Mittelstadt to Stella M. Franklin, July 8, 1913, National Women's Trade Union League of America Papers, Box 1, Library of

Congress, Washington, D.C.; U.S. Congress, Senate, Joint Committee of the Committee on Judiciary and the Committee on Woman Suffrage, *Woman Suffrage, Hearings Before a Joint Committee on Woman Suffrage*, March 13, 1912, 62d Cong., 2d sess., 1912, pp. 16-20; *Seattle Union Record*, March 3, 1917; *Chicago One Big Union Monthly*, September 1919, p. 9; Lowe to Upton Sinclair, April 20, 1919, Upton Sinclair Papers, Lilly Library, Indiana University, Bloomington, Indiana; Clayton R. Koppes, "The Kansas Trial of the IWW, 1917-1919," *Labor History* 16 (Summer 1975): 344-46; *Springfield Illinois Miner*, April 7, 1923; Death Certificate, Kansas State Board of Health, Topeka.

18. Quoted in *St. Louis Labor*, September 12, 19, October 17, 1914, August 21, 1915; " 'Triple Slaves' of Arkansas Unfurl Banners in a Dozen County Seats," unidentified clipping, April 14, 1912, *To the Working Class of the State of Arkansas* (Huntington: Privately published, 1916), p. 14, both in Freda Hogan Ameringer Papers; Benton (Missouri) *Scott County Kicker*, January 9, 16, 23, 30, 1909; *Standard Directory of Webb City, Missouri, 1911-1912* (Webb City, n.d.), p. 486; *Webb City Register*, July 8, 1909; Manuscript Population Schedule, 1900, Federal Census, Dade County, Greenfield, Missouri; *Springdale* (Arkansas) *News*, December 26, 1913; *Bolivar* (Missouri) *Free Press*, September 3, 1914; *Little Rock Arkansas Gazette*, August 15, 1913; *Little Rock Union Labor Bulletin*, July 30, 1920; *Appeal to Reason*, May 15, December 4, 1909, March 28, 1914; *S.P. Official Bulletin* 5 (March 1909): 4; *Garden City* (Kansas) *Prolocutor*, September 29, 1910.

19. Interview with Freda Hogan Ameringer, December 11, 1977, Oklahoma City; Stella Brizzolara to Freda Hogan, July 3, 1917, Freda Hogan Ameringer Papers; *Huntington* (Arkansas) *Herald*, September 9, 1910; *Fort Smith Union Sentinel*, April 10, 1914; *New Castle* (Pennsylvania) *Solidarity*, December 19, 1914; *Little Rock Union Labor Bulletin*, February 5, 1916; Freda Hogan, "The Miners of Arkansas," *International Socialist Review* 15 (January 1915): 438-40; *Chicago American Socialist*, November 21, December 12, 1914, October 2, 1915; *Malvern* (Arkansas) *Meteor*, July 19, 1912; Robert Jackson to author, May 6, 1978.

20. Quoted in Ida Hayman Callery to Phil Callery, n.d. (ca. 1916), Ida Hayman Callery Papers, Santa Barbara, California (privately held); interview with Ann Callery Baxter, July 25, 1976, Shawnee Mission, Kansas; interview with Hattie Hayman Graham, December 2, 1977, Tulsa, Oklahoma; unidentified and undated clippings, Phil and Ida Hayman Callery Papers, Pittsburg State University, Pittsburg, Kansas; *People's College News* (Fort Scott, Kansas), 1 (August 1914), p. 13; *Little Rock Arkansas Gazette*, April 3, 4, 1912; *Joplin Free Press*, April 11, 18, 1914; I. H. Callery to Carl Thompson, June 23, July 1, 1913, Socialist Party Papers, National Office Files, Duke University; *Coming Nation* (Girard), May 11, 1912; *Progressive Woman* 5 (May 1912): 6; *Chicago Daily Socialist*, April 23, 1912; *Appeal to Reason*, February 20, April 17, May 22, July 3, December 4, 1909, March 2, April 13, 1912; "Convention Notes," *International Socialist Review* 12 (June 1912): 831. The 1914 Arkansas election returns can be found in the *Biennial Report of the Secretary of State of Arkansas, 1913-1920* (Little Rock, 1921), pp. 329-32. Her spouse, Phil Callery (1880-1954), was also a labor attorney and one of the SP's stellar organizers and orators.

21. *Vinita* (Oklahoma) *Daily Chieftain*, September 12, 1906; *Cestos* (Oklahoma) *Reporter*, January 19, 1906; Benton (Missouri) *Scott County Kicker*, October 14,

1911; Neil K. Basen, "Kate Richards O'Hare: The 'First Lady' of American Socialism, 1901-1917," *Labor History* 21 (Spring 1980): 165-199.

22. Gertrude Branstetter Stone and Theresa Branstetter Taft to author, November 3, 18, 30, 1975, January 1, 1978; Taft, "Homesteading in New Mexico, 1908-1909," (unpublished ms., 1978); *Hoye's City Directory of Kansas City, Missouri, 1897* (Kansas City, 1897), p. 616; W. P. Metcalf to Winnie Branstetter, August 20, 1909, Winnie Branstetter Papers, Providence (privately held); *Appeal to Reason*, September 26, 1908; *S.P. Official Bulletin* 5 (September 1908): 2, 5 (May 1909): 3; *Socialist Woman* 2 (October 1908): 15; *Oklahoma City Oklahoma Pioneer*, March 9, 30, October 29, 1910; *Sulphur* (Oklahoma) *New Century*, February 10, 1911; "Minutes of the State Executive Committee Meeting," April 3-4, 1910, Oklahoma City, (typescript), Socialist Party Papers, Bureau of Government Research Collection, University of Oklahoma, Norman; Branstetter to Victor Berger, n. d. [ca. November 1910], Social Democratic Party Papers, Milwaukee County Historical Society; *Chicago Daily Socialist*, November 10, 1908, May 17, 19, 1910; *Progressive Woman* 6 (July 1912): 5; ibid. 6 (January 1913): 9; *Glass Worker* 10 (November 1912): 5. On Branstetter's weak leadership over the Woman's National Committee, see M. J. Buhle, "Feminism and Socialism in the United States," pp. 360-71.

23. On Block, see *United Mine Workers' Journal*, May 12, 1910; *Oklahoma City Industrial Democrat*, May 7, 1910; *Anadarko* (Oklahoma) *Democrat*, May 12, 1910; Block Family Property Deeds, County Clerk, Caddo County, Anadarko, Oklahoma; *S.P. Official Bulletin* 5 (March 1909): 2; Death Certificate, October 21, 1926, Oklahoma State Board of Health, Oklahoma City. On Merts, see *Fort Worth Light*, April 3, 1915; *Henryetta* (Oklahoma) *Standard*, April 24, 1913; *Fallon* (Nevada) *Ballot Box*, June 14, 1913; *Hallettsville* (Texas) *Rebel*, June 27, 1914; *Goltry* (Oklahoma) *News*, September 19, 1913; *Prague* (Oklahoma) *News*, April 11, 18, 1913; *Oklahoma City Social Democrat*, June 4, 1913; *Sentinel* (Oklahoma) *Sword of Truth*, March 26, 1913; *Cotter* (Arkansas) *Record*, June 5, 1913.

24. Geraldine Payne Serle to author, September 22, 1978; *Santa Barbara People's Paper*, October 20, 1906; *Los Angeles Socialist*, September 5, 1903; *Agra* (Oklahoma) *News*, May 31, 1906; W.J. Bell to Thomas J. Morgan, October 19, 1909, Thomas J. Morgan Papers, Regenstein Library, University of Chicago, Chicago; Socialist Party, *Proceedings of the 1908 National Convention*, pp. 301-02, 305; *S.P. Official Bulletin* 3 (February 1907): 3; 4 (August 1908): 8; *New Castle* (Pennsylvania) *Solidarity*, August 27, September 17, 1910, May 6, 1911; *Spokane Industrial Worker*, November 2, 1910, April 27, 1911, July 4, October 17, 1912, *San Diego Labor Leader*, April 5, 19, June 28, 1912; *San Diego Union*, January 8, 10, 11, February 9, 10, 13, 19, March 25, April 19, 20, May 27, June 10, 21, 1912, January 11, 1936; Harris Weinstock, *Report to the Governor of California on the Disturbance in the City and County of San Diego in 1912* (Sacramento, 1912), p. 7; L.P. Emerson, *The Crack of Doom* (San Diego: privately published, n.d.), pp. 13-15, 19-36; *San Diego International*, August 1, 15, 1914; Probate Records, File No. 24947, Superior Court of the State of California, San Diego.

25. On Dietz, see Melda Faye Dietz Duhon to author, September 7, 1978; *Lake Charles American Press*, March 3, 1963, clipping in Walter Dietz Papers, Louisiana State University, Baton Rouge. On Beals-Hoffpauir, see *Chattanooga News*, September 29, 1906; Lee Baxandall, "May Beals: A Voice for the Voiceless," (unpub-

lished essay, 1978); *Little Rock Arkansas Gazette*, November 4, 1906; *Maryville* (Tennessee) *Times*, July 25, 1905; *Nashville Labor Advocate*, August 12, 1904, October 13, 1905; *Chicago Daily Socialist*, November 16, 1906; *Socialist Woman* 1 (August 1907): 4; *Progressive Woman* 2 (April 1909): 7; Manuscript Population Schedule, 1900, Federal Census, Mermentau, Arcadia Parish, Louisiana. M. Beals-Hoffpauir to Upton Sinclair, May 20, 1918, Upton Sinclair Papers, Lilly Library, Indiana University, Bloomington, Indiana. For a digest of Beals-Hoffpauir's essays and poetry, see *The Rebel At Large* (Chicago: Charles H. Kerr & Co., 1906); and the 1907-1908 issues of the *Abbeville* (Louisiana) *Red Flag* and *Maryville* (Tennessee) *Southern Clarion*.

26. See for example, Ida Porter Boyer, "Oklahoma," *Woman[']s Era* 1 (May 1910]: 268-69; H. M. Sinclair, "The Real Democracy of the Socialist Party," *Harlow's Weekly*, April 25, 1914, pp. 62-63; Freda Hogan, "Women Socialists in Arkansas," *Vinita* (Oklahoma) *Daily Chieftain*, May 24, 1909; *Okemah* (Oklahoma) *Sledge Hammer*, February 19, 1914; *Carmen* (Oklahoma) *Sunlight*, December 4, 1914; *Joplin Free Press*, March 14, 1914; E. W. Perrin, "The Needs of Man," *Little Rock Union Labor Bulletin*, May 23, 1903; *American Socialist* 5 (March 1958): 17.

27. Quoted in *Abbeville* (Louisiana) *Red Flag*, October 1907; interview with Freda Hogan Ameringer, December 11, 1977, Oklahoma City; Basen, "Kate Richards O'Hare"; M. J. Buhle, "Feminism and Socialism," esp. pp. 299-311. A few Jennie Higginses were staunch prohibitionists who denounced both dancing schools and halls because they fostered white slavery and other social evils. See for example, *Alva* (Oklahoma) *Constructive Socialist*, March 12, 19, 1913.

28. Emilio Zamora, Jr., "Chicano Socialist Labor Activity in Texas, 1900-1920," *Aztlán* 6 (Summer 1975): 221-36; Walter Marion Raymond, *Rebels of the New South* (Chicago, Charles H. Kerr & Company, 1905); Donald R. Graham, "Red, White, and Black: An Interpretation of Ethnic and Racial Attitudes of Agrarian Radicals in Texas and Oklahoma, 1880-1920" (M.A. thesis, University of Saskatchewan, 1973), p. 165; conversation with Gertrude Bransetter Stone, April 10, 1976, St. Louis; interview with Freda Hogan Ameringer, December 11, 1977; Bruce Dancis, "Socialism and Women in the United States, 1901-1917," *Socialist Revolution* 6 (January-March 1976): 103-17. On southwestern SP racial attitudes, see Burbank, *When Farmers Voted Red*, pp. 69-89; Philip S. Foner, *American Socialism and Black Americans* (Westport, Conn., Greenwood Press, 1977) esp. pp. 238-53.

29. Green, *Grass-Roots Socialism*, pp. 345-83; M. J. Buhle, "Feminism and Socialism in the United States," pp. 373-76; Caroline A. Lowe to Marcet Haldeman-Julius, December 8, 1931, Haldeman-Julius Papers, Pittsburg State University, Pittsburg, Kansas; Brad Light to author, July 9, 1978. Krehbiel attended various CP-sponsored activities and events while living with her daughter in France between 1920 and 1933.

30. Telephone interview with Harvey Hardy, April 14, 1979; Ruth Jackson to author, June 12, 1978; *Malvern* (Arkansas) *Meteor*, April 5, 1922; *Eugene Register-Guard*, January 19, 1966; Ruth Anne Garrison to author, December 19, 1978; Freda Hogan to Theodore Debs, December 26, 1919, Debs Papers, Indiana State University; Hogan to Powers Hapgood, July 31, 1926, Powers Hapgood Papers, Lilly Library, Indiana University, Bloomington; interviews with Freda Hogan Ameringer, July 9, 1973, December 11, 1977, Oklahoma City.

31. Quoted in K. R. O'Hare to Samuel Castleton, September 16, 1945, Samuel

Castleton Papers, Eugene V. Debs Collection, Tamiment Library, New York University, New York; interview with Roger Baldwin, December 9, 1974, New York; K. R. O'Hare-Cunningham to Theodore Debs, March 26, 1931, Debs Papers, Indiana State University; K. R. O'Hare-Cunningham to A. James McDonald, n.d. [ca. June 1947], Frank P. O'Hare Papers, Missouri Historical Society, St. Louis; K. R. O'Hare to Nathan Fine, November 7, 1936 (carbon), Howard Y. Williams Papers, Minnesota Historical Society, St. Paul; K. R. O'Hare to Earl Warren, December 2, 1943, Earl Warren Papers, Bancroft Library, University of California-Berkeley; K. R. O'Hare, "I was Sick and in Prison," (unpublished memoirs, 1947, in author's possession), pp. 281, 292-98, 300-10, 514-19.

32. Laura Payne Emerson, *Revelation vs. Evolution or God's Kingdom on Earth* (San Diego: privately published, 1925); Geraldine Payne Serle to author, September 22, 1978; Theresa Branstetter Taft to author, January 1, 1978; telephone interview with Maynard C. Krueger, December 18, 1975; interview with Ira Finley, December 10, 1977, Oklahoma City; East Louisiana State Hospital Records, Jackson, Louisiana; Baxandall, "May Beals."

33. For the Finnish, Danish, and Norwegian patterns, see for example, Albert N. Gilbertson, "Progress of Socialism in Norway," *International Socialist Review* 5 (February 1905): 483; *The American Labor Yearbook, 1916* (New York, 1916), p. 176; *Coming Nation* (Girard), January 28, 1911; *Kristiania* (Norway) *Social-Demokraten*, December 6, 1913; *St. Louis Labor*, May 25, June 1, 8, 1907, March 5, 1910; Katharine Anthony, *Feminism in Germany and Scandinavia* (New York: Henry Holt and Company, 1915), p. 227; Finnish Diet Rosters, 1907-1913, Työväen Arkisto, Helsinki. I am indebted to Matti Simola for these illuminating data.

6

THE POLITICS OF MUTUAL FRUSTRATION: SOCIALISTS AND SUFFRAGISTS IN NEW YORK AND WISCONSIN

John D. Buenker

The Socialist and the Suffragist[1]

Said the Socialist to the Suffragist:
    "My cause is greater than yours!
    You only work for a Special Class,
    We for the gain of the General Mass,
    Which every good ensures!"

Said the Suffragist to the Socialist:
    "You underrate my Cause!
    While women remain a Subject Class,
    You never can move the General Mass,
    With your Economic Laws!"

Said the Socialist to the Suffragist:
    "You misinterpret facts!
    There is no room for doubt or schism
In Economic Determinism—
    It governs all our acts!"

Said the Suffragist to the Socialist:
    "You men will always find
    That this old world will never move
    More swiftly in its ancient groove
    While women stay behind!"

"A lifted world lifts women up,"
    The Socialist explained.
    "You cannot lift the world at all
    While half of it is kept so small,"
    The Suffragist maintained.

The World awoke, and tartly spoke:
    "Your work is all the same:
    Work together or work apart,
    Work, each of you, with all your heart—
    Just get into the game!"

Charlotte Perkins Gilman, 1912

Of all the unlikely coalitions produced during the progressive era, perhaps none seems more incongruous at first glance than the tenuous alliance between suffragists and socialists. Suffragists, in theory, regarded sexual discrimination as the most pervasive cause of society's ills and believed that its eradication would achieve social justice under the prevailing socio-economic system. Socialists assigned that same pivotal causation to class exploitation, and held that the creation of the Cooperative Commonwealth would "automatically" eliminate sexual inequities. Yet, in two states at least, Wisconsin and New York, these two groups were able to submerge their contradictory world-views temporarily and to cooperate on the enactment of women suffrage because each believed that enfranchisement would benefit its cause.

Crucial to the success of these shaky coalitions was the participation of a number of remarkable socialist women who sought to combine the feminist and socialist visions in the quest for real equality, both social and sexual. With their prodding and under the press of practical politics, suffragists accepted support from whatever quarter proferred, while socialists, despite open skepticism, gambled that the enfranchisement of women would ultimately augment their ranks. This apparent agreement, however, barely concealed major differences between suffragists and socialists, between male and female socialists, and even among women socialists themselves, differences which eventually demonstrated that woman suffrage had produced neither a unified woman's movement nor advanced the cause of socialism. Even before the ratification of the Nineteenth Amendment, however, there was ample electoral evidence that woman suffrage would not increase party membership and that women were, if anything, less likely than men to vote Socialist. Furthermore, analysis of electoral data shows that many socialists failed to support woman suffrage at the polls.

The mainstream suffrage movement consisted primarily of such organizations as the National American Woman Suffrage Association (NAWSA), the Southern States Suffrage Conference, and the National Woman's Party (NWP). Their membership consisted primarily of native-born, middle-class, Protestant women who were better educated than their sisters, possessed of more leisure time, and often desirous of pursuing a career outside of the home.[2] Since, by definition, woman suffragists could not vote, they sought allies from among those reform organizations dominated by males of similar ethnoreligious and socioeconomic backgrounds. It was this essentially native, Protestant, middle-class character of the movement that greatly limited its appeal. Increasingly, though, the ethnocentric, class-conscious strain was effectively modified in the interest of gaining additional support, both from among other segments of the female population and from a variety of hostile or indifferent, male-dominated organizations. This change in outlook brought significant numbers of working-class, immigrant-stock women into the suffrage coalition for the first time and provided the leverage for wooing men from the same backgrounds.[3]

In 1901, the newly formed Socialist party endorsed "unrestricted and equal suffrage for men and women," and pledged itself "to engage in an active campaign in that direction," a distinction it held alone until the Progressive party followed suit in 1912. There were only eight women delegates at that first convention, but their numbers increased significantly through the efforts of the Woman's National Socialist Union which helped organize women's branches and auxiliaries around the country. The party's support for women suffrage gained a new sense of urgency when the International Socialist Congress at Stuttgart in 1907 declared that "it is the duty of Socialist Parties of all countries to agitate most energetically for the introduction of universal womanhood suffrage" which should "not be conditioned by property, taxation, education, or any other qualification which should exclude members of the laboring classes from the enjoyment of this right." The 1908 convention of the SP created a Woman's National Committee (WNC), which was charged with the dual task of agitating for women's rights within a socialist framework and of trying to enlist women in the party. The WNC was a body of outstanding socialist women, many of whom had already achieved prominence within the party, the woman's movement, and wider reform and labor circles. In 1909, the WNC created Woman's Day, on which the peculiar status and problems of working-class women were recognized by parades, demonstrations, and meetings. At the 1910 Party Congress, the WNC was awarded a full-time general correspondent to carry on its organizational and propaganda efforts. Socialist women founded their own unofficial newspaper—*Socialist Woman* (later *Progressive Woman*)—in 1907, and other socialist organs, such as the *New York Call* and the *Milwaukee Leader*, began women's pages and columns. Socialist legislators consistently supported state-wide woman suffrage proposals while the party openly worked for the passage of a referendum in every state where the issue arose.[4]

The reasons for the socialists' role in the woman suffrage coalition were both practical and ideological. The possibility of converting woman suffrage advocates to the support of a wide variety of socioeconomic reforms meant the potential addition of millions of voters favorable to the "immediate demands" of the Socialist party. Moreover, like every other male-dominated organization that endorsed woman suffrage, the Socialist party fervently believed that women would be inclined toward their cause in higher percentages than men were, given the proper education and mobilization. "If the working class of the United States displayed the same intelligence that the women voters are doing," an *Appeal to Reason* editorial noted typically in 1915, "Socialism would be nearer than it is." The *Appeal* argued that the attitude of the major parties "is driving many of these suffragists to Socialism," and that once women gained sufficient political experience and savvy to hold the "capitalist" parties responsible for society's evils, "they will be ready to turn to the Socialist Party as an instrument by which to construct a government and an organization of industry that shall banish these things from the world forever." Few socialists were sanguine enough to believe that this process would be automatic, and most admitted openly that such a result would ensue only if the party engaged in massive educational and propaganda efforts, sponsored voter registration and mobilization campaigns among working-class women, and undertook the naturalization of foreign-born females. Only rarely did Socialist analysts express any overt doubts that they might actually lose ground if women were enfranchised, as when Vida Scudder noted in 1914 that "Socialism seems in less danger than the churches of being flooded with women." Even then, they generally urged that socialists support woman suffrage on grounds of justice and rely upon the same historical forces that they counted upon to convert a majority of male voters. John M. Work, an editor of the *Milwaukee Leader*, urged socialist votes on behalf of the 1912 Wisconsin suffrage referendum because "I believe that equal suffrage would hasten the coming of Socialism, but no matter whether it would hasten or delay it, we should stand for it with equal aggressiveness."[5]

On the theoretical level, socialists supported woman suffrage because it supplied a partial solution to the Woman Question which was in turn a vital segment of the Social Question that underlay all of socialism. "We Socialists do not simply say we should like to liberate them," Luella Krehbiel wrote in *Socialist Woman*, "but we have a scientific process by which it shall be done." Women, especially working-class women, were "slaves of slaves," the victims of a double, interconnected bondage forged by sex and class. Socialists posited a prehistoric "Golden Age of Women" in which the dominant modes of production were communal and women occupied a pre-eminent position known as the mother-right. During the transition from this period of "Barbarism" to "Civilization" society replaced communal organization with private property, became divided into classes, and over-threw the mother-right, an event described by Engels as "the world historical defeat of the female sex." Consequently, the same historical forces that subjected the working class to exploitation also bound women, mean-ing the liberation of one was inextricably bound up with the freeing of the other. Unlike the woman suffragists who sought only sexual equality under the prevailing socioeconomic system, socialists aimed "to remove all bar-riers that make one human being dependent upon another, which includes the dependence of one sex upon the other. This solution of the woman ques-tion is identical with the solution of the social question." Although working conditions and wages of women were initially even worse than those of male laborers, the Industrial Revolution at least released them from domes-tic servitude, made them economically free of men, and put them in a position to organize and agitate for their own deliverance. It was these working women that socialism hoped to reach with its message of double liberation and who would become "the advance guard of advanced women." The socialist woman, as New Yorker Theresa Malkiel argued, had a "double mission" to perform: "As a socialist she has pledged herself to educate and agitate for the abolition of wage slavery. As a woman she can-not very well refrain from awakening her slumbering sisters from their pro-longed lethargy." The motto of the Woman's National Committee was "to make intelligent Socialists and Suffragists of women and to secure their ac-tive membership in the Socialist Party" while one of its fundamental tenets proclaimed that "the Socialist who is not a Feminist lacks breadth; the Feminist who is not a Socialist is lacking in strategy."[6]

Beyond that general consensus, though, there were serious disagreements on both strategy and priorities which limited cooperation in achieving woman suffrage. The Stuttgart Resolution warned that "Socialist Women shall not carry on this struggle for complete equality of right of vote in alliance with the middle class woman suffragists, but in common with the Socialists Parties, which insist upon Woman Suffrage as one of the funda-mental and most important reforms for the full democratization of political franchise in general." The weakness of the SP in the United States and the consequent need for coalition building, however, necessitated that U.S. socialists work in concert with "middle class woman suffragists." But, because of their ideology and orientation, socialist suffragists stressed mass meetings, parades, petitions, rallies, foreign-language pamphlets, and support for strikers, methods which held particular promise of reaching working-class women. Their arguments were primarily a mixture of socialism and "expediency" rather than appeals to justice or sexual equality. "If I speak," *New York Call* columnist Anita Block wrote, "it must be as a Socialist, on behalf of the exploited workingwoman, my great proletarian sisterhood." Meta Berger, a prominent socialist-suffragist, described her relationship with NAWSA leaders as "pleasant enough on the surface, but underneath there was an undercurrent of suspicion and distrust, of which I was aware but which I chose to ignore," and regarded their attitude as "most undemocratic and spiteful; even going so far as to be envious of my most beautiful dress." Their unique emphasis on class differences caused woman socialists to regard feminist claims of sexual solidarity with healthy skepticism and to realize that women would likely split along socio-economic and other lines, once they obtained the franchise. This perspec-tive also caused socialists to reject the educational, property, and lengthy U.S. residency requirements for voting, devices which native, middle-class women often urged as a counterforce to male immigrant and black voters, and to emphasize naturalization and voter registration drives among the proletariat. Socialists also had problems with the suffragists' insistence upon nonpartisanship, since they were openly seeking converts to a political organization.[7]

Woman suffrage also provoked significant disagreements within socialist ranks, partly along male-female lines but also among women socialists themselves. Despite the party's official stand, it acted "without the enthusiasm it demonstrated for issues it perceived to be of serious significance." Nearly all males shared the view that the Woman Question was of far less importance than the Social Question, that suffrage was less significant than many other immediate demands, and that socialism would render most of the agitation for sexual equality unnecessary. When male socialists insisted upon the primacy of the Social Question over the Woman Question, women com-rades generally conceded that "the real freedom of man cannot be achieved before the entire social problem is solved," but insisted that "under a regime of political tyranny the first and most urgent ideal is necessarily the con-quest of political liberty."[8]

These ideological differences were reflected in organization and funding for issues of special interest to women socialists. Their male comrades were highly suspicious of attempts to set up autonomous agencies with indepen-dent or guaranteed funding, but, at the same time, they were reluctant to grant women anything like an equal voice within the party structure. There were always difficulties over the relationship between women's units and the mainstream party, over the amount and method of funding, and over the type of "approved" activities in which the unit could engage. The hand-ful of socialist women who had achieved acceptance and prominence in party ranks on their own merits sometimes rivaled males in their derision of special organizations and programs for women. Debates over separate organization and funding always found prominent women on both sides of the issue, including the discussion over the formation of the WNC in 1908 and its dissolution in 1915. Similarly the subject of cooperation with "bourgeois" suffrage organizations even drove fissures into the ranks of the militant New York contingent. So divided were socialist women on the question that the *Call*'s two women columnists, Anita Block and Meta Stern Lilienthal, regularly disagreed in print.[9] Given the complex nature of the suffrage issue, the disagreements between suffragists and socialists, and the intraparty divisions, it is not surprising that collaboration between the two movements ended in mutual frustration. The remarkable point is that Socialist legislators and electors in New York and Milwaukee lent their support to the suffrage cause for so many years.

In New York socialists and suffragists cooperated in the unsuccessful referendum of 1915, maintaining a coalition against the opposition of the two major political parties. Socialists were desirous of enfranchising the large body of women laborers who presumably were potential socialists, while suffragists were willing to accept support even from radical sources to overcome their electoral disadvantage. Following the mayoral candidacy of Morris Hillquit, the "conversion" of the two major parties to suffrage, and, above all, the divisive issues of World War I, however, the differences in outlook and motivation between the two movements came into sharper focus. Ironically the triumph of suffrage in the 1917 referendum, even though welcomed by the socialists, was accompanied by bitter exchanges between them and the mainstream suffragists and the creation of an unbridgeable chasm on ideological grounds.

New York socialists were the party's most militant advocates of remaining structurally distinct from suffrage organizations, and by 1910, the Women's Committee of Greater New York had created numerous Socialist Suffrage Clubs to bring the party's feminist message to working-class women. The membership of the Committee and of the suffrage clubs consisted primarily of women who were products of New York's unique Russian-Jewish socialist trade union milieu. For them, as for hundreds of thousands of men and women, socialism and trade unionism were "Judaism secularized," vehicles for carrying out the ethical mandates of *Hevras* and *tsedaka* (the Jewish notion of charity and distributive justice) even while rejecting the rituals and beliefs of Orthodoxy. This outlook was reinforced by the influx of Old World radicals, and by living and working conditions in the United States, where Jews and Italians of all ages and both sexes labored in the sweatshops of the garment industries. These conditions gave rise to such socialist-oriented labor organizations as the International Ladies' Garment Workers' Union, the United Hebrew Trades, and the United Cloth Hat and Cloak Makers Union, which were "not merely bargaining agencies" but "centers of social-cultural life." As a sizeable portion of the work force in the garment trades and the principal victims of such tragedies as the Triangle Shirtwaist Fire, Jewish women turned increasingly to unionism, radicalism, and political action, under the tutelage of male socialists, union organizers, settlement workers, and the Women's Trade Union League

(WTUL). Strikes and political campaigns provided the training ground for leaders, convinced many male comrades of the value of woman suffrage, and increased the sense of solidarity between working-class women and their middle- and upper-class sisters who dominated the WTUL and the mainstream suffrage associations.[10]

The closest rival to Socialist suffrage organizations was the Equality League of Self-Supporting Women, created by Harriet Stanton Blatch, daughter of Elizabeth Cady Stanton and devotee of the militant tactics of the British suffrage movement. Blatch was an ideological socialist and trade union organizer; her efforts were largely instrumental in getting the New York State legislature to propose a constitutional amendment. The two organizations worked separately and in concert to reach working-class women through rallies, parades, and mass meetings, while stressing the utility of the vote for improving working and living conditions. This increased activity among the working class called forth greater official efforts by the Socialist party in New York, although women members frequently complained of neglect and indifference on the part of their male comrades. Still, the 1912 suffrage parade featured over 5,000 socialist marchers, and the party gave significant, if sometimes grudging, support to the Socialist Suffrage Campaign for ratification of the constitutional amendment in 1915. The Women's Committee organized hundreds of volunteers, held mass meetings, distributed literature, and staged naturalization campaigns to bring immigrant women into the campaign. The party's Central Committee hired a salaried organizer and circulated suffrage petitions. To raise money, SSCC (Socialist Suffrage Coordinating Committtee) sold a Socialist Suffrage Stamp, which commemorated the "relation of ideal comradeship and perfect cooperation of men and women in the Socialist movement." The Socialist Suffragist Conference in March of 1915 attracted over 200 delegates and pledged to hold "one street meeting for every square block in the city before November 2." Exhilirated by the prospect of victory, the party's Central Committee allowed socialists to march in the 30,000-person suffrage parade, albeit by a close vote, stepped up its efforts "six-fold," and used the pages of the *Call* and the *Advocate* to encourage male socialists.[11]

Given the effort on both sides, the defeat of the referendum on November 4, 1915, proved bitterly disappointing to suffragists and socialists alike. Statewide, the amendment received approximately 42 percent of the votes cast, and it failed to carry Greater New York City by an almost identical proportion. The measure received a plurality in only four of the sixty-three assembly districts in the city, and then only by paper-thin margins. Three of those, the Sixth and Eighth in Manhattan and the Thirty-Fourth in the Bronx, were among the most socialist districts in the entire city. Since there were few significant offices at stake, it is difficult to estimate the correlation between the socialist and suffrage votes, but the general success enjoyed by the amendment in districts that were traditionally socialist strongholds and the fact that only the Socialist party endorsed ratification indicate that many male comrades responded positively.[12]

Nevertheless, the defeat of the referendum strengthened the position of party members who opposed socialist participation in the mainstream suffrage movement and special organizations devoted to women's rights. The SSCC insisted that its efforts had increased party membership in the city by 25 percent and that the amendment had carried in those districts where it had been most active. SSCC also charged that the results would have been even more successful if the Central Committee had been more whole-hearted and prompt in its support. Apparently unimpressed, the Central Committee withdrew its membership from participation in the SSCC and ceased all financial backing in March of 1916. During the next year, the SSCC continued to function on a voluntary basis, although its attention was increasingly drawn toward the war in Europe. With the resubmission of the amendment by the legislature and a referendum set for November of 1917, however, the party once again focused its attention on woman suffrage. A mass meeting was held in December of 1916 to plan strategy; the Central Committee reinstated the SSCC the following June, and the *Call* resumed its women's features.[13]

Several developments, however, guaranteed that socialist participation in the suffrage referendum would be different from what it had been in 1915 and that cooperation with "bourgeois" suffrage organizations would be almost nonexistent. The mayoral candidacy of Morris Hillquit sharpened the differences between socialists and non-socialists, making cooperation on the suffrage referendum increasingly difficult. Hillquit was the first of the four candidates to endorse the referendum, and he challenged his opponents to follow suit. Tammany Hall, sensing the imminent victory of woman suffrage, wavered between benevolent neutrality and open advocacy of ratification. Eventually Democrat John J. "Red Mike" Hylan, Fusionist Mayor John Purroy Mitchel, and Republican William Bennett all concurred, removing the issue from the arena of partisan politics and all but guaranteeing its success in the city. With the backing of the major political parties, mainstream suffragists could easily eschew socialist support and couple their advocacy of ratification with vigorous denunciations of Hillquit. This strategy was all the more appealing because the amendment's opponents tried to tar it with the socialist brush.[14]

Even more damaging to the socialist-suffragist cooperation, however, were the effects of World War I. American entry severely split the party, with many prominent members, mostly those of British-American backgrounds, openly backing the war and denouncing their erstwhile comrades as unpatriotic or worse. One woman correspondent even assured the *New York Times* that "most intelligent Socialists" were for Mitchel and that those comrades who supported Hillquit demonstrated their "mental as well as patriotic deficiency." Hillquit made the war, with its economic and civil liberties consequences, the key issue in the campaign, while his three opponents alternately labeled him as bolshevik or pro-German. Meanwhile, the New York branch of NAWSA, with whom the SSCC had successfully cooperated in 1915, had changed its name to the State Woman Suffrage party and suspended its suffrage activities in favor of war mobilization. Voicing frequent and vigorous opposition to the war, socialist women denounced the mainstream suffragists for being "so completely swamped with war work" and for neglecting the woman's cause in favor of "bandage rolling, suffrage farmeretting, census taking and various other kinds of patriotic service." The only non-socialist suffrage organization with whom the SSCC was able to cooperate was the National Woman's party, which refused to put the suffrage question in abeyance until after the war. The *Call* gave increasing space to NWP activities, applauding its militancy and denouncing suppression of its civil liberties. The absence of real cooperation between socialists and suffragists became clear when, by mutual consent, socialists refused to march in the pre-election parade in October, limiting themselves to distributing literature to spectators, and suffragists refused to invite Hillquit and Max Eastman, prominent literary radical and editor of *The Masses*, to their conference in Saratoga, despite their frequent speeches in favor of ratification. Theresa Malkiel, chief organizer of the all-out 1915 socialist suffrage effort, labeled its 1917 counterpart as "lackadaisical," chiefly due to the apathy of the male leadership and declining finances. Even so, the party sponsored a giant suffrage pageant in Union Square at which 10,000 people cheered proreferendum speeches by numerous socialist leaders and candidates. The SSCC was pointedly mandated to operate "under auspices of and in closest cooperation with the Socialist Party"; cooperation with middle-class suffrage societies was unequivocably condemned.[15]

Socialists claimed and received a good deal of credit for the referendum's success, although most of the latter came from people who were hostile to either socialism or woman suffrage. Hillquit later referred to ratification as a "very important by-product" of his mayoral campaign, claiming that it had "never been fully appreciated to what extent this Socialist campaign helped the women of the country secure the right to vote." Indeed, Hillquit could make such a claim. In Hillquit's view, "the leaders of the movement were rather pessimistic about the outlook and were preparing to curtail their campaign activities," until "the aroused public interest that marked the mayoralty campaign from the outset seemed to me to offer a splendid opportunity to serve the cause of woman suffrage." Hillquit and his fellow socialists stressed the justice of equal suffrage in order to attract those who might be repelled by the party's utilitarian arguments. As the gap widened between themselves and the mainstream suffragists, however, socialists increasingly stressed the particular value of the franchise for the working class and the Socialist party. New York socialists pointed to the immediate benefit in additional votes for labor and welfare measures, but cautioned that no one could legitimately expect women's votes to do what men's had been unable to do.[16]

On October 10, Hillquit had sent an open letter to Hylan, Bennett, and Mitchel urging them to support the amendment in "righting the age-old wrong" and asserting that the "issue of woman suffrage overshadows them all as a permanent measure of social justice and progress." Hillquit's opponents initially ignored his challenge, but Mitchel eventually replied that, although he personally planned to vote for the referendum, he did not consider suffrage to be a legitimate campaign issue. Hillquit countered that suffrage was more significant than the loyalty issue and pointedly warned them that the socialists would reap the lion's share of the benefits if the other parties failed to endorse the amendment. Whatever his motives or influence, Hillquit's stance illustrated socialism's suffrage dilemma: to be effective advocates of the amendment, they had to downplay its utility to their cause and make it a nonpartisan issue, but, in so doing, they helped to undermine its value to socialism. Hillquit publicly hailed the referendum's success even while acknowledging his own defeat and claimed that, though they deserved the credit, socialists "were satisfied with the conviction that they materially helped in the triumph of a good and progressive cause." Their lively campaign, he insisted, had increased the normal socialist vote by over 110,000 votes, more than enough to account for the amendment's 100,000 vote bulge in the city, since every socialist voted in favor of ratification. His contention was seconded by the NWP, which asserted that the 110,000 vote increase in socialist voting was enough to swing the tide to suffrage, recounted the party's efforts on behalf of the cause, and concluded that "New York state and national suffragists both owe to the *Call* and the Socialist Party obligations for the most generous service." Several prominent suffragists echoed those sentiments at a rally celebrating the referendum victory.[17]

The opponents of suffrage were also only too glad to attribute the measure's success to socialism. An antisuffragist tract published just before the election charged that "every Socialist, every Pacifist, every Feminist, every I.W.W. believes in Woman Suffrage," and that a vote for the amendment would "help the Reds of both Sexes to Russianize the greatest State in the Union" and "help the Kaiser to Prussianize the American People." The chairwoman of the city antisuffrage campaign attributed the measure's success to "the alliance between Socialism, pacifism and woman suffrage." The *New York Times* also claimed that socialists had given woman suffragists a gift, but urged women to use that present as a weapon with which to destroy Socialism. An analysis in the *Boston Herald-Journal* attributed ratification to the twin evils of Tammany Hall and socialism, noting that "the more conservative suffragists are reluctant to admit that all suffragists are Socialists, but they cannot deny that all Socialists are suffragists."[18]

The suffragists denied the claims of both socialists and the opponents of suffrage. In a detailed discussion, Mary Garrett Hay, chairwoman of NAWSA's 1917 campaign, insisted that there were only three assembly districts in Manhattan where the suffrage amendment did not poll at least a thousand votes more than the socialists polled "and that even there the difference averaged 600." In Brooklyn's three greatest socialist strongholds, she continued, suffrage also ran significantly ahead; city-wide the amendment outpolled socialism by over 80,000 votes. "No candidate for Mayor," Hay concluded, "was in the class with the amendment, though all were for suffrage." While socialists naturally accepted credit for the victory, they carefully separated themselves from any connection with the mainstream suffrage movement. The *Call* based its claim in the calculations that the amendment received a plurality of 2,392 in the ten Assembly Districts carried by socialists and only 1,034 in the fifty-two carried by candidates of the other two parties. In condescending fashion, the *Call* turned the tables on both the suffragists and the anti-suffragists:

Cheer up ladies, and calm down. Things are not as bad as they seem. The Socialists will give you a clean bill of health, and proclaim it from the housetops if you wish. It was through no fault of yours that the Socialists got the vote for you and the rest of the women in New York. You always did your very best to prevent their public espousal of the suffrage cause. But the time had come when they did what they wanted with you instead of trying to do what you wanted with them.

Socialists, the paper concluded, did not support the amendment to gain recognition or to win converts to their cause and party, but rather "because the cause of unrestricted adult suffrage is an undeniable part of their cause. In doing so, they were doing their own particular work, not yours."[19]

The validity of these claims and counterclaims are impossible to determine with complete accuracy. All the parties involved had a vested interest in asserting or denying socialist instrumentality in the election and selected their evidence accordingly. An analysis of the referendum vote, though, suggests that socialists gave the amendment substantial, but not determining, support. Eleven of suffrage's eighteen banner Assembly Districts also produced socialist majorities, while the eleven most socialist Assembly Districts provided the amendment with percentages ranging from 62 to 73 in a city that favored the measure by only 57 percent. Even granting them all the best of it, though, it is likely that socialist voters provided somewhere between one-fourth and one-third of the total vote for suffrage. Given the discrepancy between the total votes cast for the amendment and those cast for city and state office, the endorsement of suffrage by all four mayoral candidates, and the real opposition to suffrage that existed among many male socialists, it seems unreasonable to claim a more substantial figure. Despite the party's consistent support for woman suffrage, the election returns suggest strongly that about 20-25 percent of socialist voters declared against ratification while another 33 percent failed to cast a ballot in the referendum.[20]

The coalition that produced the suffrage victory in New York did not survive beyond the referendum. The split between socialists and suffragists had been almost complete during the campaign, and the subsequent debate over the magnitude of the party's contribution to the victory ensured that no reconciliation would take place. The sole purpose of their increasingly tenuous collaboration had been achieved, and it was clear that both movements had divergent plans for newly enfranchised women. Suffragists sought political influence and position under the umbrella of the two major parties, while the socialists laid plans to build a new consitituency among working-class women. In a *Call* column the day after the election, Meta Stern Lilienthal noted that socialist women, flushed with exhiliration, were greeting each other with such salutations as "Good morning, Sister Citizen" and "Congratulations, enfranchised Comrade," but she warned them not to rest on their laurels. To turn the suffrage victory into a socialist opportunity, she insisted, the party had to engage in recruitment, propaganda, and naturalization campaigns and convince working-class women to strive for "immediate social reforms of special importance to themselves and their children." This emphasis permeated the party's numerous rallies and "jollification" dinners held to celebrate the victory, and was expressed in such slogans as "the campaign is dead, long live the campaign" and in the formation of such organizations as the Naturalization Aid League. Reflecting the final break with the mainstream suffrage movement, Theresa Malkiel, organizer of the SSCC, argued that "there are no more antis, but there are still anti-socialists. So henceforth the classifications of women voters will be Socialist and anti-Socialists." Lilienthal argued that socialist women would mount an all-out effort to enroll women, but that "they will no longer do it as women, having a grievance all their own, they will do it as socialists, as members of the party."[21]

Such an orientation caused strains in the relationship with the National Woman's party; both groups could collaborate in naturalization, registration, and unionization drives among working-class women and on immediate legislative gains, but not on ultimate goals. As early as November 22, 1917, Mary Dreir of the Woman's Trade Union League and chairwomen of the Industrial Section of NWP, chided socialists for failing to do their part in an organizational parade. The *Call* continued to print favorable stories and editorials about NWP, but actual cooperation between the two became less frequent. Although New York socialists maintained their support of suffrage through the ratification of the Nineteenth Amendment, they did so from a self-consciously unique perspective and in complete isolation from the mainstream suffrage movement. This was especially true because the debate on the amendment took place during the Red Scare, just prior to the expulsion of the party's legislators from the state assembly. Socialist Assemblyman August Claesens of Brooklyn led the party's delegation in support of ratification of the amendment, but used the opportunity to express the party's peculiar view of the issue. While chiding his fellow legislators for delaying the matter so long, Claesens nevertheless charged that "voting once a year for one officeholder or another is picayune, and this measure a petty reform. These women and men," he continued, "also are demanding the right not only to vote once a year but to have a say in the management of industries in which they are employed." Under the pressure of events, socialist women generally agreed with his assessment. Anita Block argued in the *Call* that the change was ten years too late to really thrill socialist women, and that "the subject of political rights along presently accepted lines is one about which radical women have already stopped thinking. The radical woman is now looking forward to voting as it is done in the Soviet, and pure political suffrage has ceased to have interest or value for her."[22]

While the triumph of suffrage helped New York socialist women reaffirm the primacy of their class identification over their sexual one and to heal the rift between them and their male comrades, it did not entirely erase the residue of hostility and bitterness. While proclaiming that male-female differences were "a matter of history and a new leaf has been turned over," Lillienthal could not resist scoring "the unwillingness or inability of many Socialist men to recognize the importance of the work for woman suffrage." Acknowledging the party's official position on the matter and "the splendid Socialist vote" that helped produce victory, she nevertheless reminded her male comrades that "it was the work of the Socialist women within the party that forced the issue and called into being the Socialist suffrage campaigns. Socialist women, like all others, had to act upon the recognition that he who would be free himself must strike the blow." Male socialists rarely responded to such allegations; they proclaimed their continued commitment to equality, both sexual and social, and had no further need to debate the issue of separate organization or propaganda. They supported efforts to organize and naturalize women even though these apparently brought few positive benefits to the party; voter registration figures in 1918 showed that less than one-fourth of those who declared themselves socialists were women.[23]

Meta Berger. (Courtesy of Doris Berger Hursley.)

In Milwaukee, socialists and suffragists also collaborated effectively during the progressive era, only to end up at each other's throats by 1919. Socialist leaders and the party press consistently endorsed suffrage in the strongest possible terms, while socialist legislators supported every important measure. Socialists of both sexes held office in the Wisconsin Woman Suffrage Association (WWSA), socialist speakers were regularly included on suffrage programs, and WWSA stressed the endorsement of the SDP (Social Democratic party) in its campaign literature. Yet, after the defeat of the 1912 suffrage referendum, relations between the two steadily deteriorated; WWSA leaders attributed the loss partly to the poor showing of socialist voters. This decline was exacerbated by the socialists' increasing cooperation with the National Woman's party, and by the devastating impact of World War I and Americanization drives. It culminated in the bitter Milwaukee School Board election of 1919, which pitted the socialists against nearly every other element of Milwaukee society in a furious bid for the support of female voters. Just as in New York, the fundamental differences in outlook and expectations between socialists and suffragists, reinforced by the introduction of cross-cutting issues that fragmented both camps, shattered the hopes of feminists for a "woman vote" and convinced many socialists that "doubling the vote" had actually decreased their portion.

There were, however, some important differences between the Milwaukee and New York experiences. Milwaukee socialists were much more respectable and influential than their New York counterparts; they had considerable following among the city's middle class and intelligentsia, as well as among the working class and organized labor. Milwaukee first elected a socialist mayor in 1910, and party adherents occupied that position for most of the next forty years. Socialists often controlled the city council, frequently constituted a majority of the city's legislative delegation, and were always an influential minority on the School Board after 1907. Meta Berger served on the latter for thirty years, was elected its president, and retired with plaudits from much of Milwaukee's non-socialist establishment. Under these conditions, the WWSA openly courted socialist support in Milwaukee and made Meta Berger and Emil Seidel vice presidents. Berger was offered the presidency of the Association in 1915, but declined on the grounds that her socialist identification would hurt the suffrage cause in many conservative quarters, especially after she had led the fight for the union label on all WWSA publications. Significantly, she was eventually read out of WWSA because of her connection with NWP and her vocal opposition to the war and Americanization, a microcosm of the course of socialist-suffragist relations in Wisconsin.[24]

While the party in Milwaukee could not claim the active participation of the same large numbers of militant socialist women who played such an important role in suffrage campaigns in New York, there were several out-standing individuals. In addition to Meta Berger, May Wood Simons, wife of Algie M. Simons and a member of the WNC, Elizabeth Thomas, New York-born Quaker and a school board director, Annie Gordon Whitnall, wife of City Treasurer Charles P. Whitnall and a school board director, and Maud McCreery, women's editor of the *Leader* made significant contribu-tions. They distinguished themselves, however, primarily as officeholders, writers, or speakers rather than organizers of a mass movement. Mostly they served as examples to male and female comrades of what dedicated and talented socialist women could do with the franchise, if given the op-portunity.

This lack of visibility on the part of socialist women in the Milwaukee party was due partly to the high percentage of members of German heri-tage. The *"kinder, kirche, kuchen"* outlook of the German culture, even if exaggerated by outsiders, was nevertheless considerably less receptive to fe-male activism than was the milieu of New York's Russian Jews or British-Americans. Not surprisingly, the leading socialist women in Milwaukee, with the exception of Berger, were generally of Yankee or British ancestry, and they frequently scored the male chauvinism of the party's largely Teutonic leadership. Even Berger, the daughter of prominent German im-migrant who had also served on the school board, complained privately about her exclusion from socialist meetings in her own home. She married her former teacher in 1897, gave birth to two daughters, managed the household, had her own career, shared in her husband's work and trials, and maintained an affectionate correspondence with him during periods of separation. Yet her straightforward autobiography occasionally betrays evidence of resentment at being relegated to the role of *hausfrau*. The Germanness of the male socialists also affected their attitude toward suf-frage in other important ways. Even though WWSA undoubtedly over-stated their influence, the two most influential organizations which opposed woman suffrage in Wisconsin were the German-American Alliance (GAA) and the Brewers' Association. Most German socialists belonged to the for-mer and worked closely with the latter in opposition to prohibition, placing them on the horns of a dilemma between their ideology and "Kultur." When forced to choose on the issue of suffrage, German-American socialists did not all come down on the same side. Some of the most bitter exchanges in the legislative debates were those between Robert Wild of the GAA and Socialist Assemblyman Carl Minkley of Milwaukee. When the former tried to claim the opposition of all Germans to women's rights in 1913, Minkley, a GAA member, sharply replied, "I am a German and I am not a Prohibi-tionist, but I do not favor putting the beer dump ahead of women." In the same vein, Minkley argued that "four and one-half million votes have al-ready been cast in Germany for woman suffrage, and the German Alliance

does not represent the Germans of the state of Wisconsin" and that as much
as he loved beer he "would not put women's rights beneath a beer mug nor
would most of the Germans." Finally, the German identity of the Socialist
party in Milwaukee guaranteed that the issues of World War I and
Americanization would have an even more devastating effect upon their
members and on their relationship with mainstream suffrage organizations
than was the case in New York. While the latter were suspect largely on
ideological grounds, Milwaukee's German socialists bore the double burden
of ideology and ethnicity, making them anathema to all but the most
courageous or liberal-minded suffragists. Moreover, the loyalty and Americanization questions drove many British-Americans of both sexes out of
the Milwaukee socialist movement, thus depriving the party of many of its
most articulate champions of women's rights and giving German males an
even greater influence.[25]

Despite the conflicts inherent in the ethnic character of the party, Milwaukee socialists were consistent and important components of the woman
suffrage coalition in Wisconsin. As early as 1897, Debs urged the Social
Democratic party (SDP) to endorse women's rights in a speech at the West
Side Turner Hall. The following year, the SDP endorsed woman suffrage, a
stance it continued throughout the entire progressive era, despite reservations. Victor Berger occasionally betrayed skepticism about the efficacy of
woman suffrage, and usually defended party endorsement on "educational
grounds," while cautioning against allowing suffrage agitation to slow the
socialist movement. When Berger suggested, in July, 1909, that woman suffrage might even prove harmful to the SDP because women were more
socially reactionary and more church-influenced than were men, he voiced
doubts that many socialist males later expressed at the polls. The outraged
response of several socialist women and the silence of their male comrades
indicated significant divisions within the SDP. Still, the SDP was part of a
state-wide woman suffrage coalition that also included the State Teachers
Association, the Federation of Labor, the Federation of Women's Clubs,
Ladies of the Maccabees, the Grange, the Farmers' Society of Equity, the
Ministerial Association, and the Women's Christian Temperance Union.
Until the outbreak of war, none of these showed any particular embar-
rassment over consorting with socialists.[26]

Milwaukee's twelve socialist legislators were unanimous in their support
of the full suffrage amendment to the state constitution proposed by the
legislature in 1911, when even the NAWSA would have settled for presidential voting. The *Milwaukee Leader* urged ratification in the 1912 referendum and filled its pages with suffrage-related stories. SDP gubernatorial
candidate Carl D. Thompson called his party "the greatest power in favor
of woman suffrage in the world," and insisted that socialists had "stood and
fought for woman suffrage, for equal and unrestricted political rights for

over 60 years." *Leader* editor John M. Work, a long-time advocate of suffrage, admitted in his column that a "certain alleged Socialist" argued that support for woman suffrage might cost the SDP the local election. "To me," Work contended, "such a Socialist makes a noise like a Republican or a Democrat," and insisted that anyone who would "sacrifice the equal suffrage principle can not be trusted to enact the collective ownership principle." The *Leader* based its endorsement on the belief that "Socialism has no stauncher supporters than are found among the women who are devoted to the Socialist cause" and insisted that they "have shown the falsity of the contention that women have no concern in affairs outside the immediate circle of the family" and that they "would do their part in the political field for human betterment and labor's emancipation." Not content with stressing the utility of enfranchisement, the *Leader* contended that it would endorse woman suffrage even if there were no woman socialists because it could not oppose ratification "without exalting expediency at the expense of right."[27]

The 1912 referendum was defeated, carrying only about 27 percent of the vote statewide and failing to carry Milwaukee by more than two to one. Suffragists attributed the defeat primarily to the influence of the German-American Alliance and the Brewers' Association, and to their own failure to cultivate the large Scandinavian vote, but they apportioned part of the blame to the socialists. "Again we over-estimated what the Socialist vote would mean to us," Crystal Eastman Benedict reported to the Political Equality League. "I believe," she concluded, "that most of the Socialist Party members stood by their platform and voted for us, but their sympathizers did not. Thus, many of the wards in Milwaukee which gave Victor Berger enormous majorities went more than two to one against woman suffrage." Actually, 1912 was not a very good year for Milwaukee socialists. The Democrats and Republicans informally fused into what one student of the SDP has called "unofficial anti-Socialist nonpartisanship," waved the red flag, attacked the alleged inadequacy of socialism's achievements, and scored Berger for neglecting his constituency in favor of national and international affairs. The party's county officeholders were all defeated, and its assembly delegation was cut in half; the socialist proportion of the city vote ranged from 29 percent for presidential candidate Eugene V. Debs to 39 percent for incumbent Attorney General W. C. Zabel. The sufrage amendment fared even worse, receiving only about 88 percent of Deb's total and approximately 65 percent of Zabel's. Moreover, support for the amendment in predominantly socialist wards was not significantly at variance with its backing in Milwaukee as a whole, ranging between 24 and 35 percent compared to a city-wide figure of 32 percent. Four of the nine strongest socialist wards fell below the latter percentage, three exceeded it, and two equalled it. Nor was there any significant correlation between the size of the socialist vote and that for suffrage; the measure's total in the three strongest socialist wards was almost identical to its showing in the three weakest ones. Milwaukee socialists apparently behaved toward the referendum about the same as did city voters in general, meaning that about 20 percent failed to express a preference, while the remainder declared against ratification by about two to one. At most, socialists provided between 30 and 40 percent of the total suffrage vote.[28]

Whatever the position of socialist voters on the 1912 referendum, party leaders and legislators continued to press for woman suffrage in each ensuing session of the legislature. In 1913, they strongly backed another constitutional amendment, despite the overwhelming nature of the 1912 defeat. On March 20, the Assembly held a three-hour hearing on the measure at which Meta Berger joined suffrage stalwarts in speaking for the amendment, in opposition to Robert Wild of the GAA and James L. Flanders of the antisuffrage organization. Berger stressed the utilitarian argument for suffrage, charging that women were forced to accept low wages because of their disfranchisement. Citing the findings of the Illinois Vice Commission, she contended that enfranchised women would use the ballot to press for minimum wage, child labor, age of consent, and occupational health and safety laws. Attacking the presentations of Wild and Flanders, Assemblyman Minkley conceded that suffrage was not a natural right, because women, like men, had to fight for it. Taking issue with Flander's argument that voting would be too traumatic an experience for women, Minkley insisted that women could take care of themselves and that "it is the strain of thousands of women on their knees scrubbing or working in factories that ought to worry you." A week later, on the Assembly floor, Minkley charged that the men who opposed woman suffrage on the grounds of female weakness were the same ones who opposed wages and hours and health and safety legislation. He received an ovation from the suffragists in the gallery when he charged that those who opposed suffrage "belong in kindergarten rather than in the legislature." The bill passed the Senate 17 to 15 and the Assembly 47 to 26, with the unanimous support of the 7 socialists in both houses. When progressive Republican Governor Francis McGovern vetoed the bill on the grounds that the voters had just recently expressed an overwhelmingly negative opinion, the *Leader* attacked his action in strong language. Accusing McGovern of playing to the "saloon vote," of fearing for his own reelection, and of doubting the popularity of the issue, the *Leader* asserted that what the governor needed "was a greater faith in the ultimate triumph of right and less devotion to the 'practical things' that enter into our political life."[29]

Socialist legislators continued their support of woman suffrage in 1915, unanimously favoring bills granting full and presidential suffrage and county option. Minkley once again clashed with the GAA, while Socialist Assemblyman Frank J. Weber replied to an argument that suffrage would destroy the "chivalric foundation" of society by asserting that labor unions were not built upon that foundation either, but upon the belief that everyone had the same right to representation in a democracy.[30]

The rise of the NWP in Wisconsin and the outbreak of World War I revealed serious differences between the SDP and the WWSA. But, as late as January of 1917, WWSA sponsored a prosuffrage address by Max Eastman, and Theodora Youmans, WWSA's president, stated that "Mr. Eastman's powerful and eloquent address was of great value to our cause. Many of the legislators who attended were visibly impressed by it." Although the Milwaukee papers noted that the speech was "tinged to a certain extent with Socialist views and with the Socialist interpretation of the issues," one unidentified prosuffrage legislator felt that Eastman had not hurt the cause and that most assemblymen were unaffected by his socialist outlook. The *Leader* vigorously supported the NWP when its leaders were imprisoned in Washington for demonstrating in front of the White House, enjoining socialist women and men to attend a mass rally to greet a delegation arriving on the "prison special." The group's head, Bertha Moller, so impressed the *Leader* that it helped sponsor a March 6 rally for the "wives, sisters and daughters of working men," circulated a petition to free the remaining NWP members, and ran a series of profiles on the "suffrage prisoners" who would attend the meeting. The rally, held at Plankinton Hall Auditorium and addressed by Moller, Ella Reeve Bloor, Meta Bochert, a socialist candidate for the School Board, and Maud McCreery, featured the theme of the common aim of the SDP and the NWP, namely, getting the vote for foreign-stock working-class women so that "if the man workers cannot make this country safe for democracy, then let us women try and do what the men could not do." One socialist woman reported to Meta Berger that she had tried for a time "working with the Woman's Party, the WWSA or any organization which seemed to be doing effective suffrage work." By mid-1917, however, she became openly affiliated with NWP, while remaining "most desirous that the WWSA should prosper." She insisted that there was no necessary conflict between the two as there was work enough for both. She did not attend the 1917 WWSA convention "for I do not care to see the WWSA any more radical . . . but what I do want to see is a radical political suffrage organization plus many more organizations as may be needed." When Berger, a founder of the pacifist People's Council, introduced a peace resolution at the 1917 WWSA convention, Youmans "protested indignantly at my request saying, 'This is a holy war.' " Berger resigned immediately and appeared as the NWP's advocate at the Wisconsin State Teachers Convention in November; the organization refused to allow a WWSA representative to speak. Berger received a standing ovation, partly out of respect for her husband who was under indictment for opposing the war, and moved the convention to endorse woman suffrage.[31]

It was the war and the resultant loyalty and Americanization issues that created the most severe antagonism between the SDP and the WWSA. In a state with as large a foreign-born population as Wisconsin, both organizations had long recognized the importance of appeals to foreign-born males on the one hand and of the naturalization of foreign-born women on the other. Youmans noted in her "Historical Sketch of Woman Suffrage in Wisconsin" that the ethnic population made "campaigning peculiarly difficult" because "less than one voter in four has American traditions even for one generation." An Oshkosh suffrage leader, referring to an antisuffrage survey taken by her state senator and published in the *Atlantic Monthly*, wrote to WWSA headquarters that "the canvass came out exactly as any suffragist knows it would, conducted in that way, among that class of people," charging that the survey "overrepresented the views of Austrians, Hungarians, Belgians, and Russians, of whom a good many probably sympathized with the Germans in the anti-suffrage ideas." The WWSA press service, in September, 1917, issued instructions for work among the foreign born, confiding that Scandinavians, Jews, and Poles were likely to be sympathetic to woman suffrage, but that "many European nations have a deep-rooted idea of the inferiority of women," and that they "are going to vote against woman suffrage almost solidly whenever they have a chance."[32]

Earlier, during the 1912 referendum, WWSA had distributed flyers printed in German, Polish, Bohemian, Yiddish, Italian, Norwegian, and Swedish. Even so, WWSA acknowledged in 1914 that "we suffragists know very well that we have not yet reached a majority of German women of the state," and that "it was proven in the woman suffrage election in 1912, and is, I believe, corroborated by results in other states, that communities having a majority of voters native born of native parents are more likely to favor woman suffrage than communities where the foreign born and foreign parentage predominates." Socialists had, for their part, concentrated their organizational efforts among those very groups judged by WWSA to be most hostile to woman suffrage, and emphasized naturalization of women from these ethnic groups as a necessary follow-up to enfranchisement. World War I not only left the socialists open to charges of disloyalty, but isolated them in the role of defending the right of ethnic minorities to retain their identity and culture against the efforts of such organizations as the Americanization Committee of WWSA. The latter, working with the Daughters of the American Revolution, drew up a plan for the Americanization of aliens which involved classes, books, movies, slide shows, patriotic meetings, and even visitations to individual families. Much of its work was directed by May Wood Simons, who like many native-born socialists, had broken with SDP over the war and loyalty issues. Despite the pressure of this campaign, socialists championed "the unrestricted right to use any language in church services and also for the right to teach . . . any language, in public or parochial schools, that the patrons may desire."[33]

As divisions deepened, the SDP continued its own increasingly isolated efforts on behalf of woman suffrage through the ratification of the Nineteenth Amendment. The eleven Socialist legislators gave nearly unanimous support to all the suffrage measures considered during the 1917 session of the Wisconsin State Legislature. When Green Bay Republican Timothy Burke opposed a suffrage bid on the grounds that Congresswoman Jeanette Rankin had fainted after casting her vote against U.S. entry into World War I, Milwaukee Socialist Senator N. C. Zumach replied that "she voted according to the dictates of her conscience and that is more than a lot of members in this Wisconsin senate have the courage to do." In the Assembly, fellow socialists Frank J. Weber and Glenn P. Turner were among the strongest suffrage spokesmen: they and their comrades voted against all amendments designed to postpone or confuse the issue. The *Leader* also continued its editorial support of suffrage. When Congress refused to pass the Nineteenth Amendment in February, 1919, the paper printed a strong editorial headed "Pass the Suffrage Amendment," assuring readers that neither major party would dare go before the voters in 1920 with a record of opposition to the issue. Meta Berger, by now vice chairman of the Milwaukee branch of NWP, castigated the Democratic party for mocking their own pledge to "make the world safe for democracy," while praising her organization for refusing to drop suffrage agitation during the war. Seidel added that he had "nothing but contempt for such action—such men." The two Socialist Senators and thirteen Assemblymen unanimously supported a resolution requesting the U.S. Congress to pass the amendment, as well as bills for full and presidential suffrage. When Congress finally proposed the suffrage amendment, the *Leader* pledged to work for ratification in Wisconsin and carried favorable reactions from many prominent socialists. Socialists unanimously voted for ratification in the Wisconsin legislature, and when opponents tried to delay the matter, Assemblyman E. W. Knappe snapped, "We Socialists were for woman suffrage for years. It has always been a plank in our platform when other parties would have nothing to do with it, and it was a matter of ridicule. We are now opposed to these delay tactics."[34]

Even while socialists were celebrating the triumph of woman suffrage and predicting significant socialist gains as a result, however, the Milwaukee School Board election of 1919 demonstrated that enfranchisement had actually damaged their cause. Women were permitted to vote in School Board elections in Wisconsin after 1885, but they did not form a sizeable portion of the electorate until the socialist issue galvanized them into action. Socialist interest in the School Board dated from 1909 when the party elected three people to the fifteen member board—Meta Berger, Frederick Heath, editor of the Milwaukee *Herald*, and Annie Gordon Whitnall. They had campaigned against the action of Democratic Mayor David Rose in diverting a $300,000 bond issue to street improvements and pledged to make the schools a "forerunner of the socialist society." Their candidacies spawned the creation of a Citizen's Anti-Socialist Ticket which endorsed the other successful candidates with the injunction, "Do not let the Socialists control the schools." Ironically, the Citizen's Ticket unwittingly endorsed Whitnall, blissfully unaware that she was really one of the objects of their ire. These socialist board members had argued over the years for free text-books, smaller classes, health inspection, teacher pensions, nursery schools, penny lunches, the free use of school houses for public meetings, and the employment of married women teachers. They also led the struggle against the "Gary Plan" of dividing the school day into two shifts in order to econo-mize. Each ensuing election raised charges about the possible socialist "take-over" of the schools, and the onset of the war intensified the conflict, as socialist board members defended the loyalty of German Americans and party leaders while opposing efforts to turn the schools into instruments of Americanization. Berger and the other SDP members strongly opposed the collection of money in the schools, partly on the grounds that it embarras-sed the children of the working class, but also because some of the funds went to support the war.[35]

The 1917 School Board election prefigured the 1919 contest, but the issues were not debated with the same intensity. The *Leader* made special appeals to woman voters: "To vote is a simple matter. It is part of the work of municipal housekeeping. It is woman's work. Let no woman hesitate be-cause she 'doesn't know how' or 'has nothing to wear'. To go to the election booth is not a social affair—any more than going to the grocery store. Do it for the children's sake." SDP campaign manager Edmund Melms predicted that "probably more women will vote Tuesday than in any election heretofore. More of an effort is being made to get the women to the polls." The *Leader* also reported that "there was a brisk demand for registration cards for women" at socialist headquarters and charged that there was an organized campaign by city churches to mobilize women voters on behalf of the anti-socialist candidates endorsed by the Voter's League.[36]

The election of 1917 resulted in defeat for socialist candidates, and the *Leader* attributed it to a union of Catholics and capitalists which was suc-cessful in transporting an "endless chain" of "church women" to the polls "in droves," carrying anti-Socialist slips. The *Leader* contended that Catho-lic and Lutheran churches initiated an organized campaign to have every woman bring five others to the polls and that "the outpouring of women, especially after working hours, presented a spectacle never before seen in Milwaukee," insisting that women outnumbered men three to one in some voting lines. In one precinct, the number of women voters had increased from 25 in 1917 to 117. Attributing the SDP defeat to the fact that "the Socialist women did not vote in any large numbers," the *Leader* argued that working-class women were often reluctant to vote, but, more significantly, acknowledged that "the importance of her vote has not been sufficiently emphasized in our party" and pledged that "the failure to enlist the Socialist women in our school elections must be recognized and remedied."[37]

The 1919 School Board election was held in the aftermath of the loyalty hysteria of World War I and during the Great Red Scare, conditions which sharply intensified the divisions that had already been apparent in 1917. The socialists ran five candidates in the March 19 primary, including one woman, Meta Bochert, on a platform seeking better educational facilities, the elimination of school collections, opposition to military training, and higher teachers' salaries. Since they already had four holdover candidates on the fifteen member board, the SDP made a major effort to achieve majority control of the body. They hit particularly hard at the Americanization campaign in the schools, which was organized by the Americanization Committee of the Milwaukee County Council for Defense and the Wisconsin Loyalty League, under the direction of erstwhile Socialists Algie and May Wood Simons. The program, strongly backed by most churches, business leaders, and the Milwaukee *Journal*, screened teachers, required loyalty oaths, and dropped foreign languages from the curriculum. The school system supplied teachers for Americanization courses in factories, while allowing a heavy infusion of vocational courses.[38]

The SDP created a Woman's Agitation Committee to combat the organizational activities of their opponents, and the *Leader* devoted a great deal of space to energizing the woman socialist vote. It assured women that they would be protected by police and that "a Socialist teller or inspector in every booth will make it his business to be particularly kind to women voters." Noting that their opponents had launched a telephone canvass, the paper urged socialist women to do the same, or to go door to door. It urged socialist males to take their wives, daughters, mothers, and sweethearts to the polls and see to it that they voted. Much of the party's propaganda was directed at reporting the mobilization efforts of the anti-socialists, whom it referred to variously as the "bonton women," the "silk stocking element," and the "hol(e)y cause." Many of the latter were members of such organizations as the County Suffrage Association and the National League for Women's Service, with whom the socialists had previously cooperated on woman suffrage. The paper predicted a heavy voter turnout for the primary, estimating as much as a tripling of the women's vote, which would make it the deciding factor in the election.[39]

With the anti-socialist vote spread out among twelve candidates, the socialists easily took five of the first six places in the primary, carrying fourteen of the twenty-five city wards. The *Leader* pointed with pride to the substantial increase in women voting, and contended that the five socialists had polled pluralities ranging from six to ten thousand more than the Voter's League candidates who would oppose them in the general election of April 1. Party analyses stressed the crucial importance of the woman's vote, with Berger insisting that "we must educate our women to do their duty as citizens on election day" in order to eliminate race hatred in schools. The *Leader* proclaimed that its slogan until April 1 would be "every woman an agitator" in order "to make the good showing of the Socialist women's vote at the primary still better at the election."[40]

The campaign was carried on in apocalyptic terms on both sides and completed the process of dividing the city's woman voters into two hostile camps, leaving the socialists with the smaller portion. The anti-socialist candidates were endorsed by the Voter's League, the Good Government League, and the Loyalty League. The Milwaukee *Journal*, chief organ of the nonpartisan candidates, kept up a steady barrage of anti-socialist appeals aimed especially at the women of Milwaukee. Charging that the socialists were antiwar, anti-Americanization, and in favor of foreign languages, the paper warned that "the other women of Milwaukee face a grave responsibility" because "the danger that they will win the school board election is great in view of the large number of women who will vote for their candidates." Algie Simons lent his voice to the campaign, labeling the socialists tools of "Bourbons, Bolsheviks, and boche," while the *Journal* contended that the SDP candidates would "devote the evening schools and recreation centers, now Americanizing agents, to Socialist propaganda." The Good Government League claimed to have over 500 women canvassers who would help to refute "the base label of unthinking men that the women didn't care for the ballot," while the woman president of the Milwaukee Teachers Association claimed that "the majority of teachers have worked and will work for the non-partisan candidates for the school board."[41]

The *Leader* also made women the special target of its preelection propaganda, urging socialist and working-class women to outvote the "wealthy" women backing the nonpartisan candidates. While nonpartisan propaganda featured the two female candidates on its slate, the socialists stressed the qualifications of Meta Bochert, "a real daughter of the revolution" who was the first female member of the twenty-second ward SDP committee. At an enormous rally on the eve of the election, Maud McCreery insisted that the "fate of the children of the working class is at stake, and every wife and mother must live up to her responsibility and take advantage of the great opportunity." The *Leader* predicted a doubling of the woman vote over 1917, while Elizabeth Thomas urged her sister comrades to equal or match the nonpartisan women by bringing ten others to the polls. Perhaps the only undecided women in the city were the adherents of the Wisconsin State Association Opposed to Woman Suffrage who were on the horns of a dilemma produced by their hatred of socialism on the one hand, and by their opposition to women voting on the other.[42]

Election day witnessed a dramatic increase in voter turnout over both the 1917 School Board election and primary. The socialists doubled their total vote from the 1917 election, but still fell far short of victory by an average of over 13,000 in each election. The party's all-out effort had nearly doubled its primary total for each of the five candidates, but the five nonpartisan favorites had more than tripled theirs. In their five strongest wards, Socialist School Board candidates mustered majorities varying from 62 to 72 percent, while, in their five strongest wards, nonpartisan candidates polled from 76 to 86 percent of the total vote. In the election for School Board, the city's non-socialist voters, galvanized by the socialist success in the primaries, united behind the nonpartisan candidates. Significantly, the difference between the all-male vote for municipal judge and that for the School Board indicated that the nonpartisan ticket had attracted an almost two to one majority among the over 38,000 women voters. Nearly every precinct in the city reported a much heavier female turnout than usual, most of them carrying cards and newspaper clippings from the *Leader* or *Journal* to insure that they voted correctly, a strong indication of the number of first-time voters.[43]

According to the *Journal*, the "majority apparently came with their minds made up and voted quicker than many men." Many male voters had to drop out of lines to go to work, and the city determined to redraw several precinct boundaries in anticipation of the enactment of full woman suffrage. Women comprised about 44 percent of the total vote cast in the School Board election, reflecting the special efforts on both sides, but nonpartisan candidates clearly derived the greatest benefit. In the five strongest socialist wards, women voters comprised anywhere from 40 to 48 percent of the total, while in the five strongest nonpartisan wards, they constituted over 60 percent in all but one, where they were just less than one-half. In the five socialist wards, the SDP captured between 59 and 74 percent of the woman vote, whereas in the five nonpartisan wards, anti-socialists garnered between 80 and 90 percent of the woman vote.[44]

Socialists claimed that the city's churches had worked in conjunction with the Good Government League, the Loyalty League, and industry to transport women to the polls. The *Journal* ecstatically reported that the election "turned the faces of Milwaukee's fairest maids and matrons, those whose names are often seen in the society page accounts of the most exclusive social functions, toward the polls," and printed quotations from many of them which, ironically, corroborated socialist interpretations. The *Wiscon-*

sin State Journal reported that "many a male opponent of woman suffrage in Milwaukee was forced to admit that the lesson of the election last Tuesday is that when the women of Wisconsin get the full right of the ballot, they will form a decisive force for the cause of good, straight, clean government on the American plan in this city, where such a force is notoriously and emphatically needed." Socialists alternated between denouncing the actions of their opponents and pledging themselves to greater efforts among women voters in the future. "Quite a few Socialist women voted," the *Leader* confessed, "but by no means all of them. We must see that they do the next time." In a major test, only about one-third of Milwaukee's most politically active women had been willing to accept socialist candidates. The "woman vote" in Milwaukee had clearly divided along partisan, socioeconomic, and ideological lines to the ultimate detriment of the socialists.[45]

In Wisconsin, as in New York, then, the tenuous coalition between socialists and suffragists on behalf of woman suffrage ended in mutual frustration. The press of practical politics and the efforts of dedicated and able socialist women had temporarily harmonized two conflicting world-views and even submerged the significant disagreements which existed over the issue within the Socialist party. The electoral evidence, however, eventually caused suffragists to question socialist commitment, while leading the latter to doubt that they had actually doubled their portion of the vote. The triumph of woman suffrage quickly revivified the differences between the two components of the coalition, and placed them in competition for the allegiance of the newly enfranchised. Above all, the outbreak of World War I and the resultant conflicts over loyalty and Americanization created an unbridgeable chasm between socialists and non-socialists, foreclosing any possibility of cooperation. Without a doubt, it was the socialist women who felt the greatest frustration of all, rejected by suffragist sisters for their radical ideology and chastised by male comrades for their militant feminism. Perhaps Theresa Malkiel expressed their dilemma best: "I have often been accused of being a womanist," she told the 1910 Party Congress, "my contention is that I am a Socialist first to last, but a woman nevertheless."[46]

Notes

1. Charlotte Perkins Gilman, "The Socialist and the Suffragist," *Life and Labor* 2 (1912): 61.
2. The literature on the woman suffrage movement is large and growing. See especially Aileen Kraditor, *The Ideas of the Woman Suffrage Movement, 1890-1920* (New York: Columbia University Press, 1965); Eleanor Flexner, *Century of Struggle: The Woman's Rights Movement in the United States* (New York: Atheneum Publishers, 1968); David Morgan, *Suffragists and Democrats: The Politics of Woman Suffrage in America* (East Lansing: Michigan State University Press, 1972); Ross

Evans Paulson, *Women's Suffrage and Prohibition: A Comparative Study of Equality and Social Control* (Glenview, Ill.: Scott, Foresman and Company, 1973); Anne F. and Andrew M. Scott, *One Half the People: The Fight for Woman Suffrage* (Philadelphia: J. B. Lippincott, 1975); William O'Neill, *Everyone Was Brave: The Rise and Fall of Feminism in America* (Chicago: Quadrangle Books, 1970); J. Stanley Lemons, *The Woman Citizen* (Urbana: University of Illinois Press, 1973); and Alan Grimes, *Puritan Ethic and Woman Suffrage* (New York: Oxford University Press, 1967). On the Southern States Suffrage Conference, see Paul E. Fuller, *Laura Clay and the Woman's Rights Movement* (Lexington: The University Press of Kentucky, 1975). On the difference between NWP and NAWSA, see the exchange between Abby Scott Baker of NWP and State Senator Helen Ring Robinson of Colorado in Scott and Scott, *One Half the People*, pp. 132-41.

3. Kraditor, *Ideas of the Movement*, pp. 43-75, 96-162; Flexner, *Century of Struggle*, pp. 229-332; Vida Scudder, "Women and Socialism," *Yale Review* 3 (1914): 454-70; May Walden Kerr, *Socialism and the Home* (Chicago: C. H. Kerr, 1901); Susan W. Fitzgerald, "Women in the Home" in Scott and Scott, *One Half the People*, pp. 114-15; Morgan, *Suffragists and Democrats*, pp. 25-26, 69-104; Flexner, *Century of Struggle*, pp. 229-61; Sharon Hartman Strom, "Leadership and Tactics in the American Suffrage Movement: A New Perspective from Massachusetts," *Journal of American History* 42 (1975): 296-315; John D. Buenker, "The Urban Political Machine and Woman Suffrage: A Study in Political Adaptability," *The Historian* 33 (1971): 264-79; Joseph P. Mahoney, "Woman Suffrage and the Urban Masses," *New Jersey History* 87 (1969): 151-72.

4. The most thorough study of socialist women and their interaction with the party and suffrage organizations is Mari Jo Buhle, "Feminism and Socialism in the United States, 1820-1920," (Ph. D. diss., University of Wisconsin-Madison, 1974). I am grateful to Professor Buhle and her mentor, Professor John Cooper, for the opportunity to read her manuscript. I have relied heavily upon it for my discussion of the interaction between the two movements in the next several pages.

5. *Appeal to Reason*, April 15, 1916; Scudder, "Women and Socialism," pp. 459-60; *Milwaukee Leader*, October 6, 1912; *New York Advance*, November 16, 1917.

6. Luella Krehbiel, "Women and Socialism," *Socialist Woman* 2 (1908): 7; Frederick Engels, *The Origins of the Family, Private Property and the State* (New York: International Publishers, 1970); August Bebel, *Women Under Socialism* (New York: Schocken Books, 1971); Josephine Conger-Kanecko, "Socialism and the Sex War," *Progressive Woman* 3 (1909): 9; Lida Parce, "What Is The Woman Question?" *Progressive Woman* 2 (1909): 3; *New York Call*, May 17, 1914; Gertrude Breslau Hunt, "Socialist Women in the Garrick Theater," *Socialist Woman* 1 (1908): 11; Charlotte Perkins Gilman, *Women and Economics: The Economic Factor Between Men and Women As A Factor In Social Evolution*, Carl N. Degler, ed. (New York: Harper and Row, 1966).

7. Algie M. Simons, "Report on the Stuttgart International Socialist Convention," *International Socialist Review* 8 (1907): 129-43; Sally M. Miller, "Americans and the Second International," *Proceedings of the American Philosophical Society* 120 (October 1976): 378; *New York Socialist*, July 18, 1908; Meta Berger, "Unpublished Autobiography," State Historical Society of Wisconsin (SHSW), Madison, n.p. On the Socialist attitude toward NWP, see for example, *New York Call*, December 5,

1917, and *Milwaukee Leader*, February 14, March 3, 4, 7, 1919. On the attitude of NAWSA toward NWP, see *The Wisconsin Citizen: Monthly Bulletin of the Wisconsin Woman Suffrage Association*, November, 1917, and Wisconsin Woman Suffrage Association (WWSA) *Press Service*, July 14, 1917, both in WWSA *Reports*, SHSW, Box 26, Folder 4.

8. Miller, "Americans and the Second International," p. 378; Scudder, "Women and Socialism," p. 456; Victor Berger to Morris Hillquit, February 13, 1910, Morris Hillquit Papers: General Correspondence, SHSW, Reel 2; *New York Advance*, November 9, 1917; Meta Berger, "Unpublished Autobiography," SHSW, n.p.; Lena Morrow Lewis, "Women and the Socialist Party," *Chicago Daily Socialist*, May 10, 1907; Eleanor Haynes, "Socialist Women in the United States," *Socialist Woman* 1 (1907): 10; Theresa Malkiel, "Where Do We Stand On the Woman Question?," *International Socialist Review* 10 (1909): 159-62.

9. Buhle, "Socialism and Feminism," especially chapters 4-9; John Spargo, "Women and the Socialist Movement," *International Socialist Review* 8 (1908): 449-55; Lena Morrow Lewis, "Woman Suffragists and Woman Suffrage," *Socialist Woman* 1 (1908): 3. For a full discussion of the issue of the WNC and its relation to the party and its cooperation with suffrage organizations, see Socialist Party, *Proceedings of the 1910 National Congress*, pp. 180-250; *Chicago Daily Socialist*, May 10, 1907; December 22, 1909; February 2, 14, April 6, May 31, 1910; S.P., *Official Bulletin*, November 1911; Jesse E. Molle, "The National Convention and the Woman's Movement," *International Socialist Review* (1908): 688-90, *Socialist Woman* 1 (1908): 5; Josephine Conger-Kanecko, "Notes on the Congress," *Progressive Woman* 4 (1910): 4; *New York Call*, December 12, 20, 1909. The columns by Block and Lilienthal appear mainly in October of 1915 and 1917, just prior to the woman suffrage referenda in New York.

10. Irving Howe, *World of Our Fathers* (New York: Harcourt Brace Jovanovich, 1976), pp. 101-15, 267-416; Ronald Sanders, *The Downtown Jews: Portraits of an Immigrant Generation* (New York: Harper and Row, 1969), pp. 56-96; Moses Rischin, *The Promised City: New York's Jews 1870-1914* (Cambridge, Mass.; Harvard University Press, 1962), pp. 51-94, 144-235.

11. Morgan, *Suffragists and Democrats*, pp. 85-86; *New York Call*, December 23, 1910; January 4, 21, February 1, 8, 14, 1911; November 17, 1912; March 29, 1913; March 30, April 2, 5, 6, 20, May 2, 17, 24, June 13, December 15, 1914; January 10, 12, 22, February 2, 19, 21, March 6, 8, 22, April 13, 17, May 31, September 5, October 16, 25, November 3, 1915; Mary Oppenheimer, "The Suffrage Movement and the Socialist Party," *New Review* 3 (1915): 359-60.

12. Percentages based upon my compilations of data taken from *New York Times*, November 4, 1915. Data on the ethnic makeup of the Ninth Congressional District are from Arthur Goren, "A Portrait of Ethnic Politics: The Socialists and the 1908 and 1910 Congressional Elections on the East Side," *Jewish Historical Quarterly* 50 (1961): 202-38.

13. Oppenheimer, "Suffrage Movement," pp. 359-60; *New York Call*, March 31, May 1, June 9, 10, 1916; February 25, 1917.

14. Hillquit Papers, SHSW, Reel 2; Morris Hillquit, *Loose Leaves From A Busy Life* (New York: Macmillan, 1934), pp. 204-10.

16. Hillquit Papers, SHSW, Reel 2; Hillquit, *Loose Leaves*, pp. 208-15; *New York*

Advance, October 5, 26, 1917; *New York Call*, November 2, 3, 6, 1917; *The Call Magazine*, November 4, 1917, p. 5; *New York World*, November 4, 1917.

17. *New York Call*, November 6, 8, 1917; Hillquit, *Loose Leaves*, pp. 208-19; *The Call Magazine*, November 4, 1917, p. 12; December 2, 1917, p. 13.

18. *The Call Magazine*, November 4, 1917, p. 12; *New York Call*, November 8, 1917; *Rochester Herald*, November 8, 1917; *Boston Herald-Journal*, November 12, 1917; *New York Tribune*, October 25, 1917; Susan B. Anthony, Carrie Chapman Catt, and Ida Husted Harper, *History of Woman Suffrage: 1900-1920* (New York: Arno and the *New York Times*, 1969), 5: 580-84; *New York Times*, November 8, 1917.

20. Anthony, Catt, and Harper, *History of Woman Suffrage*, 5: 584. Voting analysis is based upon my calculations from data supplied by *New York Times*, November 7, 1919.

21. *New York Call*, November 8, 9, 12, 17, 19, 22, 28, 1917.

22. *New York Call*, November 22, 1917; June 5, 7, 18, 1919; *Albany Evening Journal*, June 7, 1919.

23. *New York Call*, November 28, 1917; WWSA, *Press Service*, July 14, 1918; WWSA *Reports*, SHSW, Box 26, Folder 5.

24. The best account of Milwaukee Socialism in this period is Sally M. Miller, *Victor Berger and the Promise of Constructive Socialism, 1910-1920* (Westport, Connecticut: Greenwood Press, 1973) and her "Milwaukee: Of Ethnicity and Labor," in Bruce M. Stave ed. *Socialism and the Cities* (Port Washington, N.Y.: Kennikat Press, 1975), pp. 41-71. See also Marvin Wachman, "History of the Social Democratic Party of Milwaukee, 1897-1910," in *Illinois Studies in the Social Sciences*, 28, 1 (Urbana: University of Illinois Press, 1945) and Frederick I. Olson, "The Milwaukee Socialists, 1897-1941"(Ph. D. diss., Harvard University, 1952). The account of Meta Berger's relations with WWSA and NWP is in her unpublished autobiography, SHSW, Madison, n,p.

25. *Milwaukee Journal*, March 20, 1913. On Milwaukee socialists and the loyalty question, see Miller, *Victor Berger*, pp. 145-248; Wachman, "History of the SDP," p. 74; Olson, "Milwaukee Socialists," pp. 249-385; and Gerd Korman, *Industrialization, Immigrants, and Americanizers: The View From Milwaukee, 1866-1921* (Madison: State Historical Society of Wisconsin, 1967), pp. 184-217.

26. Olson, "Milwaukee Socialists," pp. 171-91; Wachman, "History of SDP," pp. 17-27; *Milwaukee Social Democratic Herald*, July 24, 1909; *New York Call*, May 19, 1911; *Milwaukee Leader*, March 6, 1912; Ada James to Mary Summer Boyd, April 16, 1917, WWSA *Correspondence*, SHSW, Box 26, Folder 4.

27. Meta Berger, "Unpublished Autobiography," SHSW, Madison, n.p.; Wisconsin Legislature, *Senate Journal, 1911*, pp. 456-57, 814, 815; *Assembly Journal, 1915*, pp. 806-07, 1033; Wisconsin, Secretary of State, *Wisconsin Blue Book, 1911* (Madison: State Printing Office, 1911), pp. 738, 772-74; *Milwaukee Leader*, October 6, 1912.

28. *Milwaukee Leader*, October 1, 6, November 2, 1912; Olson, "Milwaukee Socialists," pp. 272-75; Crystal Eastman Benedict, "Why We Lost in Wisconsin," WWSA *Reports*, SHSW, Box 26, Folder 2. Analysis of the election returns are my computations based upon data provided by the *Milwaukee Journal*, November 6, 1912.

29. *Wisconsin State Journal* (Madison), March 13, 20, May 7, 1913; *Milwaukee Journal*, March 20, 1913; *Milwaukee Leader*, March 20, May 27, 1913; *Senate Journal, 1913*, pp. 401-02, 811-12; *Assembly Journal, 1913*, p. 942; *Wisconsin Blue Book, 1913*, pp. 640, 671-75.

30. *Milwaukee Leader*, April 14, 1915; *Wisconsin State Journal*, April 14, 1915; *Woman Suffrage Advocate* (Milwaukee), November 18, 1915; *Senate Journal, 1915*, pp. 794-95, 810, 869-70, 926; *Assembly Journal, 1915*, pp. 572, 798; *Wisconsin Blue Book, 1915*, pp. 490, 521-25.

31. *Milwaukee Free Press*, January 17, 1917; *Milwaukee Journal*, January 17, 1917; *Milwaukee Leader*, February 14, March 3, 4, 7, 1919; Meta Berger Papers, SHSW, Box 1, Folder 4, November 2, 1917; Meta Berger, "Unpublished Biography," SHSW, n.p.

32. Theodora Youmans, "Historical Sketch of Woman Suffrage in Wisconsin," WWSA *Reports* 18, SHSW, Box 26, Folder 2; Letter from WWSA, Rachel S. Jastino, Chairman, Legislative Committee, May 1, 1916, WWSA *Correspondence, 1910-1919*, SHSW, Box 26, Folder 5; WWSA *Press Service*, September 14, 1917; WWSA *Correspondence*, SHSW, Box 26, Folder 1.

33. Letter from Mary R. Plummer, Public Policy Petition Committee, NAWSA, to WWSA, September 7, 1912, WWSA *Correspondence*, SHSW, Box 26, Folder 3; WWSA, *The Wisconsin Citizen: Monthly Bulletin of the WWSA*, February, 1918; WWSA *Reports*, SHSW, Box 26, Folder 1; Miller, *Victor Berger, pp. 59-60*.

34. *Milwaukee Leader*, April 10, 11, 12, 20, 26, May 3, 1917; February 7, 11, May 16, June 5, 10, 11, 1919; *Senate Journal, 1917*, p. 446; *Senate Journal, 1919*, pp. 148, 276-77, 540-43, 1394-97, 1546-48; *Wisconsin Blue Book, 1917*, pp. 506-07, 537-41; *Wisconsin Blue Book, 1919*, pp. 463, 476, 489, 491-96.

35. Olson, "Milwaukee Socialists," pp. 169-71; Meta Berger, "Unpublished Autobiography," SHSW, n.p.

36. *Milwaukee Leader*, March 21, April 3, 1917.

37. Ibid., April 4, 1917.

38. Korman, *Americanization*, pp. 171-90; *Milwaukee Leader*, March 17, 1919.

39. *Milwaukee Leader*, March 17, 18, 1919.

40. Ibid., March 19, 20, 1919.

41. *Milwaukee Journal*, March 22, 23, 26, 28, 30, 1919.

42. *Milwaukee Leader*, March 22, 31, 1919; *Milwaukee Sentinel*, April 1, 1919.

43. *Milwaukee Journal*, April 1, 2, 1919; *Milwaukee Leader*, April 1, 2, 1919.

44. Electoral analysis is based upon my computations of data found in the *Milwaukee Journal*, April 2, 1919.

45. *Milwaukee Journal*, April 1, 2, 1919; *Chicago Tribune*, April 2, 1919; *Wisconsin State Journal*, April 19, 1919; *Milwaukee Leader*, April 2, 1919.

46. Socialist Party, *Proceedings of the 1910 National Congress*, p. 185.

7

WOMEN SOCIALISTS AND THEIR MALE COMRADES: THE READING EXPERIENCE, 1927-1936

William C. Pratt

Most published scholarship on women and American socialism has been concerned with the national picture in the decades before World War I—the era when the Socialist party (SP) was a viable political alternative in many American cities and towns.[1] These works collectively provide us with a good understanding of how male socialists often felt about their female comrades and what role these female comrades were able to acquire for themselves within the party. But perhaps a shift in focus might help us develop a fuller understanding of both how women participated and what American socialism looked like as a social movement. By examining the activity of women socialists at the local level, we may be able to uncover a clearer or less abstract view of what women socialists did, and how they fit into the overall picture. This study explores the experience of women in the Reading, Pennsylvania, socialist movement, concentrating on the years from 1927 to 1936, the peak of strength for this local movement. While 1927-1936 is much later than the time frame studied by earlier scholars, it was during this period that the Reading party was most successful and furthermore, at this time, Pennsylvania women could vote. In other words, we will be examining the role of women in a specific socialist movement at a time when it enjoyed political success and when these women could legally participate as equals in the political process.

Reading socialism's political success in the late 1920s and 1930s was certainly atypical, but it was built upon a strong pre-World War I foundation. Across the country in the 1900-1917 period, there were numerous socialist

enclaves or "island communities."[2] These pockets of socialist strength frequently flourished until World War I, when most of them suffered grave
setbacks from which they never recovered. A few, however, survived and
went on to enjoy later electoral success or at least a political revival. Milwaukee and Reading were among the surviving "island communities."
Eventually they, too, would succumb to more conventional politics, but that
would not occur until substantially later than was the case elsewhere. The
Milwaukee party took control of city hall in 1910 and, after a short interval,
elected and reelected Daniel Hoan as mayor until 1940. While it did not control the city council during the postwar era, this party remained an important force in local politics.[3] Its counterpart in Reading, although it never
controlled city government prior to 1928, played a relevant political role
from 1910 until 1947. Between 1927 and 1936, the Reading socialists took
over city hall on two separate occasions, and elected the city's two state
legislators to three consecutive terms. As late as 1943, they managed to elect
a popular standard bearer to a third term as mayor. Their party was primarily a working-class movement with strong labor union connections and
reflected the dominant Pennsylvania Dutch culture of the area. These two
aspects of their social base gave the Reading socialists an advantage that
American socialists elsewhere frequently did not enjoy and account for
much of their success.[4]

Women participated actively in the Reading movement before they obtained the vote, but they clearly had a secondary role. The Reading SP's
first political success came in the elections of 1910 and 1911. In 1910, it
elected one of the city's two state assemblymen and, in the following year,
lost a closely contested mayoralty election, but elected five city councilmen
(under the old system of ward representation).[5] Clippings from the daily
press report that socialist women participated in the party caucus which
selected the SP slate and marched in a large campaign parade:

A genuine surprise was sprung upon the spectators when several hundred women
comprising an entire division were seen. There was no special uniform worn by the
women, although they were conspicuous carrying the small red Socialist emblem
and the Stars and Stripes. The women ranged in age from 10 to probably 50 years. If
ever an enthusiastic delegation of women paraded on local streets it was Friday evening when these Socialist women affiliated themselves with the men in making the
demonstration the most successful ever attempted by the local Socialist party.[6]

The significance of such participation should not be exaggerated. The
involvement of women in fund-raising activities for the local movement
was probably a more important function in the pre-World War I era. As
early as 1903, the Women's Socialist Educational League was established.
According to the local party weekly years later, it "was started as a mere
auxiliary organization," and initially "confined itself to fund-raising activi-

ties and its members worked unselfishly at the tasks of preparing luncheons, assisting at picnics and in any other way by which the party could be furnished with finances."[7] The party paper listed these functions, and it is probably fair to conclude that women had "a mere auxiliary" role in the local socialist movement in those years.

In 1915, however, the Reading SP nominated a woman as one of its candidates for school director. Though defeated, Amanda Woodward-Ringler drew more votes than her two male socialist running mates, and apparently she was the first local woman candidate for a city-wide public office. Her candidacy proved to be an anomaly, however, as the SP did not run another woman until after 1920, when Pennsylvania women were enfranchised. But the Woodward-Ringler candidacy offered a hint of things to come. She was the wife of the state secretary of the party and a former schoolteacher.[8] In the future, women Socialist candidates often would be related to prominent local male socialists, and like Woodward-Ringler, often they either were not traditional housewives or had had previous experience in another occupation.

A state-wide referendum on woman suffrage was also on the ballot in 1915. This referendum lost, primarily due to the opposition in the Pennsylvania Dutch counties situated in the southeastern part of the state. Although the measure lost almost 2 to 1 in Berks County, it came within 1,300 votes of passing in Reading itself.[9] According to the official history of the suffrage movement, in Pennsylvania "[t]he Washington party [the Progressive party in Pennsylvania] and Socialist watchers were universally helpful" during the 1915 referendum.[10] In Reading, the local SP provided considerable support for the measure. According to the *Reading Eagle* (one of the local daily newspapers): "The only party really in favor of woman suffrage in Berks County is the Socialist organization, which actively espouses the cause of women . . . ." Two women socialist speakers, one sponsored by the Women's Socialist League, the other by the German Branch, were brought to the city to speak in favor of woman suffrage; the *Labor Advocate* (the Socialist weekly) ran several stories on the topic; and local socialists urged support for the measure in the fall campaign. At the same time, the matter apparently was seldom mentioned at old party (Democratic or Republican) gatherings. Thus, in 1915, the Reading SP assumed a much stronger public position for woman suffrage than did the old parties.[11] (That this measure was on the ballot may have been a factor in the decision to run a woman candidate that year.)

In 1920, when Pennsylvania women finally received the franchise, the local party appointed a Woman's Organization Committee. According to the SP paper, this action was "at the request of the women comrades."[12] This move was taken, in part at least, because of the need to mobilize women voters and resulted in the formation of the Berks County Association of

Women Workers. This group sponsored a variety of activities for several years, including lectures by Margaret Sanger on birth control. In 1921, the SP nominated two women candidates at its caucus, though one of them subsequently withdrew. Locally, it proved to be a good year for women candidates—several were nominated and one of them was elected to the school board on the Republican ticket.[13]

But socialist attempts to involve women at this time had little effect on party fortunes. The local organization had been weakened by the wartime experience and repeated electoral defeat. It may have had a membership of over 2,000 in 1911, but by the early and mid-1920s its numbers had dropped significantly. In early 1921, the local party claimed 522 members; by 1927, its membership had fallen to approximately 100. A local newspaper account reports that 50 members participated in the 1927 nominating caucus, and that 2 of them were women.[14] That gathering was a far cry from the 1915 caucus in which Amanda Woodward-Ringler was nominated, when the Labor Advocate could say: "In the audience there were many women." The party was in poor shape in 1927, and one of its most prominent figures said later that it had seemed "pretty well shot."[15] However, such an evaluation did not take into account the shortcomings of the SP's opponents.

The incumbent Democratic administration was saddled with a very unpopular tax assessment as well as a general "spendthrift" image. Assessments had been raised substantially the previous year, and thousands of homeowners had appealed. Though Reading had a predominantly working-class population, almost 60 percent of its families owned their own homes, and it was to these voters that the socialists pitched their campaign in 1927, promising a revision of the assessment and economy in government. On the eve of the election, SP advertisements in the daily press included the following: "Protect your home. Play safe—Win with the Socialists" and "Avoid debts, high taxes and unfair assessments."[16]

Getting out the potential socialist vote had been an ongoing problem for the party. The Labor Advocate claimed: "In the past, thousands of male Socialist voters failed to register. And in many hundreds of Socialist homes the men of the house were the only ones to cast ballots." This alleged failure of working-class women to vote was frequently discussed both in the party weekly and by SP spokesmen in the 1927 campaign and those of the next several years.[17] In 1927, it was felt that the assessment issue was particularly helpful with women voters. Said the Labor Advocate's editor:

It is encouraging to note the large number of women who are attending Socialist street meetings this year. The wife and mother is the money spender of the family and, as such, feels the results of the new assessment much more keenly than does the man of the house. Every dollar taken by the tax collector means one dollar less to spend on good food and stylish clothing and, evidently, the women are resentful of the fact that council has decided that workers' wives and children shall eat less, wear less and enjoy fewer movies this year than last.[18]

The unpopular assessment proved to be the chief issue of the campaign and most observers agreed that it was due primarily to this issue that the SP won the election. Few should have disagreed with a *Literary Digest* headline which read: "NO, READING HAS NOT GONE RED!"[19] In fact, the socialists had come to power by exploiting their opponents' weaknesses and the conservative temperament of all the electorate. They elected the mayor, two city councilmen, the city controller, and two school directors. All were men (as had been the entire ticket), but the 1927 election would be the last municipal contest for a decade without at least one woman socialist candidate. This victory provided the momentum for rapid party growth, which in turn led to increased participation of women at several levels within the party organization. Party membership climbed to 881 by October of 1928, and new branches were established in unorganized sections of the city, as well as in some parts of the county.[20] The Reading party was on the move again.

While women socialist activity increased, much of it tended to be the same kind in which women had been involved earlier. The Women's Socialist League began scheduling weekly meetings at the party's Labor Lyceum: "Like every other party activity, the League has been gaining in interest and membership since the November election. The decision to meet at headquarters rather than in the homes of members, as heretofore, was rendered necessary by the constantly growing attendance."[21] In early 1928, the League sponsored a lecture by Mary Winsor, a prominent woman socialist from Haverford, Pennsylvania, who had just returned from a trip to the Soviet Union. Her topic was "Woman's Status in Russia" and the meeting was limited to "women only."[22] While the League might occasionally sponsor this type of program, it was most noted for its auxiliary role. Throughout its history it had sponsored card parties, and its members had worked at party picnics. These gatherings served both to raise funds for the local socialist organization and provide recreational activity for its membership. A survey of the *Labor Advocate* during the period under consideration in this study reveals the extent to which the local socialist movement depended upon its women comrades for such activities. A supplementary report at the 1928 national convention reinforces this impression. National secretary William H. Henry, after crediting the recent Reading victory with encouraging party members elsewhere "to greater activity," discussed the importance of local party organization. The recent Reading and Milwaukee triumphs showed

the fact . . . that intensive, continuous organization work is essential. Particularly in connection with the Milwaukee victory, we call attention to the fact that social activities prove very beneficial in our movement. In this connection, it might be mentioned that the Milwaukee women comrades are constantly keeping the movement alive by their social activities .·. . .[23]

Among the most important of the auxiliary activities in the Reading movement were the party picnics held at local picnic groves. These gatherings were usually opened to the general public and raised money for other party functions. Games for children, other recreational activities, entertainment, including band concerts, plenty of food, and socialist orators of both local and national prominence were regular features.[24] Women volunteers prepared lunches and desserts for these picnics, and the *Labor Advocate* often printed appeals for such assistance. In June of 1928, the chairman of the picnic arrangements committee was quoted in a front-page story: "and don't forget to tell the ladies that we are looking for the very kind of layer cakes they know how to bake." The writer added: "So shine up the mixing bowl, girls, and prepare to get busy." Two weeks later, a front-page advertisement for the coming picnic ended with: "And OH, Ladies, Bring Cakes!"[25]

In 1929, the party rented and later purchased a twenty-two acre picnic grove six miles outside the city. Renamed "Socialist Park," it quickly became one of the movement's proudest possessions.[26] Thereafter, party picnics probably became an even more important institution than before. Substantial improvements were made on the park's facilities after the socialists took it over. All the work done at Socialist Park was provided by volunteer labor and, while rank-and-file men (or "Jimmie Higginses") built or painted, women comrades provided meals prepared in the park kitchen. During the picnic season in the early and mid-1930s, crowds numbering perhaps as high as 25,000 attended these party affairs and a crew of women cooks was usually on duty. Socialist Park, which was also rented to other groups when it was not in use by the party, was an important institution within the Reading movement and one in which women played a major role.[27]

At the 1928 SP national convention, an attempt was made to increase woman's activity in the socialist movement. A resolution was passed establishing a committee to develop a plan for the party's National Executive Committee (NEC) that would encourage women to work in the forthcoming presidential campaign.[28] This action led to the formation of a National Women's Committee by the NEC in May of 1928. The new committee was given the job of "special propaganda work among the women of the working class" and was chaired by Reading's Lilith Martin Wilson. A prominent figure in the local movement, Wilson had just been elected to the NEC at the recent convention. Chairing this committee proved to be a thankless task. It prepared and distributed five different leaflets during the 1928 campaign and attempted to encourage "the organization of women's committees of locals and branches, and clubs of sympathizers . . . ." But few local organizations expressed interest in the committee's plans, and further attempts to stimulate similar interest after the 1928 campaign were also disappointing. Wilson found the work frustrating and resigned in September of 1929.[29] Subsequent efforts on the part of others also proved unsuccessful, and a 1934 national convention memorandum concluded: "The previous record would seem to indicate that new methods must be used in interesting women."[30]

But while national propaganda work failed in Reading, efforts to involve more women in party activities met with some success as we already have seen. A National Woman's Committee report of 1929 noted: "The most active women's groups at present are those of New York City and Reading, Pa."[31] Soon after the national committee attempt began, the Reading organization elected a nine-woman committee, the Berks County Women's Political Committee, at its monthly meeting.[32] The *Labor Advocate's* coverage in July, August, and September suggests that this committee was very active. Socialist women's groups (which initially were called clubs) were organized in the various city branches and some of the county units as well. We find the following comment in the party weekly:

The organization of the women Socialists of Reading is an activity which should challenge the fullest cooperation of the men. Every man in the movement should exhaust all honorable means to interest his wife, daughter or mother in this movement. The time has come to realize that women are good for something more than silent partners in Socialism. They can be developed into active party workers who will give invaluable service during campaigns and on election days. Help the women to organize and double the strength of the Socialist party of Berks.[33]

Much of the motivation for organizing women at both the national and local level at this time came from the desire to gain their support in the coming election, as *Labor Advocate* coverage indicated. Frequently, the newly organized women's groups would have male socialist speakers. For example, Charles Sands spoke to the Northwest group on the topic, "Women's Place in Politics." According to the party paper,

Comrade Sands declared that the possession of the ballot now removes all barriers to women's advancement . . . [and] expressed the belief that the women's movement in Reading is the beginning of a political awakening on the part of women citizens which will force professional politicians to conduct public affairs *in the interest of the home* rather than for the advancement of personal ambitions.[34]

Women did come to play an important role in political campaigns. According to the National Woman's Committee report cited earlier, women socialists in Reading "were engaged in active campaign work, and served on election boards and acted as pollmen on election day."[35] Other sources indicate that women continued this involvement in local socialist campaigns in the years after 1929.

While the initial objective behind this organizational effort probably was to increase the vote of working-class women, it had an additional and per- haps more lasting impact. It helped to bring a larger number of women into active participation within the party and also served to strengthen the non- political aspects of the movement. But not all attempts at organizing were successful. In October of 1932 the Eighteenth Ward women were organized, but by December of the following year, the *Labor Advocate* reported that "meetings of the women's auxiliary of the 18th Ward Branch will be discon- tinued. However, all Socialist women are urged to attend the regular branch meetings. . . ."[36] Throughout much of the 1930s, however, four of the city branches and one or two of the county branches were able to maintain separate women's groups. Though these groups were separate from the in- dividual branches, they were identified with the branches and apparently were not intended to be *alternative* socialist organizations as had been the case with some socialist women's groups in the pre-World War I era else- where in the country.[37] Reading socialist women were welcome (at least in theory) to attend the regular branch meetings, as well as the monthly Local meeting, and also were eligible to serve on party committees. When a for- mer participant was asked about the separate women's group, she replied, "We wanted our night out too."[38] Among other attractions, the separate women's organizations provided some of its members with an opportunity to get away from their families one night a week.

Like the regular branch meetings, these gatherings often featured an ed- ucational program. The *Labor Advocate* frequently reported on speakers and other educational activities (though its coverage of such topics became less thorough after the initial 1928 organizational effort). Soon after it was organized, the Sixth and Fifteenth Ward Branch women's group conducted a discussion based on a National Woman's Committee leaflet, *Electricity in the Home*. Later, this group discussed Shaw's *The Intelligent Woman's Guide to Socialism and Capitalism*.[39] On other occasions, women's groups heard talks on such topics as "The Task for Socialist Women" and "The Real Truth about George Washington." Throughout the late 1920s and early 1930s, Mary B. Nelson gave talks to socialist women and others on birth control. A registered nurse, she had helped organize Pennsylvania's first birth control center in Reading.[40] (Mary Nelson was not the only birth control lecturer available, however. In early 1930 socialist alderman V. James Roslin addressed the Central Branch women. As his wife had just given birth to their sixth child, Roslin concluded with: "Don't do as I do, but do as I say.")[41] It should also be noted that women's group meetings of- ten were devoted almost entirely to socials and entertainment. It was not unusual for the *Labor Advocate* to report the following type of activity:

"Last Thursday night the women of the Central Branch gathered at the home of Mrs. Charles Hoverter and they're still talking about the good time—especially the good eats—which they enjoyed."[42]

Each individual socialist branch sponsored fund-raising activities such as card parties, cake sales, strawberry and ice festivals, dinners and hoe-downs, and these affairs obviously required substantial volunteer labor from women members. The Reading SP social calendar became quite crowded as the movement grew in the late 1920s and early 1930s. The following are social events scheduled for one week in February of 1934:

1. A card party at Labor Lyceum on Saturday night, sponsored by the Young People's Socialist League with pies baked by the women of the Southern Branch.
2. A card party on Saturday night, sponsored by the women of the Northeast Branch.
3. A cake sale on Saturday, sponsored by the Laureldale Branch.
4. A "Washington Social and Card Party" on Saturday night, sponsored by the West Reading Branch.
5. A "hokum and card party" on Tuesday night, sponsored by the women of the Northeast Branch.[43]

On some occasions, the various women's groups would conduct special fund-raising affairs to help the local party reach its quota for a national drive or to meet expenses at the park. The *Labor Advocate* greeted one 1931 joint effort with typical enthusiasm: "When the men of Local Berks need cash the women of the Socialist party always come to the rescue; it's wonderful how the 'weaker' sex always comes up strong toward the finish. Let's help them do the job in a big way."[44]

This comment (along with others cited from the male-edited *Labor Advocate*) suggests that women tended to be assigned a purely auxiliary role in the local movement even after it had made special efforts to organize them. Since no minutes of any branch women's group have been discovered, these newspaper accounts provide many of the details available on women's activities. We may, however, obtain some additional insight about the role of women through examining some of the branch minutes which usually were kept by their male colleagues. Most of the following discussion is based on the minute books of two city branches—the Central Branch and the Northeast Branch—at various times in the late 1920s and 1930s.[45]

First, it might be noted that there is not very much discussion specifically referring to women. These branches discussed organizing women and their organizations, but their minutes do not indicate that these were major ongoing concerns. Women speakers addressed the branches infrequently, but we do find Ethel Hofses (the wife of the *Labor Advocate* editor) speaking on "World peace and disarmament" and Annie Zechman discussing "Socialism, women, and affairs of today" at the Central Branch.[46] Although former participants testify that women attended and participated in regular branch meetings, the minutes themselves do not provide very much evidence on this matter.[47] What they do suggest is that the regular branch and the women's group were separate and that a formal system of communications existed between the two organizations. For example, the Northeast Branch minutes of August 1932 contains the following: "It was moved and sec. that a committee be appointed to go to the Women meeting and streighten [sic] out the missunderstanding [sic] with this branch." Subsequently, plans were made for a joint meeting, announced in the *Labor Advocate*, which was held in early September. The minutes reveal nothing concerning the nature of the misunderstanding, and the joint meeting appears to have been conducted according to the regular branch format.[48]

In March of 1935, this branch voted to invite "women to attend Branch meetings." The following week, however, it was reported that "Women [were] unfavorable to meeting with men." Though branch meetings were not sexually segregated, this episode and some others suggest that that tendency might sometimes be present.[49] Regular branch meetings were not "men only" affairs, but apparently some women did not feel entirely comfortable attending them. Several years after the period under study in this essay, a perceptive male socialist in the Reading movement wrote: " 'Men's meeting'! That is what women are calling Branch meetings." He went on to say:

It is discouraging and lonesome to be 'the only woman' in a meeting. Husbands and wives should attend together wherever possible. Branches must include women as officers and as members of their committees. Women need to be encouraged to participate in discussion; meetings can be made interesting to women as well as men."[50]

These words were written after the local movement had peaked and was declining, but they may have some relevance for the earlier period as well. Most of the women's group members had spouses who were also socialists. For example, in mid-1934, the Central Branch had 198 members, 50 of whom were women. All but 9 of them had spouses who were socialist men.[51] Apparently, many socialist couples were not attending branch meetings together. Separate meetings gave both the husband and the wife a night out.

Though some women shied away from the "men's meeting," others attended and participated in its affairs. Since the branch was the primary party unit in the local movement, the record of women's participation at that level should help us determine the overall significance of their involvement in the Reading Socialist organization. And the fact that women played an active auxiliary role within branches, it should be noted, did not preclude a more influential role for some. Each year, the branch would elect its officers, and these typically consisted of an organizer, a recording secretary, a financial secretary, and a treasurer. In addition, at the outset of each meeting, a chairman would be elected. In the period studied, neither the Central Branch nor the Northeast Branch elected any permanent women officers and apparently none was ever elected to chair a meeting. (One woman did serve as temporary financial secretary of the Northeast Branch in 1928.)[52] While women did not serve as branch officers, they were occasionally elected to branch committees, served as delegates to conventions, and were even elected to the party's county committee. We find the Northeast Branch appointing "a Com[mittee] of five ladies" to serve as "an Entertaining Comm." in April of 1928. One of its members had resigned by the next meeting, perhaps indicating that she had not been present when she had been selected.[53] In addition to such assignments, a few women were elected to more important committees, including Esther Auman, who was elected to the Northeast Branch's Fund-Finding Committee in late 1933 and again the following year.[54] Yet the minutes do not report many branch committee assignments for women, and, considering the propensity of both of these branches to work through temporary committees, that suggests a limited role for women within these branches.

Perhaps the most significant committee assignment at this level was that of the county committee. Each branch was entitled to representation on this body, though the basis of that representation changed from time to time. In 1928, the Northeast Branch elected four women and thirteen men to the county committee. After that, however, its allotted number of representatives was reduced substantially. (In 1929, this branch only had four to elect.) Between 1929 and 1935, only one woman from this unit, Esther Auman, was elected to the county committee, and she was elected as a replacement in 1935. (By this time, in addition to other responsibilities, she was financial secretary of the Local.)[55] An episode involving the Central Branch and its county committee representatives is worth noting. At a late 1935 branch meeting, it was mistakenly announced that the branch was entitled to thirteen seats on the county committee. It was decided that the branch would elect ten committee men and that the women's group could elect the other three at its own meeting. The branch then proceeded to elect ten men to these positions. When the error was discovered however, the minutes of the next meeting report how the matter was resolved: "Motion carried comm.[unication] from Com. Bigony that we have 2 more Co. Comte. members than we are entitled to be recd & *that 2 of the women be dropped*[.]"[56]

At the branch level, then, it appears that women's participation was often limited. Men usually served as branch officers and speakers, assumed branch committee assignments, and represented the branch at state conventions and the county committee. Though we have seen some exceptions—

women did serve as speakers, were elected as delegates, and did actively participate in meetings—many of them may have felt more at home in their separate organizations.[57] The regular branch meeting, at least for some, was perceived as the "Men's meeting." Most active socialist women channeled their efforts into the "auxiliary activities": they worked at the card parties, cooked at the park, and waited on tables at the fund-raising affairs. Though some of the rank-and-file women (along with their male counterparts) might be nominated for minor political offices at the precinct level, generally speaking, they performed the anonymous role that women have usually been assigned. Yet there were a few exceptions who did not act out that role. Within the local movement, a small number of women acquired prominence, serving on important Local committees and being nominated for public office.

Theoretically, the party membership was governed by the monthly Local meeting. Here, both standing and ad hoc committees were chosen, recommendations from the branches and committees were acted upon, and new policies were enacted. This gathering also served as a forum for both the leadership and the rank and file. Influence at this level could result in important committee assignments and would indicate that an individual was accorded respect and esteem from his or her colleagues. The nature of women's participation at the Local meeting and in the committees that were selected by it provide considerable insight into the overall significance of their involvement in the Reading party. A statement from a recent study on women in a different social movement may be of relevance here.

If women only sat on the back benches during Alliance meetings, listening silently while men discussed the great economic and political issues of the day, their membership would have been insignificant. If, on the other hand, women actually helped to run the organization and helped contribute to its success, even if they were not equal in every respect to men, then the Alliance was an important departure . . . .[58]

The minute of the Local meeting seem less ambiguous in regard to women's participation than those of the two branches examined earlier. Though men seem to have done most of the talking, some women also took part in the discussion. (It should be noted, however, that the minutes usually do not identify the speaker or the maker of the motion.) One of the more unusual entries in the Local minutes relates to a motion made by a woman Socialist school director in March of 1933. Hazelette Hoopes had moved "that we congratulate President elect Roosevelt for appointing Francis [sic] Perkins [h]is Secretary of Labor."[59] In this case, the motion failed as the local party refused to congratulate a capitalist politician. But while some women spoke up at Local meetings, they usually were not elected as officers. Between 1928 and 1936, the Local had an average of five officers each year. Men held all of the posts in five of these years, and only one woman was elected as an officer for each of the four remaining years. In 1930, Lilith Wilson served as secretary, and Esther Auman held the post of financial secretary from 1934 through 1936. Apparently Wilson was the only woman who ever chaired a Local meeting (and that occurred only once), but women were almost always elected to some standing committees.[60] As was the case at the branch level, much of the Local's business was handled by ad hoc committees that would be chosen throughout the year. Although these were frequently staffed entirely by men, it was not unusual for women to serve on them as well. In July of 1928, Ethel Hofses, along with three men, audited the books of the financial secretary and the treasurer.[61] An ad hoc committee was chosen in the summer of 1935 to deal with a Picnic Committee controversy. The minutes read: "that Comte of 5 be elected, 2 of whom shall be women, to investigate purchases of Picnic Committee." Though women often were selected as secretaries by their committees, this time a man served in that function.[62] The minutes also testify to the auxiliary role that women frequently played in Local Berks. We find reports of $60 and $100 contributions which were raised by Women's Socialist League activities.[63] Yet this role does not appear to be emphasized.

In late 1931, the local party established the Women's Committee,[64] which was intended to coordinate the activity of the various branch women's groups in the county. This committee coexisted with the Women's Socialist League for a few years before the League was phased out. Its organization suggests a more serious attempt to mobilize women for active duty within the movement. A 1934 committee report stated: "While there is a little work of social nature carried on occasionally by this committee, most of its duties are of an educational, political, and propaganda character."[65] The Local meeting voted to "donate $50 to the committee for organization work" in March of 1933 and later that year refused to make the committee "a part of the Women's League."[66] Though this body also played an auxiliary role as numerous articles in the *Labor Advocate* testified, it was a standing committee of the Local and sponsored a wide range of activities. The organization of this committee contributed to the growing strength of the local movement in the early and mid-1930s, and its existence may have made it more likely that women could contribute outside their traditional auxiliary role. Yet, the work of this committee tended to be confined to women's activities and did not involve as much interaction with their male colleagues as did participation on other committees.

Participation on the Local's standing committees may help us gauge the extent of women's influence. As already noted, though the Local meeting made policy, many responsibilities were delegated to the committees. Following the 1927 victory, an Executive Committee was established, which was "to have full authority to represent and to act for the Local, between meetings of the Local including authority to act in an advisory capacity to elected Socialist public officials . . . ."[67] (Subsequently, the division of labor between this committee and the county committee, which was made up of elected members from the various branches, was made more clear.[68]) In addition, each year, at the December meeting, the Executive or Advisory Committee was elected by the Local membership. This committee played a prominent role and elections to it were frequently competitive. Other standing committees included the Picnic Committee, the Lecture Committee, and the Referendum Committee. During the 1928-1936 period, the number of standing committees increased, as did the number of committee assignments.[69]

The following table, based on the annual committee elections, indicates the opportunity women actually had to participate in such committee work. The figures in this table do not take into account elections to committees, standing or otherwise, which were conducted at other meetings during the year.

ANNUAL COMMITTEE ELECTIONS

Year of Service	Male Committee Members	Female Committee Members
1928	9 (9)*	1 (1)
1929	13 (10)	0 (0)
1930	21 (12)	4 (1)
1931	45 (16)	3 (1)
1932	44 (10)	15 (3)
1933	45 (8)	16 (3)
1934	52 (12)	17 (3)
1935	58 (9)	12 (2)
1936	63 (15)	12 (2)
Total	350 (101)	80 (16)[70]

*The figure in parentheses represents the number of that sex holding seats on the Executive or Advisory Committee.

Throughout the entire period, as these figures show, men filled the vast majority of committee slots. At first, it might seem that 1932 represented a major breakthrough for women since their committee positions increased from three to fifteen. Yet the explanation for this increase is simply that the Local elected an eleven-person Women's Committee at the 1931 December meeting. Aside from the eleven on this body, the committee assignments for women again were few in number. Ethel Hofses, Bertha Tyson Weidner, and Mary Nelson were elected to the Advisory Committee along with ten men, and Weidner was also chosen for the Lecture Committee. On the remaining seven committees there was no women's representation.

Later, the size of the Women's Committee was reduced to five members, so that women's representation actually did increase in some of the years after 1932. At the December 21, 1933 meeting, for example, Annie Zechman, Bertha Weidner, and Ethel Hofses were elected to the Advisory Committee, and Zechman and Weidner received other assignments as well. Two other women, including Lilith Wilson, received two or more committee positions apiece. But 1933 proved to be the high point in women's representation. Constituting approximately 32 percent of the party's membership, women held almost 25 percent of the committee posts.[71] Over the entire period 1928-1936, however, women received less than 19 percent of these assignments. And an examination of the sexual composition of the Executive or Advisory Committee, the most important body elected at the December meeting, reveals that the representation of women was even smaller. A total of 95 individuals served on this committee between 1928 and 1936 and out of that figure fewer than 14 percent were women.

This tabulation of women committee assignments is at best a crude measure of their influence in local party affairs, but it does suggest that some women were afforded an opportunity to participate in a directive capacity. Though they did not hold as many committee posts as their numbers might justify, it seems that their representation in later years went beyond that of tokenism.

And who were the women chosen to serve on the standing committees? A total of twenty-two different women were elected to these bodies at the December meetings between 1927 and 1935. Of that total, eleven were never chosen for any committee other than the Women's Committee. Five different women were elected to the Executive or Advisory Committee: Lilith Wilson (two terms), Mary Nelson (one term), Ethel Hofses (four terms), Bertha Tyson Weidner (five terms), and Annie Zechman (four terms). Wilson was the most prominent woman in the local movement. Prior to moving to Reading in 1921, she was already well known in the national party. She was a graduate of the party's Rand School in New York City and had served as a SP organizer and lecturer. In 1921, she was elected to the party's National Executive Committee (NEC). Later that same year, she came to Reading and married L. Birch Wilson, a prominent figure in the local movement. (Between 1928 and 1936, he served on the Executive or Advisory Committee seven times.) She was a frequent candidate for public office and was elected to the state assembly for three terms, beginning in 1930. Since all elected socialist officeholders were *ex officio* members of the committee, she was not eligible to be elected to it after she became a legislator. She continued, however, to serve on other Local committees. In 1928, she was again elected to the NEC and continued serving on that body until 1934.[72] Ironically, in the same year that she returned to the NEC, she was defeated for Local Berks' Executive Committee. Wilson did not usually participate in local women's group functions, though she had helped organize some of them in 1928.[73]

Ethel Hofses, Bertha Weidner, and Annie Zechman, on the other hand, played active roles in the women's groups, and their involvement was frequently reported by the party paper. Hofses was the wife of the *Labor Advocate*'s editor, Raymond Hofses, who held several other party posts and was a school director from 1927 to 1933. Zechman had been an officer of her branch women's unit and helped reestablish another branch's group in mid-1931: "The reorganization of the Northeast women was effected largely through the efforts of Mrs. Annie Zechman, a member of the Northwest Women's organization, who made a number of personal visits to interest the women of the Northeast section in political activities."[74] Both Zechman and Weidner served on several other committees, including the Picnic Committee, and no other women served on as many as they did between 1928 and 1936.

If we exclude those who served only on the Women's Committee, we find that few other women had comparable committee assignments. Mary Nelson, for example, served on the Advisory and Women's Committees in 1932, as well as two others in previous years. Esther Auman, active within women's organizations, was elected to the Women's Committee from 1932 through 1935. In 1934, she also served on the Auditing and Organization Committees. Another individual active on the Women's Committee was Emma Sands. She was elected to this body five consecutive years and frequently was one of its officers. Her only other committee assignment, however, was the Education Committee in 1934. Like Wilson and Hofses, her husband was a prominent figure in the Reading organization and served four terms on the Advisory Committee from 1932 to 1935. Their daughter, Clara Mosteller, was also very active in the party. In 1936, she served on both the Auditing and Organization Committees.[75]

A few women, in addition to serving on Local committees, were nominated as SP candidates for public office. In 1930, Lilith Wilson was elected to the state assembly, becoming "the first Socialist woman to be named to any legislative body in the United States." She was reelected in 1932 and 1934, and it probably was in this forum that she made her greatest contribution to the local movement. The record that she and her Reading SP teammate, Darlington Hoopes, compiled in Harrisburg is beyond the scope of this study, but it drew strong support from organized labor and was one of the party's greatest assets during the early and mid-1930s.[76]

In the eyes of the general public, Hazelette Hoopes may have been the second most prominent socialist woman in Reading. Like Lilith Wilson, she was not a native of the area, but had moved there in adulthood. She was a 1924 graduate of Boston University and had been a YWCA secretary in Norristown, Pennsylvania, prior to marrying Darlington Hoopes. At the time, he was state secretary of the party and one of the few socialist attorneys in the state. When the socialists won in 1927, the Hoopeses moved to Reading. Both Hazelette Hoopes and Lilith Wilson were nominated as two of the party's three school board candidates in 1929, and Hoopes was elected. Six years later, she was reelected in the 1935 socialist victory.[77]

Neither Wilson nor Hoopes was especially active in the local women's groups. One socialist woman later remarked to the effect: "We were more a social group; they had more important things to do." Both of them had helped in the initial organization of the separate women's groups in 1928, and Hazelette Hoopes occasionally participated in women's programs and also worked in the kitchen at Socialist Park. Intellectually inclined and not of the local Pennsylvania Dutch culture, the two of them seemed to have little in common with the average Reading socialist woman who, more likely than not, was of a working-class background. Hoopes relates that several men told her that they "were glad they had a college graduate for the ticket."[78] The fact that both women had spouses who were prominent local socialists probably also played a role in their nominations.

Bertha Weidner, Annie Zechman, and Mary Nelson were also Socialist candidates in the early and mid-1930s. Weidner was nominated for school director in 1931, while Nelson had one of the SP's nominations for poor director that year. Zechman ran twice, but was defeated both times. In 1933, she sought a poor director post and two years later again tried for that position.[79] Another woman nominated by the Socialist caucus was Gertrude Hiller. An officer in her county branch at least once, Hiller was nominated for the poor board in 1935. She narrowly defeated one of her male socialist running mates and became the first and only woman socialist to hold a county office in Berks.[80] The following is a list of socialist women candidates in Reading and Berks county, and the outcomes of their candidacies:

1921	Ella Welfley	defeated for school director
1923	Lilith Wilson	defeated for school director
1929	Hazelette Hoopes	elected school director
	Lilith Wilson	defeated for school director
1930	Lilith Wilson	elected state legislator
1931	Bertha Weidner	defeated for school director
	Mary Nelson	defeated for poor director

1932	Lilith Wilson	reelected state legislator
1933	Annie Zechman	defeated for poor director
1934	Lilith Wilson	reelected state legislator
1935	Hazelette Hoopes Gertrude Hiller Annie Zechman	reelected school director elected prison inspector defeated for poor director
1937	Mabel Lausch	defeated for school director
1938	Bernice Hoverter	appointed city treasurer
1939	Bernice Hoverter	defeated for city treasurer
1941	Hazelette Hoopes	defeated for school director[81]

The local socialists had a better record on nominating women candidates than either of the old parties. Between 1921 and 1936, the SP selected a total of thirteen women candidates, while the combined figure for the Republicans and Democrats was ten.[82] Neither of the old parties nominated a woman for a post higher than school director. Part of the explanation for the socialists' record lies in their method of selecting candidates. The socialists picked their ticket at a party caucus and then simply ratified those choices in the primary. The old parties, however, chose their tickets through the primary and although party leaders may have wanted certain individuals nominated, it was not always easy to arrange that outcome. At the same time, however, we should acknowledge that the Socialist caucus was an open process for dues-paying members and by the mid-1930s may have had as many as several hundred people participating in it. That the socialists ran more women candidates was also due to the availability of women who were willing to stand for office and the willingness of their colleagues to nominate them.[83] With the exception of the state assembly, however, the posts for which they were selected between 1921 and 1936 seem to have been relatively minor ones.

We should also examine the opportunity that the Young People's Socialist League, or "Yipsels," provided for women's involvement. According to one former Yipsel leader (admittedly a man): "There was a difference as Day & Night between the Y.P.S.L. & the S.P. as far as the Role of women." The Yipsels had been reorganized in Reading in late 1929 and enjoyed rapid growth along with the rest of the party in the early 1930s. At their peak, they had over ten circles and 200 to 300 members.[84] Young women played a very active role in this group, serving as circle organizers and on the county executive committee. In late 1933, the *Labor Advocate* reported that Circle #1 had elected an entire slate of women officers. The following year, the county organization elected women to three of its seven offices.[85] While we also can find examples where all the Yipsel officers were men, it seems that women did have more opportunity here than in the parent organization.[86] The Yipsels, however, had little influence within Local Berks. Many of the older party members, including some leaders, were not sympathetic to the Yipsels and saw them as a nuisance. By the mid-1930s the Yipsels were on the decline and the number of active circles dropped to three or four.[87] Within their remaining ranks, however, were energetic individuals who felt that the party leadership was too conservative and who would join forces with other dissidents.[88]

Such battles came out into the open in 1936. That year marked the beginning of the end of the Reading socialist success story when a devastating split occurred disrupting the party's political operations and its social structure. Socialist officeholders would finish out their terms, but only one other would ever again be elected, and that would not occur until 1943.[89] Reading socialism's civil war was related to the controversy that tore the national organization apart the same year, but had local causes as well. While the national movement had been divided into "old guard" and "militant" factions for several years, these labels did not appear in Reading until late 1935.[90]

The internal upheavals that wracked the local socialist community were not "men only" affairs, since some women took a very active part in them. Though the old guard retained the loyalty of almost all local Socialist officeholders at the city and county level, a considerable number of "Jimmie Higginses" and active women were found within the militant group. Clara Mosteller, Bertha Weidner, Annie Zechman, Minnie Pike Hurley (Zechman's younger sister), and Gertrude Hiller, a newly elected prison inspector, were active in the militant cause. Even before the 1935 election, they had begun to caucus with other dissidents to determine strategy and to decide who should receive jobs in the new city administration.[91] The old guard, on the other hand, was led entirely by men, many of whom had led the local movement for decades. Lilith Wilson, who had been identified with the old guard on the national level while on the NEC, had become seriously ill in mid-1935 and died in July of 1937.[92] In the spring of 1936, each faction drew up a slate of its delegates for the national convention and sought support for its slate among the membership. The old guard slate did not list any women either as a delegate or an alternate. On the other hand, the militants listed several: Weidner, Mosteller, and Hiller were among its seven delegates, and four more, including Zechman and Hurley, were listed as alternates. An inflammatory militant pamphlet, *Rule or Ruin*, lists both slates. Following the militant names, it reads: "Look this list over. It contains the names of seven women comrades (not a single woman is named on the 'Old Guard' slate) . . . ." The old guard was more successful, however, as the membership elected fourteen of its delegates and only three militant men.[93]

Throughout much of 1936, the local movement was preoccupied with the old guard-militant controversy. Then, in August, the state party disaffiliated with the national organization and lined up with the old guard. This step led to a local split and the emergence of two local socialist parties, one identified with the state organization and the other with the national group. The once united movement now became a battlefield where former colleagues fought each other for control of the local membership and its property holdings.[94] Conversations with former party workers on both sides some thirty-five years later reveal that the split was a very traumatic episode for them. Though the old guard ultimately prevailed, the leftists continued a well-publicized campaign against their socialist opponents for the next several years. One immediate consequence of the split was to destroy socialist chances in the November election when every Socialist candidate was decisively beaten.[95]

The old guard was able to reorganize six city branches and several county units, though with a considerably smaller membership.[96] Some of the branches continued their women's groups, and the *Labor Advocate* coverage indicates a substantial amount of socialist women's activity over the next several years. In 1941, the Women's Socialist League was revived. But the local movement had lost its forward momentum during the 1936 troubles and was never able to regain the initiative.[97]

And what of the women who went with the smaller leftist group? Their fate as socialists proved to be sadder than that of their former comrades. (Many supporters of their faction became disillusioned after the split and subsequently dropped out of left-wing politics altogether.) Though the leftist colleagues, and most of them probably ended up in the Democratic party by 1940. Gertrude Hiller sought a nomination for county commissioner on Their branches did sponsor some social activities, but their membership dwindled rapidly.[98] After the split, the leftists were sometimes referred to as the "Mostellerites" (after Clara Mosteller, the group's treasurer). In 1938 and 1939, they endorsed Democratic candidates against their former socialist colleagues and most of them probably ended up in the Democratic party by 1940. Gertrude Hiller sought a nomination for county commissioner on the Democratic ticket, but lost in the primary. Other leftists who attempted that route for city-wide or county office also were defeated at the primary level.[99] (Twenty years later, however, a former leftist would make it— Minnie Hurley was elected to the lucrative post of county treasurer as a Democrat in 1959.)[100] No longer using the socialist label, the leftists slowly

International Women's Day, Reading, Pa., March 5, 1933.

International Women's Day. Women's Committee, Local Berks, 1933.
(Courtesy of Eugene Haag, Reading, Pennsylvania.)

faded out of the Reading socialist picture. But much ill-feeling and bitterness between those who had been in the two groups continued as a legacy of the 1936 split.

Local socialist women had enjoyed their greatest days when the SP was at its peak in the early and mid-1930s. Yet even after the split, they had some bright spots. Their social activities continued, and Socialist Park remained a viable institution after the SP political machine had broken down. And perhaps one of the most significant events concerning socialist women occurred after the split, when in late 1938, the Socialist administration appointed Bernice Hoverter as city treasurer to fill a vacancy left by her father's death. William "Shorty" Hoverter had been one of the inner circle of local leaders since the beginning of the century, and his wife, Emma Hoverter, was active in women's affairs and was one of the founders of the original Women's Socialist League. So, when their daughter was appointed to this post, part of the motivation probably was to help "Shorty" Hoverter's family. Moreover, Bernice Hoverter may have been at least as qualified for the job as her father had been. She had studied accounting at a business school and, at the time of his death, was a clerk in his office.[101] Two months following her appointment, Socialist mayor J. Henry Stump commented: "I want to point out that this is the first time the women of Reading have been recognized by an appointment to a high and important municipal office." At the 1939 party caucus, all of the current Socialist officeholders were renominated, including Bernice Hoverter. The *Labor Advocate* quoted the party's county chairman as saying: "In deciding to keep her on the job for a full term the socialist rank and file demonstrated their belief that women should have an equal chance with men to fill positions for which they are qualified." That year, however, the voters rejected the entire socialist ticket, and Bernice Hoverter's tenure as city treasurer ended after slightly more than one year's service.[102]

For many observers today, it seems an exaggeration to claim that the Reading socialist men felt "that women should have an equal chance with men to fill positions for which they are qualified." Or, they may think, perhaps more significantly, that many socialist men did not believe that women were qualified for as many types of positions as men were. In the eyes of many men, women in the party were expected to support their husbands by voting the SP ticket, helping to get out the party vote, and working in their auxiliaries. Special appeals to women voters usually were limited to their roles as working-class mothers and homemakers and, then, frequently in condescending tones. Despite the successful candidacies of Lilith Wilson and Hazelette Hoopes, as well as the substantial percentage of women members and the loyal service that many of them provided, women tended to be assigned a subordinate role in the movement. In 1941, when the Women's Socialist League was revived, the *Labor Advocate* announced that it "will again act as an auxiliary to the party organization in activities *for which women are especially fitted.*"[103] But we should also acknowledge that the presence of women on influential committees such as the Executive or Advisory Committee and the county committee suggests that they "actually helped to run the organization . . . ."[104] Women in the local party may not have been in the first line of leadership, but some of them clearly functioned outside an auxiliary role.

Many of the observations of this study are consistent with those of Buhle's article on the pre-World War I movement at the national level and add credence to the view that socialists found it easier to break with the prevailing economic system than the traditional role of the sexes.[105] Despite their frequent reformist and even conservative rhetoric during municipal campaigns, the local socialists sought to replace the capitalist system and denounced New Deal proposals as inadequate. Yet most of them, male and female, were not inclined to question male domination of either their movement or their homes. They were part of a basically working-class movement that represented the dominant culture of the area in several respects. Whatever the political advantages of this situation, it certainly affected the ways in which women were viewed in the party. Conservative, Pennsylvania Dutch cultural norms prevailed within Local Berks.[106] Hazelette Hoopes recalls when she arrived in Reading in the late 1920s: "I had never lived in such a male place."[107] For many if not most of the local socialist women, however, such male domination was probably seen as part of the natural order. We might also note that this traditional view toward women often involves a certain amount of deference on the part of men. A recent comment by Frank Zeidler in regard to women in the Milwaukee socialist movement may be helpful here: "The males treated the Socialist women with considerable deference and gene[r]al affection." He adds: "This might now be considered patronizing . . . ."[108]

The traditional view continued to be expressed by the local party, but we have seen some examples of a modification of this view as well. Male socialists had supported woman suffrage, equal pay, birth control, and had encouraged the increased participation of women in the movement. On the matter of nominating women for public office, as indicated, the SP had a better record that either of the old parties. As late as 1968, the Reading *Eagle* reported: "Curiously, each woman who won or held a top elective office in Reading and Berks County was associated with the Socialist party."[109] But then it is easier to run a few more women candidates than it is to change age-old assumptions about women. It is not a simple case, and all the implications of this ambivalence are not yet apparent.

We should also note the concerns of the time in which we are studying this particular socialist movement. During the 1930s, the United States suffered the worst depression in its history. This situation, at least briefly, presented the American left with opportunities, but also greatly affected its priorities. Demands for immediate relief, organization efforts among the un-employed, and, even more importantly, among the unorganized workers, took priority over social questions involving blacks and women. Foreign policy considerations from 1933 on further complicated the situation. Probably to most left-wingers at the time, these priorities seemed appro-priate. At the same time, there was no clamor on the part of women to change such priorities. In response to a 1932 questionnaire which the SP national office mailed out to socialist women, "the majority of the approx-imately 100 replies received indicated no interest in special work among women and a feeling that it was unnecessarily duplicating effort. They felt that special literature for women was unnecessary."[110] This situation stands in marked contrast with that of the pre-World War I era when the National Woman's Committee assumed an active role. In the case of the Reading movement, its priorities included the strengthening of an already viable political machine. That it was more interested in organizing women than many other local socialist organizations of the time was due in part to its perceived need to attract more women voters. The concerns of the 1930s were somewhat different from those of today and affected the way in which women were viewed within the American left. To cite the dominant econo-mic and foreign policy concerns then is not to excuse socialist men for their views on the Woman Question, but to suggest that these concerns may have helped reinforce the traditional view of the role of the sexes. Advances on social matters seem to be more likely in a time of prosperity or relative affluence than in a time of economic deprivation. We cannot blame the depression for the way in which women were treated by their male socialist colleagues, but perhaps it may help explain why their advances came as slowly as they did in the 1930s.

Similar studies of other local socialist movements probably will not yield results entirely different from those of this exploration. It does not appear that social democratic parties have had an exceptional record in regard to women. A recent study dealing with the German Social Democrats states: "While German Social Democracy was officially committed to the women's struggle, a critical analysis . . . compels a less positive appraisal of the de-gree to which women achieved equality in the socialist world."[111] It is likely that other studies will find the situation to be similar to that of the Reading movement (and of the national movement in the pre-World War I era): the majority of women performing a subordinate and supportive role, with only a relatively small number of them achieving more prominent posi-tions. Of those who achieved such prominence we might also find that they were frequently related by blood or marriage to prominent male socialists. Taking into consideration the prevailing assumptions of male supremacy, the deeply held notion maintained by a majority of women that their place was at home, and the limited time that married women with children have had historically to devote to nonemployment activities outside the home, it does not seem very realistic to expect the situation to be much different.[112]

At the same time, however, the strong probability that most women in the left-wing movements usually performed an auxiliary or supportive role should not inhibit historians from making a thorough examination of that role. After all, the majority of active men in such movements have been "Jimmie Higginses," and their function has also been a supportive one. Women's auxiliaries of organizations deserve scholarly attention and such studies should add further dimension to both women's history and the history of society generally. Auxiliaries and the rank and file of social movements are among the missing components of our historical understanding, and further research in these topics will enable us to construct a fuller picture of the collective past of men and women.

Notes

1. Ira Kipnis, *The American Socialist Movement, 1897-1912* (New York: Monthly Review Press, 1972), pp. 260-65; James Weinstein, *The Decline of Socialism in America, 1912-1925* (New York: Monthly Review Press, 1967), pp. 53-62; Mari Jo Buhle, "Women and the Socialist Party," *Radical America* 4 (February 1970): 36-47, 50-55; Bruce Dancis, "Socialism and Women in the United States, 1900-1917," *Socialist Revolution* 6 (January-March 1976): 81-144.

2. The "island communities" conceptualization is borrowed from Robert H. Wiebe, *The Search for Order, 1877-1920* (New York: Hill and Wang, 1968), p. xiii.

3. For scholarly accounts of the Milwaukee Socialist movement, see Sally M. Miller, "Milwaukee: Of Ethnicity and Labor," in Bruce M. Stave, ed., *Socialism and the Cities* (Port Washington, New York: Kennikat, 1975), pp. 41-71; Frederick I. Olson, "The Milwaukee Socialists, 1897-1941" (Ph.D. diss., Harvard University, 1952).

4. For scholarly accounts of the Reading Socialist movement, see Henry G. Stetler, *The Socialist Movement in Reading, Pennsylvania, 1896-1936* (Storrs: Privately published, 1943); William C. Pratt, "The Reading Socialist Experience: A Study of Working Class Politics" (Ph.D. diss., Emory University, 1969); Kenneth E. Hendrickson, Jr., "The Socialists of Reading, Pennsylvania and World War I—A Question of Loyalty," *Pennsylvania History* 36 (October 1969): 430-50; "The Socialist Administration in Reading, Pennsylvania Part I, 1927-1931," Ibid. 39 (October 1972): 417-42; "Triumph and Disaster: The Reading Socialists in Power and Decline, 1932-1939—Part II," Ibid. 40 (October 1973): 381-411.

5. Some local Socialists felt that their 1911 mayoralty candidate had been "counted out." (Personal interview with Raymond E. Kiebach, August 12, 1976.)

6. Clippings, Benjamin A. Fryer, "Fryer's Berks County Political Scrap Books," vol. 18, p. 67; vol. 19, p. 202, Historical Society of Berks County, Reading, Pennsylvania.

7. *Reading Labor Advocate*, July 28, 1933.

8. *Reading Eagle*, September 1, 1915; November 3, 1915. A woman had sought a school board post at least as early as 1898, when such representation was on a ward basis. (Ibid., December 30, 1897.)

9. *Reading Eagle*, November 3, 11 and 12, 1915. "The southeastern end of the state of Pennsylvania will be the battlefield for the suffragettes in the next five years, for it is the Pennsylvania German settlement that administered a defeat to equal suffrage at the polls this month." The article went on to say: "Not one of the purely Pennsylvania German counties gave suffrage a majority." The "Pennsylvania Dutch" are descendants of German immigrants, and the phrases "Pennsylvania Dutch" and "Pennsylvania German" can be used interchangeably. See William T. Parsons, *The Pennsylvania Dutch: A Persistent Minority* (Boston: Twayne Publishers, 1976), Preface, n. p.

10. Ida Husted Harper, *The History of Woman Suffrage* vol. 6 (New York: National American Woman Suffrage Association, 1922), p. 556. The author also noted that "in many cases the Democratic and Republican watchers gave assistance." (Ibid., pp. 556-57.)

11. The *Eagle* stated that the socialists felt that woman suffrage "is a means to an end and that it will greatly enhance their party numbers." (*Reading Eagle*, August 3 and 12, 1915; September 13 and 22, 1915; October 20-22, 28, 1915.) Local suffragists, including several women socialists, worked "at the various polling places handing out cards on election day . . . ." (Ibid., November 30, 1915.) The *Labor Advocate*, in a post-election editorial, said: "The Socialists endorsed Woman Suffrage; in fact Socialism is Woman Suffrage." (*Reading Labor Advocate*, November 6, 1915.) The local SP did not own this paper until 1918 (and then it was through a holding company of individual party members), but its earlier owner was a party leader. (Ibid., January 5, 1918; Stetler, *The Socialist Movement in Reading*, pp. 60-61, 63.)

12. Minutes of Local Berks County Socialist Party, April 1, 1920, p. 15, in Darlington Hoopes Papers; *Reading Labor Advocate*, April 3, 1920. The Hoopes Papers are available on microfilm at Pennsylvania State University and from Rhistoric Publications.

13. This group sponsored at least two Sanger lectures. (*Reading Eagle*, December 4, 1920; February 8, 1921.) Despite its efforts, the SP paper complained that "only one woman comrade [was] present" at a recent Local meeting. (*Reading Labor Advocate*, June 4, 1921.) For 1921 election results, see *Eagle*, November 9, 1921.

14. *Reading Eagle*, November 3, 1911; L. Birch Wilson testimony, "In Re. Dissolution of the Labor Lyceum of Reading, Pa.," Berks County Court House, Reading, Pennsylvania; Minutes of Local Berks, January 6, 1921, p. 33. Of this 1921 number, "108 members [were] from 6 mos to 1 yr in arrears. . . ." The 1927 caucus is reported in clipping [April 26, 1927], Fryer Political Scrap Books, vol. 41, p. 75.

15. *Reading Labor Advocate*, May 29, 1915; "Address of Mayor Henry J. [sic] Stump of Reading, Pennsylvania," Socialist Party Papers, Duke University. This collection is now available on microfilm from the Microfilm Corporation of America. I have not followed its suggested citation form as much of my research in that collection was done at Duke.

16. The 1927 campaign is covered in Hendrickson, "The Socialist Administration

in Reading, Pennsylvania," pp. 419-26; Pratt, "The Reading Socialist Experience," pp. 67-93. For SP advertisements, see *Reading Eagle*, November 5, 1927.

17. *Reading Labor Advocate*, January 1, 1927. Socialist spokesmen had talked of a low women socialist vote as early as 1920, the first year women voted in Pennsylvania. One SP leader said after the 1920 election: "In the Socialist strongholds in Reading, an examination of registration figures will show that only a comparatively few women registered under the party banner. This made the women Socialist vote very light and gave the Republicans a tremendous advantage with their large number of women voters." (*Reading Eagle*, November 3, 1920.)

18. *Reading Labor Advocate*, September 3, 1927. Prior to the caucus, the party had appointed a *man* as "special organizer of the women of the Socialist party of Reading. . . ." (Ibid., March 19, 1927.)

19. "No, Reading Has Not Gone Red!" *Literary Digest* 95 (December 10, 1927), p. 14. Mayor-elect J. Henry Stump explained to an audience of New York Socialists: "We went out on the street corners and talked assessments for 10 weeks. We rallied our forces around the issue of special privilege, and despite the fact that the politicians tried to divert our campaign to theoretical questions we kept on the issue we picked and emerged with victory." (*New York Times*, December 12, 1927.)

20. Minutes of Local Berks, October 4, 1928, p. 150; *Reading Labor Advocate*, July 21, 1928.

21. *Reading Labor Advocate*, January 21, 1928.

22. Ibid.

23. William H. Henry, Supplementary report to report of Committee on Ways and Means, Socialist Party *Proceedings of the 1928 National Convention*, p. 74e.

24. For example, see *Reading Labor Advocate*, June 5, 1915; July 10, 1915; August 14, 1915.

25. *Reading Labor Advocate*, June 16 and 30, 1928.

26. For a history of Socialist Park through 1932, see George M. Rhodes, "A Brief History of The Socialist Park," ibid., November 18, 1932; November 25, 1932; December 2, 1932. The park was actually owned by a holding company of individual party members.

27. "The Northwest Women's organization will serve a free dinner to all who help with the work of grading the Park on Sunday. Last Sunday a happy crowd of about 70 workers enjoyed a sour krout [sic] dinner as the guests of the Women's Socialist League. . . ." (*Reading Labor Advocate*, May 29, 1931.) For a discussion on the local party's rank and file, see William C. Pratt, " 'Jimmie Higgins' and the Reading Socialist Community: An Exploration of the Socialist Rank and File," in Stave, ed., *Socialism and the Cities*, pp. 141-56. I have not used the name "Jennie Higgins" in this study to refer to the active rank-and-file woman member. Though some local socialists did use it, I have found several who were not familiar with the name and it was not used in the party paper. When I asked one former woman member about it, she responded to the effect: "I guess we were 'Jimmies' too." (Personal interview with Catherine E. Tomlinson, July 25, 1973.) In 1930, the national party conducted a "Jimmy Higgins Contest." After "only one woman comrade . . . entered the contest," a special announcement was made to point out that women were eligible for the contest. At least in the *Labor Advocate*, this piece has the following sub-heading:

"JIMMIE CAN BE A WOMAN!" (*Reading Labor Advocate*, September 19, 1930.)
  28. S.P., *Proceedings* of 1928 National Convention, p. 30e.
  29. *Reading Labor Advocate*, May 26, 1928; "Convention Memo #10: Women's Work," in *Report* of the NEC to the National Convention, June 1, 2, 3, 1934, p. 32, (Hereafter cited as Report to 1934 Convention.) For resignation, see Lilith M. Wilson to National Executive Committee, September 14, 1929, Socialist Party Papers.
  30. *Report* to 1934 Convention, p. 34.
  31. Lilith Wilson, "Annual Report of the National Women's Committee From May, 1928, to January, 1929," Socialist Party Papers.
  32. Minutes of Local Berks, July 5, 1928, p. 142.
  33. *Reading Labor Advocate*, July 21, 1928.
  34. Ibid., September 15, 1928. Italics added.
  35. Wilson, "Annual Report," Socialist Party Papers.
  36. *Reading Labor Advocate*, November 4, 1932, December 22, 1933.
  37. See Dancis, "Socialism and Women in the United States," pp. 103-07.
  38. Tomlinson interview.
  39. *Reading Labor Advocate*, August 4, 1928; December 8, 1928; November 27, 1931; March 26, 1932.
  40. Ibid., December 19, 1930; April 3, 1931; February 19, 1932; *Reading Eagle*, January 11, 1922; *Planned Parenthood Center of Berks County—40th Anniversary 1927-1967* (local Planned Parenthood pamphlet).
  41. *Reading Labor Advocate*, January 4, 1930.
  42. Ibid., March 1, 1930.
  43. Ibid., February 16, 1934.
  44. Ibid., July 31, 1931. "When Local Berks sends its quota of $500 to the National Campaign Fund headquarters a goodly share of the money will have been raised by the women of Local Berks. That the Socialist women of Reading will play their part in carrying the message of Socialism to the less-strongly organized sections of the nation was assured last Thursday night when, at a meeting of the Women's Socialist League [it was] decided to hold a monster card party and luncheon on the three floors of Labor Lyceum." (Ibid., May 6, 1932.)
  45. The Central Branch Minutes have been surveyed from February 24, 1929 (when the branch was organized) to March 23, 1936. Those of the Northeast Branch have been surveyed from November 14, 1927 through August 26, 1935. Both sets are in the Hoopes Papers and were examined on microfilm. In the case of the Northeast Branch, the minutes were not always easy to read. As a result, the election of branch officers for 1929 was not examined. The Central Branch did not have a women's group initially, but had one by the end of 1929. (Minutes of Central Branch, April 7, 1929, p. 43; *Reading Labor Advocate*, December 7, 1929.) The women's organization of the Northeast Branch was reestablished in July of 1931. (Ibid., July 10, 1931.)
  46. Minutes of the Central Branch, February 1, 1932, p. 167; August 15, 1932, p. 197.
  47. Tomlinson interview; Eugene Haag to author, February 22, 1978.
  48. Minutes of the Northeast Branch, August 22, 1932, p. 110; September 6, 1932, p. 112; *Reading Labor Advocate*, September 2, 1932.
  49. Minutes of Northeast Branch, March 18, 1935, p. 229; March 25, 1935, p. 232. When the *Labor Advocate* had announced the joint meeting of the Northeast Branch

discussed above, it referred to "the *men's* and *women's* organizations." (*Reading Labor Advocate*, September 2, 1932. Italics added.)

50. Elwood Keppley, "Party-torial," *Reading Labor Advocate*, February 11, 1944.

51. Central Branch Dues Report, June to September, 1934, Hoopes Papers. Approximately 89 percent of the women socialists of the five city branches had socialist spouses. (Branch Dues Reports, June to September, 1934, Hoopes Papers.)

52. Minutes of the Northeast Branch, September 10, 1928, p. 159. The Southern Branch, however, elected women as treasurer and as one of its trustees, and the Southwest Branch elected a woman as recording secretary when they were first organized. (*Reading Labor Advocate*, May 4, 1929; February 14, 1936.)

53. Minutes of Northeast Branch, April 16, 1928, p. 128; April 23, 1928, p. 130.

54. Ibid., December 11, 1933, p. 260; December 10, 1934, p. 176.

55. Ibid., February 13, 1928, pp. 111-12; December 30, 1929, pp. 247-48; February 25, 1935, p. 222; Minutes of Local Berks, December 20, 1934, p. 100.

56. Minutes of Central Branch, December 16, 1935, pp. 180-81; January 13, 1936, p. 182. Over two years earlier the following oblique statement was recorded: "Motion that communication from Women's Branch, Central Branch be received and vacancy in seats at County Committee be considered when vacancies occur carried." (Ibid., October 23, 1933, p. 55.)

57. It was not unusual for women to be nominated for precinct posts. In 1931, for example, when the city ticket was defeated by a fusion ticket, the socialists still managed to elect some candidates to ward and precinct posts, including several women inspectors of elections in Sixth Ward precincts. (*Reading Eagle*, November 13, 1931.)

58. Julie Roy Jeffrey, "Women in the Southern Farmer's Alliance: A Reconsideration of the Role and Status of Women in the Late Nineteenth-Century South," *Feminist Studies* 3 (Fall 1975): 78.

59. Minutes of Local Berks, March 2, 1933, p. 11.

60. Ibid., December 5, 1929, p. 196; December 21, 1933, p. 42; December 20, 1934, p. 100; December 5, 1935, [133]; November 7, 1929, p. 191.

61. Ibid., July 5, 1928, p. 143.

62. Ibid., July 3, 1935, p. 125; August 1, 1935, p. 127.

63. Ibid., November 7, 1929, p. 191; April 4, 1929, p. 171.

64. Ibid., December 3, 1931, p. 265.

65. Emma M Sands, "Report of the Women's Committee of the Socialist Party of Local Berks—Reading, Penna. Year of 1933-34," Socialist Party Papers.

66. Minutes of Local Berks, March 2, 1933, p. 10; December 21, 1933, p. 45.

67. Ibid., December 1, 1927, pp. 119-20. This motion also stated: "That public officials elected to city-wide offices shall be ex-officio members of said committee, with voice and vote; That three years continuous membership in the Party, at time of nomination shall be required for eligibility to membership on said Executive Committee."

68. Within the County Committee, there was some opposition to the new committee. At the June 7, 1928, Local meeting, the County Committee recommended "that the Executive Committee be abolished and its functions be turned over to the County Committee. . . ." Later, such a motion was voted on, and lost. (Minutes of Local Berks, June 7, 1928, p. 139.) By the end of 1929, it had become the Advisory Committee.

69. The 1935 constitution provides for ten standing committees. Only the Cam-

174   William C. Pratt

paign Committee was not elected at the December meeting. *Constitution of Local Berks County Socialist Party* (Reading, 1935), pp. 4, 10-14, in author's possession. In late 1933, the composition of the Women's Committee was changed. Each of the five city branches had one of its members elected to the committee at the Local meeting, and then all branches in the Local were entitled to elect two representatives. (Minutes of Local Berks, December 21, 1933, p. 46.) The following discussion is limited to those women elected by the Local.

70. Minutes of Local Berks, December 1, 1927, p. 120; December 6, 1928, pp. 155-56; December 5, 1929, pp. 196-98; December 4, 1930, pp. 223-25; December 3, 1931, pp. 262-65; December 1, 1932, p. 301; December 21, 1933, pp. 43-46; December 20, 1934, pp. 101-04; December 5, 1935, pp. 133-36.

71. This calculation is based on incomplete dues-reports for July-September, 1934. (The dues-reports for several of the county branches are missing. For this calculation, the membership at large is treated as a separate branch.) Of the 1,285 members listed, 413 of them (32.1 percent) are women. By examining the names in the twelve branches in which it is relatively easy to ascertain married couples, I have found that approximately 91 percent (285 out of 312) of the women members had socialist spouses. This percentage was even higher in the county branches, where 122 out of 131 women members were in this category. (Dues-Reports for Local Berks, June-September, 1934.) According to a Local report prepared in late 1935, 541 members (or 26.7 percent) of a total membership of 2,025 were wives of socialist men. ("Fourth Quarterly Report Showing the Standing of all Members at the Close of 1935,") Socialist Party Papers.

72. Lilith Wilson to Comrade Barnes, October 25, 1929, Socialist Party Papers; *Reading Eagle* clipping [August 1934], Fryer's Political Scrap Books, vol. 53, pp. 251-52; *Reading Eagle*, July 9, 1937. She had been the party's candidate for governor in 1922.

73. Minutes of Local Berks, December 6, 1928, p. 156; Tomlinson interview; *Reading Labor Advocate*, July 21 and 28, 1928; August 11, 1928.

74. *Reading Labor Advocate*, December 23, 1932; July 10, 1931.

75. Auman served as an officer of both the Women's Committee and the Socialist Women's Chorus. (Ibid., June 23, 1933; January 5, 1934; January 26, 1934; January 17, 1936.) Sands was secretary of the Women's Committee at least three times. (Ibid., January 13, 1933.) In 1934, the Local nominated both Sands and Mosteller for the National Women's Committee. (Minutes of Local Berks, October 4, 1934, p. 92.) Mosteller also had served as secretary to the county committee. (*Reading Eagle*, January 18, 1935.)

76. *Reading Eagle* clipping, Fryer's Political Scrap Books, vol. 53, p. 251; *Reading Eagle*, July 9, 1937. For a short summary of the Hoopes-Wilson legislative record, see Pratt, "The Reading Socialist Experience," pp. 187-93. In 1934, *Black News*, a publication of the Pennsylvania Federation of Labor, the Railroad Brotherhoods and the Pennsylvania Security League, gave Hoopes and Wilson a 100 percent rating on twenty-seven key measures. (*Reading Labor Advocate*, November 2, 1934.)

77. Hazelette Hoopes to author, August, 1973; *Reading Eagle*, November 6, 1929; November 5, 1935. She had been elected to the Local's Educational Committee soon after the 1929 election. (Minutes of Local Berks, December 5, 1929, p. 197.)

78. Tomlinson interview; Hoopes to author. Both Wilson and Hoopes were mem-

bers of the Eighteenth Ward Branch, whose women's group broke up in late 1933. The 1933-34 local Women's Committee report testified to the strong Pennsylvania Dutch makeup of the Reading movement, saying at one point: " . . . Local Berks is made up of mostly the Pennsylvania German element. . . . "

79. *Reading Eagle*, November 4, 1931; November 10, 1933; November 5, 1935.

80. *Reading Labor Advocate*, December 16, 1932; December 13, 1935. Hiller had been elected to the Referendum Committee twice. (Minutes of Local Berks, December 20, 1934, p. 102; December 5, 1935, p. 135.)

81. *Reading Eagle*, November 9, 1921; November 7, 1923; November 6, 1929; November 5, 1930; November 4, 1931; November 9, 1932; November 18, 1933; November 7, 1934; November 5, 1935; *Reading Labor Advocate*, December 13, 1935; *Reading Eagle*, November 3, 1937; December 21, 1938; November 8, 1939; November 5, 1941.

82. Totals calculated from an examination of primary and general election returns in *Reading Eagle* and Fryer's Political Scrap Books, 1920-1941.

83. To participate fully in a nominating caucus, a party member had to be "in good standing for the immediately preceding twelve months. . . . " Those "in good standing for . . . six months" could vote for minor candidates such as those at the borough or ward level. (*Constitution of Local Berks*, pp. 15-16.) Close to 450 members participated in the 1935 caucus which lasted over twelve hours. But both the number of participants and the length of the meeting were unusual. (Minutes of Local Berks, May 26, 1935, pp. 116, 124.) Hazelette Hoopes noted that "sometimes women declined" and the minutes of the 1935 caucus indicate that Bertha Weidner declined nomination for two posts. (Ibid., pp. 122-23.)

84. Austin E. Adams to author, March 1978; Minutes of Local Berks, December 5, 1929, p. 197; clipping [December 1933], Fryer's Political Scrap Books, vol. 53, p. 63; Stetler, *The Socialist Movement in Reading, Pennsylvania*, p. 62.

85. Adams to author; Eugene Haag to author, February 22, 1978; *Reading Labor Advocate*, December 29, 1933; *Reading Eagle*, July 2, 1934.

86. See *Reading Labor Advocate*, November 21, 1930; September 25, 1931.

87. Haag to author; Brown interview, July 28, 1973. In September of 1935, three Yipsel circles were holding regular meetings and in January of 1936 there were four. (*Reading Labor Advocate*, September 13 and 20, 1935; January 3 and 17, 1936.)

88. Brown interview, December 23, 1967. Said a Yipsel column: "We may say that Reading needs more Socialist education and a little less of Socialist-sponsored socials. Card parties and socials may develop a fine feeling of friendship, but Socialism is a fight that can be won only by real work and study." (*Reading Labor Advocate*, January 17, 1936.)

89. J. Henry Stump was elected mayor for a third term in 1943. (*Reading Eagle*, November 5, 1943.)

90. For discussion of the national split, see David A. Shannon, *The Socialist Party: A Political History* (Chicago: Quadrangle Books, 1967), pp. 212-17, 234-44; Bernard K. Johnpoll, *Pacifist's Progress: Norman Thomas and the Decline of American Socialism* (Chicago: Quadrangle Books, 1970), pp. 77-177. The first reference I have found to old guard and militant factions in the local movement is in Mark L. Brown to [Jack] Altman, October 4, 1935, Socialist Party Papers. For a discussion of the causes of the local split by a participant, see Mark L. Brown, "Flood Tide to Suicide:

An Account of the 1936 split in the Socialist party of Berks County" (manuscript in Brown's possession in Reading, Pennsylvania).

91. The first militant caucus is reported in Brown to Altman, October 4, 1935; Darlington Hoopes' Notes on the State Executive Committee Investigation, [August 23, 1936], Hoopes Papers. Mosteller's father, Charles Sands, was elected to a two-year term on city council in 1935 and later was acknowledged as a militant leader. An old guard leader outside Reading referred to "[t]he Sands forces" in a March, 1936 letter. (Emil Limbach to Jim Oneal, March 3, 1936, Socialist Party Papers.) Another figure prominent in militant circles in Reading was Ralph Bigony, the Local organizer. Years later, he and Mosteller would marry. Several former participants of the local movement believe that jobs played an important role in the split. (Brown and Clayton Mengel interview, March 31, 1968; George M. Rhodes interview, April 6, 1968; Darlington Hoopes interview, July 8, 1971.)

92. Brown feels the local leadership was "a closed corporation." (Brown interview, June 14, 1968.) For Lilith Wilson, see Johnpoll, *Pacifist's Progress*, p. 126; *Reading Eagle*, July 9, 1937.

93. *Rule or Ruin—An Appeal to Rank and File Socialists* [April, 1936], Socialist Party Papers; Eugene Haag to "Milt," May 8, 1936, Socialist Party Papers. In previous years, the Local had not nominated many women as delegates to the national convention. Lilith Wilson had been the only local woman nominated as a delegate in 1928, 1932, and 1934. In 1932, the Local had voted on a state-wide slate, nominating two other women out of the twenty delegates, but they were not from the Reading area. Annie Zechman had been elected as one of the eight alternates in 1934. (Minutes of Local Berks, February 2, 1928, pp. 126-27; January 7, 1932, p. 269; April 5, 1934, p. 58.)

94. See *Reading Eagle*, August 15 to September 1, 1936 for daily front-page coverage on split. The old guard-controlled city council fired several leftists from city jobs, including Mosteller and Weidner in early September. (Ibid., September 9, 1936.)

95. *Reading Eagle*, November 4, 1936.

96. See *Reading Labor Advocate*, September-October, 1936. The *Labor Advocate* complained of "Leftist" interference at Socialist Park. A scheduled activity "was made impossible by the tactics of the leftist disruption group, a majority of whom were on the picnic committee. . . . During the past week the leftists have raided the kitchen and removed all necessary equipment and furniture from the kitchen and dining room." (Ibid., September 18, 1936.) The old guard group was run by a "Committee of 18" while it was being reorganized. Mabel Lausch, a relatively new party member, was the only woman to serve on this body. The following year, she would be one of the Socialist candidates for school director. (*Reading Eagle*, August 27, 1936; Minutes of the Committee of 18 [in possession of Margie Rhodes, Pennside, Pennsylvania]; *Reading Labor Advocate*, July 30, 1937.)

97. The *Labor Advocate* referred to three women's groups in late 1939. At that time, the local party still had six city branches and seven in the county. By then, party membership had dropped to 678. (*Reading Labor Advocate*, November 17, 1939; November 24, 1939; December 29, 1939; State Executive Committee Minutes, February 16, 1940.) Four years later, membership would drop to 370. (Ibid., January 20, 1943, Hoopes Papers.) For stories on Women's Socialist League, see *Reading Labor Advocate*, April 25, 1941; May 16, 1941; June 13, 1941; April 30, 1943; April 21,

1944. In 1950, the SP paper said that the Women's Socialist League was "just about the most active sub-division of Local Berks" and as late as 1955 party records note that the League raised $18.70 for the *Socialist Call* newspaper through a bingo party. (Ibid., March 10, 1950; Minutes of Local Berks Executive Committee, May 20, 1955, Hoopes Papers.)

98. Personal interviews with Alice, Ruth, and Frank Hoffman, August 19, 1972; Brown interview, July 28, 1973. For leftist social activities, see *The Loyal Socialist*, vol. 1, no. 1 (November 1936); vol 1, no. 5 (January 1937), Socialist Party Papers. According to national party records, there were only 116 leftists in the entire state by February of 1937. Shannon, *The Socialist Party of America*, p. 250. Yet, in April of 1938, 14 branches were listed for the leftist Local Berks. "List of Branches in Pennsylvania, Socialist Party," (April 1938), Socialist Party Papers.

99. "Since their secession from the local party, the Mostellerites have functioned chiefly as a 'hate' unit." (*Reading Labor Advocate*, December 30, 1938.) Her name was frequently mentioned in stories on a long, drawn out court battle for control of the old SP's $3,000 treasury. (*Reading Eagle*, June 9, 1939.) The *Eagle* referred to "Mrs. Mosteller and her group." Results of the leftist support for Democratic candidates included a bolt by twenty-eight members who eventually were reunited with the other local socialists, and the loss of the leftist group's charter. (Brown interview, December 23, 1967; *Reading Labor Advocate*, February 17, 1939; March 3, 1939.) A 1939 *Eagle* story related: "The Left Wingers, a majority of whom were reported by their officers to be registered now as Democrats and active in behalf of that party, held a reunion at Lesher's Hotel . . . ." The story also reported that a committee, which included Bertha Weidner, had been appointed "to arrange for the 1940 reunion." (*Reading Eagle*, September 25, 1939.) For Hiller candidacy, see ibid., September 13, 1939. Two years later, she sought a Democratic nomination for prison inspector, but again was defeated in the primary. (Ibid., September 10, 1941.) Several former leftists, including Mosteller's father, received city jobs after the Democrats took control of city hall in 1940. See *Reading Labor Advocate*, January 19 and 26, 1940; February 2 and 9, 1940; March 29, 1940.

100. *Reading Eagle*, November 4, 1959.

101. *Reading Eagle*, December 21, 1938; *Reading Labor Advocate*, October 17, 1947; personal interview with Darlington Hoopes, July 11, 1973; Brown interview, July 28, 1973.

102. *Reading Labor Advocate*, February 24, 1939; July 7, 1939; *Reading Eagle*, November 8, 1939.

103. *Reading Labor Advocate*, April 25, 1941. Italics added.

104. Quotation from Jeffrey, "Women in the Southern Farmers' Alliance," p. 78.

105. Buhle, "Women and the Socialist Party."

106. William Parsons writes: "On the status of women and their achievements within the framework of Pennsylvania Dutch society, the Dutchman has been ambivalent. He assumed that a male-dominated social order was proper and that women had special responsibilities only in certain areas which he called *Kinner, Kich un Karrich* ('children, kitchen and church'). Of course the husband ran the farm, operated the mill, and concerned himself generally with economic enterprise." In addition, he also notes: "[o]ver the years a few individual women of the Pennsylvania Dutch have achieved prominence on the historical scene. . . . But they have been his-

torically anonymous for the most part, and so they remain." Parsons, *The Pennsyl-vania Dutch*, pp. 222, 225.

107. Hoopes to author.

108. Frank Zeidler to author, March, 1978.

109. *Reading Eagle*, January 28, 1968.

110. *Report* to 1934 Convention, p. 33. "[N]early 1,000 copies of . . . [this] questionnaire were sent out. . . ." According to the questionnaire, it was "sent to a cross section of women Party members." ("Questions for Socialist Women," Socialist Party Papers.)

111. Jean Helen Quataert, "The German Socialist Women's Movement 1890-1918: Issues, Internal Conflicts, and the Main Personages" (Ph. D. diss., U.C.L.A., 1974), p. 5.

112. That Lilith Wilson, Clara Mosteller, Bertha Weidner, and Annie Zechman were childless probably enabled them to have more time to participate in party activities than the average Reading socialist woman. (Mosteller and Weidner were no longer married by the mid-1930s. Brown interview, July 28, 1973.) Hazelette Hoopes, on the other hand, had children and, because her husband frequently was away from home on party or legislative business, was often left alone with them. Running the household and fulfilling her school board responsibilities left her with little time to participate in many party activities. (And if a cooperative neighbor had not taken care of her children, she would not have been as active as she was.) She also mentioned that sometimes other women would ask why she missed certain meetings and that they did not always understand how busy she was with her school board tasks. (Hoopes to author.)

COMMENTARY

Sally M. Miller

The seven original essays in this collection have explored the subject of American socialism and feminism from the 1890s to the 1930s, most focusing on the Socialist party of America in the years from the turn of the century to the First World War. The several authors have provided further support for the view that Marxists who committed their lives to a struggle for an egalitarian social order were nevertheless traditionalists in their attitudes and behavior concerning the respective roles of men and women. Even among those socialists who were overt feminists, almost without exception they supported life styles and goals that were indistinguishable from bourgeois feminism. A feminist such as the anarchist, Emma Goldman, whose women's liberation philosophy focused on and questioned the whole texture of people's lives, is not found among the women (or men) of these pages. Instead, these essays demonstrate that, within a variety of responses to the Woman Question, a narrowness of approach was characteristic, and that the ambiguities and tensions inherent in the socialist-feminist nexus resulted in the subordination of feminism.

The essay entitled "Daniel DeLeon and the Woman Question" by L. Glen Seretan is a brief, suggestive prologue to the essays which follow. This study of a leading American Marxist is an exercise in intellectual history rather than a biographical or institutional history. As a result, Seretan treats DeLeon's ideas somewhat in a vacuum rather than attempting to relate them to the policies and practices of the Socialist Labor party which he dominated. The author demonstrates that while DeLeon was renowned as a champion of groups somewhat neglected by other socialists, whether racial, ethnic, or occupational, and did not hesitate to attack fellow socialists who compromised with egalitarianism, his record on women as an exploited group belied that pattern. For aside from ideological statements on behalf of sexual equality, DeLeon's language, attitudes, and life style betrayed disinterest in basic components of the Woman Question and, indeed, an obliviousness to its fundamentals. The contradictions in his posture reflect those of most orthodox and revisionist Marxists.

DeLeon's Socialist Labor party has been much less the focus of scholarly scrutiny than has the Socialist party. Its record on feminism has not yet been examined at all, and therefore an institutional study of the SLP might well analyze this issue. Women such as Anna B. Touroff, Dr. Anna Reinstein, and Olive M. Johnson were active in the party. The autonomous women's group called the Socialist Women of Greater New York was loosely tied to the SLP through overlapping memberships. It attempted to build bridges to the international socialist women's movement, as did the women of the Socialist party, through systematizing an exchange of publications and interaction at international conferences. But the activities, values, goals, and even identity of these women have yet to be researched.[1]

The essay entitled "Women in the Party Bureaucracy" by Sally M. Miller serves as an introduction to the internal workings of the Socialist party, its structure, and the interaction regarding women functionaries. This overview traces the development of the woman's sector of the party, its accomplishments and weaknesses, and its dealings with the party leadership. Thus, it begins to flesh out the workings of the national party, but it is lacking in details and only suggests the marked regional differences that existed. The socialist press, both the national publications and local newspapers, offers a wealth of information. For example, the press regularly published motions of the National Committee and the endless countermotions. Such printed matter offers many insights into attitudes as well as policy making, yet this material has tended to be neglected in favor of the minutes of the National Executive Committee and the proceedings of the national conventions. Since the strength of the movement rested upon the local efforts and activities, probing these measures submitted by National Committee members from across the country will suggest a great deal about the relationships, attitudes, and ideas of the women and men of the party. A monograph developing these materials would be useful.

The biographical studies of May Wood Simons by Gretchen and Kent Kreuter and of Lena Morrow Lewis by Mari Jo Buhle are both overdue and, therefore, most welcome. May Wood Simons was an educated young woman who, like so many other socialist women, was aided in her political growth and awareness by her husband for whom, of course, political and educational opportunities were greater. Wood Simons became both the

major woman theorist of the Socialist party and, as well, a leading woman
activist through her essays and her central role in the Woman's National
Committee. Her Marxist writings, while no more theoretically creative than
those of other American socialists, demonstrated an understanding of
socialist classics and of economics, and also a willingness at least to explore,
like Charlotte Perkins Gilman, the ways in which community services
might render women's family responsibilities less burdensome. Further, she
was perhaps the major party figure to maintain that the exploitation of
women under capitalism differed in dimensions from that of men. But, unlike so many socialist-feminists, May Wood Simons chose her version of
feminism over socialism when a choice seemed necessary to her after fifteen
years in the Socialist party. While the authors stress the great psychological
price she paid for attempting to balance her active career as a professional
woman and a party activist against domestic obligations, other avenues
might be explored to probe more fully the choice made by this particular
socialist feminist. Her abandonment of the Socialist party occurred upon the
eve of American entry into the First World War, when she and Algie, living
in German-dominated Milwaukee, came to believe that they had to choose
between the allied war effort and their party. Like so many Anglo-Saxon
Protestant leaders of the Socialist party, they fled, charging the party with
pro-German policies because of its antiwar position. It is possibly this
trauma that pushed Wood Simons, never having resolved her psychological
dilemma, out of socialist activism. Or, the way may have been prepared for
her decision as early as the party's termination of the woman's sector in
1915, thus clarifying the limited degree of importance party officials attached to the Woman Question. Whether Wood Simons' decision was
motivated by her own psyche to a great extent, or by the institutional developments of the era, might yet be explored further.

The essay on Lena Morrow Lewis analyzes the career of a woman who
was more liberated than many of her sister socialists. Morrow Lewis had
converted to socialism after her own emergence to leadership in the major
women's reform movements of the late nineteenth century and, thus, had
not been nurtured along politically by a male friend or husband. She had
hewed her own path. Ironically perhaps, given her roots in the woman's
network, her feminism was even more ambivalent than was Wood Simons's.
Morrow Lewis assigned her loyalty to socialism rather than to feminism,
supporting to struggle for women's rights but not for the woman's sector. The
class struggle was paramount to her, and she was willing and able to function within the male-dominated Socialist party for the liberation of all men
and women. On behalf of that issue, she sacrificed the home life that, in
contrast, May Wood Simons saw as life's primary commitment.

These two women, sharing the same middle-class, midwestern, and educational background and yet so different in the routes they followed, illus-

trate the identical principle. Women socialists had to make choices and to
decide priorities, and apparently always at some personal cost. It was not
possible to be a socialist woman untouched by tensions and clashing loyalties. But both these prominent activists present the reader with the familiar
phenomenon of the achiever or the exceptional woman. Thus, neither essay, however important an addition to the historiography, gives us a
glimpse of the rank-and-file socialist woman who organized her neighbors,
sold party leaflets outside the local factory, served as secretary to the
woman's committee of her local, and made her own judgment about life's
options.

The essay by Neil K. Basen on socialist women in the southwestern states,
Kansas, Arkansas, Oklahoma, Texas, and Louisiana, focuses on the grass-
roots rank-and-file socialist woman. Demonstrating that both middle-class
and working-class women were active in the movement in the southwest,
with the former more often assuming higher levels of leadership, the essay
presents a picture of greater opportunity for women in these state parties
than in the national organization. While the author describes these state
bureaucracies as more integrated vehicles for the socialist women, he admits
that important and influential policy positions were closed to them. Nevertheless, a more open party environment for women committed to the cause
seems evident, and reasons for a somewhat receptive atmosphere are
suggested or implied. The greater fluidity of the social and political structure in some of the newest states of the Union is an important variable leading to attitudinal differences, which others have offered as one explanation
for the early enfranchisement of women in the western states. But the suggestion of a greater receptivity by native-born white Protestant male party
leaders to women comrades than by foreign-born male leaders, although
not entirely new, needs exploration. This essay, opening a new area of
inquiry, raises perhaps more questions than it answers, while inviting the
reader to recognize the diversity among white women party activists and
also the regional differences in male party members' behavior toward
women comrades. The logical adjacent area of research needing exploration
is the role of immigrant women and black women in socialist locals, the
diverse cultural factors shaping their political radicalization, and attitudes
of party policy makers toward these women.

The essay entitled "The Politics of Moral Frustration: Socialists and Suffragists in New York and Wisconsin" by John D. Buenker explores the
tenuous but important alliance between suffragists and socialists con-
structed in the two states. Such partnerships between bourgeois and socialist feminists for purposes of the enfranchisement of women were attempted
in other states, all of which were east of the Mississippi River, since by the
time of the emergence of the Socialist party, women west of the Mississippi
were generally enfranchised. Additional studies must document those cam-

paigns prior to the passage of the Nineteenth Amendment at the end of the
First World War. New York and Wisconsin were not representative states,
as both of them featured urban enclaves of large immigrant populations
which presented different kinds of challenges and possibilities to those campaigning for support for woman suffrage. Thus, it is highly probable that
the pattern of building socialist-suffragist alliances as well as the details of
the campaigns themselves differed markedly in those states which were
more rural-dominated and native born in their population base. The reader
is cautioned to avoid generalizing from the New York-Wisconsin case studies until their typicality or exceptionalism is documented.

The final original essay, "Women Socialists and Their Male Comrades:
The Reading Experience, 1927-1936" by William C. Pratt, is another
example of the type of case study necessary before generalizations can be ap-
propriately attempted. This study of the Reading socialists, covering a later
period in the history of the socialist movement, traces the policies, attitudes, and interaction of the women and men of the local party. This suggestive effort needs to be emulated by authors focusing on other locals in
rural and urban centers, both those which approached political responsibility and those which did not. This particular study offers the additional advantage of tracing the careers of prewar activists like Lilith Martin Wilson
into the later period when the issues differed and the entire ambience of the
times and the movement itself varied from the prewar period. Thus, it sup-
plies insights into the question of how some women activists remained loyal
to the party in a less optimistic period when so many abandoned it. At the
same time, however, because this essay deals with the years after the peak
of party vitality, some of its nuances should not be applied to the earlier
period.

This collection of essays as a whole has indicated how women functioned
in a radical context, their own conflicting options and priorities, the institutional constraints upon them, and the ways in which the particular institutional structure operated at a distance from women's life styles. Yet an even
more systematic study of party structure and its ramifications is needed
since this was the framework in which these women chose to commit their
efforts.[2] That structure, which at times permitted special machinery to support a woman's movement and at other times did not, established the para-
meters of the activities and the effectiveness of female (and male) feminists.
Accordingly, structure shaped the functioning of these activists: whether
feminists primarily sought to convert more women to socialism, or to increase the percentage of women in party offices, or to promote discussion
and commitment to issues a social democratic party did not typically emphasize but which held inherent interest for women. In the absence of party
machinery supportive of a woman's movement, an inevitable dilution of the
possible outreach to women occurred on the basis of a classical and tradi-

tional emphasis on the class struggle. A party relatively aloof from issues such as family planning, day-care centers, the double burden of outside employment and household responsibilities, and female health and safety issues determined the effectiveness of members sensitive to those factors.

As these crucial matters become better understood, a next task will be the discovery of the unorganized woman, the woman who was not necessarily the object of any institution or reacting to any particular bureaucracy. Historians are always much more comfortable when they focus on institutional settings, for reasons that are both data-inspired and temperamental. Yet to limit our understanding to those whose lives suggest a relationship to specific organizations is to omit the lives of most people. Therefore, whatever knowledge has been and will be gleaned from the institutional approach should next be followed by studies of independent women and isolated women, whether critical thinkers or individuals who coped as they could and made decisions as shaped by their own values and other cultural experiences.

Finally, it is necessary to analyze in greater depth the very beginning point of this study: one must still understand the phenomenon of the existence of sexism in the radical context. A deeper exploration of formative experiences within a more psychological orientation will inevitably be required in order for historians to clearly comprehend why movements, intellectuals, and activists who dreamt, planned, and plotted to implement social revolution, nevertheless assigned to men and women the very same roles that they had seemed to play traditionally. As William Pratt notes, ". . . Socialists found it easier to break with the prevailing economic system than [with] the traditional role of the sexes." In the long run, it is this central question that must still be address.

Notes

1. See *Report* of the Socialist Women of Greater New York to the International Socialist Congress, Copenhagen, August 28-September 4, 1910. Copy at the International Institute of Social History, Amsterdam.

2. The author is indebted to Professor Drude Dahlerup of the University of Arhus for insights into the wide ramifications of party structure in her as yet unpublished work on the Social Democratic party of Denmark.

APPENDIX: WOMAN
AND THE SOCIAL PROBLEM

May Wood Simons

The socialist movement of today means not only a transformation in industry but as well in all those things having their roots in economic conditions—art, education, ethics and politics. It means not alone a revolution in the position of the laboring man but a complete change for woman, economically, socially, intellectually and morally. The vital influence of socialism upon woman's condition and the influence in turn that she may exercise on the socialist movement have been subjects receiving only a secondary attention thus far.

Since the present social problem is a political one and since woman has no power in politics it has been presumed that her influence is too small to need reckoning with.

This is a serious neglect of the truth on the part of the socialist workers and means that a force in society that might be utilized to good purpose may, from lack of proper consideration, become a difficult body to deal with, or before we are aware, be led over to the side of our opposition.

Woman constitutes in society a conservative reactionary body and having little initiative can therefore be better used by those opposed to revolutionary changes. So well is this fact recognized that it has become a rule of interpretation in studies of comparative sociology, that if in any society, since the introduction of private property, and the consequent degradation of woman, any custom is found to prevail among women which is not common to the whole of society, it is taken as positive proof that the custom was at one time universal, but is now being or has been superseded by a more modern process.

An illustration of this fact today is seen in the persistence of a great number of industries such as baking, washing, sewing, etc., in the home where they are done in a much more primitive and wasteful manner than existing inventions would permit them to be done elsewhere. This conservatism, as it exists today, is but the result of a long series of conditions that have worked together to make women physically weak, mentally narrow, politically powerless.

In no other country has capitalism utilized so extensively the economic power of women as in America. In no other country has she to so great numbers entered trade, manufacturing industries, clerkships and professions. To a certain extent she is filling industry at the expense of men, especially in manufacturing and mechanical industries and in trade and transportation. She is today not alone a factor in industry that must be reckoned among other industrial forces, but at the same time she exerts a powerful influence on society through the home. To neglect this large and powerful body merely because it has no vote means the loss of what could be used for the most effective propaganda work for socialism. It means further that when socialism is once realized we shall have a vast part of the population still in a backward stage. This will hinder the realization of the best art and literature and science. The future society would find itself unable to produce the best family life; and this inferiority of woman would bring the degeneration of the race. Thus looked at from a broader view the inclusion of woman in the socialist program and propaganda means far more than the advance of woman alone, but the advancement of the whole race as well. Any system of society that would secure the advancement of humanity must stand for the social equality of all its members, and not give over the training of its young to those either socially or mentally inferior.

Many have contended that the work of propaganda among women requires essentially different methods than those used among workingmen. So it was said shortly ago that the work among agrarian populations must be carried on differently than for the town proletariat. This has been proven erroneous, and the same principles are found to apply in both cases.

So with woman—it is necessary to point out her economic condition, the effects of capitalistic industry upon her and the changes that socialism would make in her position.

Her Economic Condition

To understand fully the economic state of woman today we must go back in history and even into pre-historic times and trace briefly the changes through which she has passed. It is to woman in the state of savagery that we must look to find the beginnings of all industry. She first gathered the bark and branches and made a shelter for herself and offspring, thus being the first of the architects and builders. She sewed together the skins of animals killed in the hunt or wove the animal and vegetable fibers and clothed her family. With clay she shaped the first rude bowls, laying the foundation of our present great pottery making. Even the desire to beautify these articles of use seems to have originated with her, and the early wares of the Mexicans and Peruvians are still standards of artistic beauty in their field. She loosed the soil with a clam shell or a pointed stick, planted the grain, and thus became the earliest of the agriculturists.

In this stage of society, woman, strong physically, journeyed with the men on their trips and provided food and clothing for herself and children. As the human race advanced into barbarism she became less the companion of man, but still procured much of her own food. She stood at one time at the head of the matriarchal family and from her her children took their names and through her reckoned their descent. With later barbarism life grew more settled. Herds and flocks were kept. These were tended by the men and gradually they also took over to themselves the agriculture.

These new conditions resulted in woman finding more of her material support in man. Her work became now almost wholly confined to the home, and thus savagery and barbarism gave birth to and slowly developed her economic dependence. Civilization brought this to full growth.

With the introduction of private property the headship of the family was transferred from the mother to the father. This marked the first great economic and social change for woman. It meant that she now became a secluded being, entirely dependent on man for subsistence, and since her life in the open air was gone, she was no longer his physical equal. She ceased to be actively engaged in industry, and child-bearing was henceforth her chief occupation. The opinion, therefore, began to prevail that this was her sole function to perform in society.

Morgan in his "Ancient Society" says of the Greek woman: "Abundant evidence appears in the Homeric poems that woman had few rights men were bound to respect." The virtuous women were doomed to a life of absolute seclusion. Turning next to the Roman family he says: "The condition of woman was more favorable, but her subordination the same."

Lecky in his "History of European Morals" points out that the Roman matron had at one time gained political equality, but this was soon lost through economic dependence. Women of the patrician class at this time knew nothing of useful toil, the care of their children even being almost wholly undertaken by slaves. With the latter Roman Empire, there being no middle class, we see woman occupying one of two positions, either an appendage to a degraded manhood, economically dependent on him, or a slave dependent on a master.

Through the years of the Middle Ages history refers only incidentally to woman. This was the time when her secluded life continued for long periods, made her the narrow inferior being she is today.

The year 1760 marks the beginning of a revolution of greater importance to mankind in general than was ever opened by the victories of any king or conqueror. To woman this change was of supreme importance. It was with the opening of the industrial revolution brought about by the introduction of steam power that her pure economic value became utilized.

Under the old domestic system each little cottage was a factory in which the master workman and his apprentices using their own tools wove the cloth and manufactured shoes. In this work woman assisted only in the minor processes, such as dyeing.

For man the industrial revolution did not produce a complete change. Toward the close of this period these home factories had begun to produce for a wider market of exchange. For woman, who had produced only for consumption in the home, the change was revolutionary. She stepped at once from domestic seclusion into the industrial world as a producer for commercial exchange.

Heretofore the clumsy tools had been too heavy for her to use and lack of physical strength had thus barred her from competing extensively in the labor market. The new machines with their power of steam required only a guiding, and this could be furnished quite as well by women as by men. Thus the labor power of a woman under the new system equaled that of many men working after the old methods.

The present century has in this way changed for a vast number of women economic dependence from husband or father to employer and made her problem more identical with that of the laboring man.

We are able to see something of the present numerical industrial strength of women in the fact that from government reports it is found that the proportion of women employed in all occupations has risen in relation to the whole number from 14.68 percent in 1870 to 17.22 percent in 1890, the number of men having decreased from 85 percent to 82 percent. In the different occupations her numbers have increased in agriculture, mining, fishing, professional services, trade, mechanical and manufacturing industries and have decreased only in domestic and personal service.

It is seen that today in the United States there is scarce an industry, from the heavy farm work of the South or the canning establishments of the West, to the factories of New England, that has not been recruited from among women until now near four million not counting the thousands of wives employed in home work, are actively engaged in industry.

But it is not the number of women employed in industry that gives us an idea of their actual industrial position. It is necessary to examine their wages and the amount of organization existing among them.

Capitalism that finds a source of strength in the great body of unemployed men who compete with each other in the labor market has reached out to the women to yet further increase this struggle, and has found in them an extremely valuable economic factor from the fact that they can be compelled to accept a lower minimum wage than man.

The minimum wages of all labor being determined by the subsistence point, that is, the smallest amount of which in any given social stage, a man will live and perpetuate his kind, it is taken for granted by the employer that this must be higher for man than for woman. Man's wages must include the support of wife and child. Woman, whether true or not, is looked upon as having no dependents on her work, and from her known ability to live more cheaply than man is marked as the lowest of the laborers—the "downmost man."

However, an instance of the manner in which capitalism uses the working women against the working men and vice versa is afforded by the railroad employees. Women working in the offices have invariably been paid lower wages than the men who preceded them. Now the R.R. employers are discharging the women and filling their places with men working at the same, or slightly higher, wages than the women received. Shortly we shall look to see the women coming back at a still lower wage and being again displaced until the limit of existence is reached.

Statistics show that in 781 instances in which men and women work at the same occupation performing their work with the same degree of efficiency, men receive higher wages in 595, or 76 percent of the instances; women greater pay in 129, or 16 percent, while in 57 cases, or 7 percent, they receive the same pay for the same work. Woman's average wage in the United States is about $5 per week, while many receive but $1 or $1.50. This is not a living wage, and many women are forced to choose between existence and a life of prostitution.

Next, the lack of organization, or the inclination for organization among women industrially employed, is at once apparent as a source of weakness. She is not a good Trade Unionist. Various reasons are offered for this: her extreme individualism, prejudice and unwillingness to tell her wages. It must be noted, however, that few women enter industry expecting to remain in it permanently. Most think to eventually enter a home. This explains partly the lack of interest in Unions. But first it must be remembered that the whole training of women hitherto has been such that economic movements, Trade Unions, or politics have not entered her range of vision. Her environment has been wholly domestic and she still sees with a shortened eye. This is, therefore, one of the obstacles that socialism will meet in its work among women. To many it is much like bringing to them a new science, the very terms of which are foreign.

Thus far we have looked only at woman in industry. As an industrial worker her problem and its solution is the same as that of the working man. There is no difference in the way in which capitalism exploits men and women. In the economic fight it has been the one maintaining life on the barest necessities, who had at the same time little power of resistance, who has been pushed soonest to the wall, whether man or woman. In industry, before the machine, in the view of capitalism men and women are looked upon merely as producers, as human attachments to the piles of steel and iron they guide; hired by the piece, without regard to sex.

The same laws of competition, oversupply, etc., hold with the laborer whether man or woman. As pointed out by John A. Hobson, "It is not difference of sex which is the chief factor in determining the industrial position of woman. Machinery knows neither sex nor age, but chooses the labor embodied in man, woman or child which is the cheapest in relation to the degree of its efficiency."

A large portion of the women, however, are not actively engaged in industry. They are the wives of laboring men and must look to them for their livelihood. This makes them none the less dependents, economically and in a double sense, since they are dependents of wage slaves.

But capitalism in the thousands of cases has not left these women in the home to care for the children. While the father looks for work the mother is forced into the labor market. Thus we find in many New England towns the father caring for the house and small children while the mother and older children become the bread winners.

Until recently the working women have been entitled to be called the "working girls." The majority began work at fifteen years and the average of all was less than twenty-three. At the present thirteen out of every 100 women in the labor world are women with families.

Some Effects of Capitalism

The entire economic situation stands in the relation of cause to the conditions found in the homes and health of women. Modern industry appears as a gigantic Moloch into which are fed the lives and health of the laboring class. One need not go back to the horrors of the early factory days in England. Present society has horrors of its own. The foul "sweat shop," the crowded factory, the cheap laundry, the box making establishment, the tobacco trade, and the shops all today make a profit from underpaid female labor. Long hours, bad sanitary conditions, the "speeding up" of machinery are a strain under which the laboring class is fast deteriorating physically. Of the vast number of working women in the United States, it is found, according to the report of the commissioner of labor, that one out of every three are living in houses that are classed as "very poor," while one out of every ten are working in shops designated as "neglected and unhealthful."

The reports of labor on "Working Women in Large Cities" show that out of every 100 women interviewed who entered work in good health, eleven at the time of the investigation were in bad health. Making all due allowance for other causes, much of this is traceable to overwork in small, ill-ventilated rooms, especially among women who take work to their homes. All this, however, does not represent the true condition. It does not take into account the great number that every year are compelled to drop out of the industrial ranks through complete loss of health. This affecting the children born to these women means that the next generation will have less of strength and vitality.

This is the point of first importance to socialism. The future proletarian forces are in this way being gradually weakened and losing their power for intelligent revolt.

One has but to live in the slum of a modern city like Chicago or London to see how hopeless is the work of Socialist Propaganda among a slum proletariat. And these are far ahead of the next generation for a large part are country born and of still fairly strong physique, while their children are weak and pallid.

The socialists of other countries have recognized the danger of this physical degeneration to the laboring class movement. Knowing that a spiritless, indifferent proletariat is most to be dreaded, they have used their political power whenever they have come into control of cities, to carry out plans for feeding the school children.

A further proof of this fact that the laboring class is becoming physically less robust is seen in the constant lowering year after year by the European powers of their standards of measurements for soldiers. These, coming mostly from the laboring population, can no longer in sufficient numbers come up to the former standards.

On the home and family life even the most superficial observer must have noted that the present capitalistic system exerts a baneful effect.

First as to marriage. The supposition exists that marriages today are founded on the mutual regard of two individuals. In fact, however, they are principally made for economic reasons. The girl toiling the factory or shop thinks she sees in marriage an escape from her slavery.

With this for a reason and with comparatively little acquaintance, it is not remarkable that when economic troubles arise the man and wife are driven apart. In Chicago today the divorce courts dissolve one-fifth as many marriages as are made.

Thus has capitalism dug a pit at the beginning of the home by bringing two people to live together for no other reason on the part of woman frequently than that she wishes to obtain support. To the socialist this seems but legalized prostitution. It is likewise for support that the prostitute nightly sells herself. Affection and respect enter frequently no more into the one than the other.

After having begun the family on this unstable foundation capitalism adds yet other things that all result in destroying family life. The man is frequently forced to stand to one side and see his wife driven into the factory, until in the East we have our "she villages" and on the other hand in the mining regions our "stag towns."

In the crowded districts of our great cities the home is turned into a "sweat shop." The father, mother, with the neighbor and the mere babies work from daylight until far into the night for a starvation wage.

Thus after building the family on an economic basis and destroying it through industrial conditions, capitalism goes yet further and says that for thousands no homes shall exist at all.

The young man earning a few dollars a week, with little hope of ever getting more, knows he cannot on that amount support himself and a family. To him family life is forbidden, and society reaps the whirlwind of illegal sexual relations. A careful view of society must convince one that never, even among savages, did promiscuous relations of the sexes exist more than in our civilization of today.

All of the older nations have for years maintained large standing armies, where great numbers of men in the prime of manhood are brought together in barrack life away from their homes. The evils resulting from this are too apparent. Capitalism reaching full growth among us today demands such an army in the United States, and sends back our young men unfit to become either husbands or fathers.

But capitalism comes in yet other ways to destroy home life. It takes the father away from the home in the morning before the children are awake; he returns at night when they are again in bed. He never knows his own children. It is a horrible farce to call the existence of the average laborer family life.

On none today do the sufferings arising from the small overcrowded quarters that capitalism has forced its wage-earners to live in fall so heavily as upon the women. Confined continuously in one or two small rooms, that serve for kitchen, bedroom, laundry, dining and sickroom, little wonder that the mother is ill and fretful and the work half done.

There is no opportunity before or after marriage for the woman of the laboring class to obtain an education. She enters the factory or shop before she has finished the grammar school in order that she may help to support the family. She has time to read neither book nor newspaper after marriage, the care and work for the family extending far into the night. If she fails to understand quickly the principles of socialism is it not because our industrial system has well nigh crushed out the power of thought?

Changes Socialism Would Bring

It is to socialism alone that the home life must look for its rescue and purification.

By assuring to every member of society the opportunity to work under conditions healthful and pleasant it would remove the evil of marriages formed for economic purposes only and put it upon its true basis of mutual affection and respect. It would give some time for acquaintance before marriage and thus secure adaptability of disposition.

A great amount of the drudgery now connected with the home would be done away with. The domestic service is still in the Dark Ages and all the discoveries of science have done little for the work of the home.

The laundry work, the cooking when put in the hands of scientifically trained cooks, which would greatly increase the general good health, and the sewing could all be done far better in co-operative establishments. This in no way implies that each housewife may not if she so desire [sic] still bake, cook and scrub for herself, but there would be few who would fail to see the advantages of the co-operative method.

It would secure to every individual the opportunity for education and to every mother a chance to spend a few hours of the day at educative work and social gatherings, sending her back to her child strong physically and mentally to care for and train it.

Since she would perform services for society either in bearing and rearing citizens or working in the improved and beautiful shop or factory, or in producing works of art, she would no longer be an economic dependent upon man.

Woman's economic equality, however, is not imaginable without political freedom. Socialism will mean the complete political equality of women.

Many advocates of woman's suffrage have but seen in part. They look only for a sex emancipation and fail to perceive that the present working man has a vote, but that his condition is not that which the well being of man demands, because thus far he has not used his vote for the interests of his class. So woman with political power would be equally as oppressed unless aware of the fact that her vote must be used to bring about an industrial revolution, that would likewise give her economic freedom.

Socialism alone recognizes the full significance of equal suffrage for men and women. It sees that a large body in society, politically powerless and politically ignorant, who yet exercise a wide influence, will in time become a dangerous factor.

This movement for equal suffrage meets its opponents in the capitalist class that would restrict the right of the ballot as far as possible, that disfranchises the negro, talks of property and educational qualifications, and sees a menace in extending the vote to women.

Women recognizing the extent to which, because of this lack of political power, they are bound and their consequent less ability to effectively aid the socialist movement, will use every opportunity to gain for themselves the ballot.

The Social Problem

It remains now to examine the problem that society is facing today, its solution, and its relation to woman.

History has recorded the movements that freed the slave from his master, the serf from the land, and the struggles of the bourgeoisie with the nobility for political equality.

The social movement that is going on at present is a proletarian movement; that is to say, it is the effort of the laboring class to bring into being a form of society founded in the interests of that class and at the same time of society as a whole.

Looking at society we see it composed of two classes, a ruling class whose continuance depends solely on the stability of the present industrial system, and the strength of which arises from its monopolization of the means necessary for human well being.

On the other hand, the laborers owning none of these great instruments of production—machines, factories, mines, etc.—are in complete dependence on the possessors of these for the privilege to work, and hence the means to live.

These two, employers and employed, are opposite in their interests, and no relation can exist between them that will ever mean justice and equality of opportunity to the exploited class.

This movement is international and has everywhere followed close upon the steps of capitalism. Japan, but a few years old in capitalistic industry, having not yet destroyed all the old "domestic workers," is already struggling with its labor problem, while the latest American colonial possessions have thus soon felt the weight of capitalistic rule.

This present class movement has come to be consciously conducted. J. S. Cairnes has said that "A time arrives in the progress of social development when societies of men become conscious of a corporate existence, and when the improvement of the conditions of this existence becomes for them an object of conscious and deliberate effort."

Such a time has been reached in the laboring class, and they are class-consciously seeking to direct society in its industrial evolution.

The laborers believe their movement to be in accord with the development of society and the social stage to which it leads to be the natural outgrowth of the present.

Following the course of social progress from the early part of the 18th century, the mercantile system is found still prevailing in the dealings of nations. Along with this were to be seen the small hand manufacturers jealously guarding their particular trade. In economic history this is known as the "domestic system."

The close of the century marks the beginning of the great inventions, the rise of the factories and a change of policy to that of laissez faire. Side by side with this came the passing of the small masters into wage earners and the removal of the tools from the users to the owners of factories.

With increasing growth and concentration of industry the wage earners grew to such proportions that before the first half of the present century had passed, Karl Marx, having foreseen already much of the trend of social development, was calling the laboring men to unite.

To the last quarter of this century has been reserved the final feature in the growth of the present industrial order. Corporation, trust and monopoly mark the latest phase of concentrated capital.

Accompanying this is the great body of workers shut out from the instruments of production, or using them only with the consent of those who have become their owners, and securing for their labor but a part of what they produce.

"The remainder," Lester F. Ward says, "finds its way into the hands of a comparatively few, usually non-producing individuals whom the usages and laws of all countries permit to claim that they own the very sources of all wealth and the right to allow or forbid its production."

Working men have at last recognized that so long as the privilege to obtain access to the means to work lies entirely in the hands of a class to whose interest it is to exploit the worker, nothing but a complete change of the system can bring the liberation of the proletariat.

Furthermore, they realize that it must be through their own ballot that this shall be accomplished. They see that the next stage of society will mean the abolition of private property in the means of production and its transfer to the hands of the users.

The agent in the transformation will be the working man himself. Concerning this Karl Marx wrote: "The emancipation of the working class must be achieved by the working class itself and, therefore, involves a class struggle which, on the side of the workers, is not for class privileges and monopolies, but for equal rights and duties and the abolition of all class rule."

Woman's Part in the Socialist Movement

Having thus stated the social question, the working woman will see that to her this movement is of vital interest.

This is essentially an economic movement. We have seen to what extent woman has become an economic factor, how that equally with man she is exploited by the ruling class, and that in no way does she as a wage earner differ from the working man.

In but one place is there being an intelligent effort made to secure equal rights for women and men. That is in the socialist movement. This movement stands for a condition in which classes on an economic basis cannot exist. It does not demand especial privileges for the laborer—only equal opportunity for all and that all shall be required to work for what they receive. As said by Liebknecht, today, "Riches are the portion of the idle, poverty the reward of the worker."

Woman has an active part in this proletarian movement. She is still unlearned in social matters, and has little conception of the present step in industrial evolution and has failed to take her part in the guiding of its development.

This lack of active part in the social development is the result partially of a psychological condition among women that has arisen from her economic position.

Biology shows that the parent mother stood originally at the head of the race as bearing and rearing the young. She was not inferior either mentally or in function. Her confined life during ages has constituted the cause of her present inferiority. An organ unused tends to degenerate. Woman's intellect has been little used. On the other side, she had had much to exercise her feelings and has thus become almost entirely a creature of emotion.

Her ideas have been confined to the home, family or relatives. She has scarce ever been broad enough to reach beyond into the neighborhood, never into the greater social world or to unborn generations.

Many of our working women far behind the body of working men have not a glimmer that a social question exists. This movement emphasizes the preparation of the workers to take an intelligent part in the co-operative commonwealth. The measure of the advance of civilization or society lies not in the culture or education of a class or sex, or in the number or completeness of material inventions, but in the equality with which these things are distributed and within reach of all. The claim sometimes heard that equalization of woman with man politically and economically would be detrimental to her performing the function of mother in the race and is unnecessary for the advance of society, can no longer be considered by the fair minded or intelligent.

This, however, must be no sex movement alone. The economic equality of woman can be accomplished only through the economic liberation of the working class.

Already the laboring men, conscious of their interests, are organizing themselves in the socialist movement.

They have behind them the experience of years spent in political struggles and trade unions.

Shall we to whom this movement means more than to any other body in society today remain inactive?

No new organization should be formed. The socialist party to which men and women are admitted on an equality already exists.

The time is ripe for the laboring women to unite with the laboring men in this struggle for economic freedom.

BIBLIOGRAPHIC ESSAY

Research into the history of the Socialist party must begin with an examination of the voluminous manuscript collection housed at Duke University Library, the Socialist Party of America Papers. For a generation, scholars and students have made the pilgrimage to Durham, North Carolina, to peruse these papers which rather miraculously found their way to Duke after being discarded by the party's National Office. In the last few years, however, the availability of these manuscript materials on microfilm, well indexed, has decreased the numbers who research among the actual papers and documents. The collection covers the years from the founding of the party to the 1960s, and is strongest in the period after 1920. Of special interest for those concerned with the role of women in the Socialist party are the published leaflets and various other documents of the Woman's National Committee which may be found in the National Office Papers of the Duke collection. The two dozen leaflets commissioned by the Woman's National Committee on subjects held to be of interest to women were authored by many of the prominent women leaders, and were widely circulated by the party. As a result, copies of the leaflets are available in many of the major archival collections across the country. Guides to manuscript sources are Gerald Friedberg, "Sources for the Study of Socialism in America, 1901-1919," *Labor History* 6 (Spring 1965): 159-65, and Bernard K. Johnpoll, "Manuscript Sources in American Radicalism," *Labor History* 14 (Winter 1973): 92-97. A useful guide to secondary sources published over the last generation is Clifton Jones, "The Socialist Party of the United States, A

Bibliography of Secondary Sources, 1945-1974," *Labor History* 19 (Spring 1978): 253-79. The journal, *Labor History* publishes frequent lists of articles in the field, and thus offers handy compendia.

Key Marxist works dealing with the Woman Question include *The Holy Family* and *The German Ideology* by Karl Marx and Frederick Engels, available in many editions, and also, by Engels, *The Condition of the Working Class in England* and *The Origin of the Family, Private Property and the State*. August Bebel's *Woman Under Socialism* should also be consulted, and its 1904 edition, translated by Daniel DeLeon, is available through Schocken Paperbacks in a 1971 publication. Also of interest is Paul LaFargue, "The Woman Question," *International Socialist Review* 5 (March 1905): 547-59.

The essay on Daniel DeLeon and the Woman Question draws essentially on the writings of DeLeon. Thus, while the *Weekly People* may be consulted for an overview of DeLeon's thought, a more selective approach to this topic should emphasize the following titles: Daniel DeLeon's *Abolition of Poverty*, published in 1911 and available in a 1945 edition published by the New York Labor News Co., and his *Socialist Reconstruction of Society*, a 1905 publication reprinted in 1968 by the New York Labor News Co. See also Daniel DeLeon and James Connolly, "Wages, Marriage and the Church: A Discussion Initiated by James Connolly and Answered by the Editor of the *People*," in *Weekly People*, April 9, 1904. Secondary accounts of DeLeon, few of which touch upon the Woman Question, include Louis Fraina, "Daniel DeLeon," *New Review* 2 (July 1914): 390-99; David Herreshoff, *American Disciples of Marx* (Detroit: Wayne State University Press, 1967); Arnold Petersen, *Daniel DeLeon: Social Architect*, 2 vols., (New York: New York Labor News Co., 1941-53), and L. Glen Seretan, *The Life and Career of Daniel DeLeon, 1852-1914: An Interpretation* (Cambridge: Harvard University Press, 1979).

The essay on the party bureaucracy and women draws essentially on the National Office Papers of the Socialist party collections and on the various national party newspapers of the period. The National Office Papers do not appear to have been retained in their entirety, but the party press frequently reprinted the *Minutes* of the Woman's National Committee meetings and also the *Minutes* of the National Executive Committee. Thus, it becomes possible to trace discussions in the woman's sector and to follow them when matters were referred to the party's executive. The Socialist party publications which should be consulted are the *Official Bulletin*, 1904-1913, the *Party Builder*, 1912-1914, and the *American Socialist*, 1914-1917; the issues of the first year of the *American Socialist* featuring heated debates concerning the eventual demise of the Woman's National Committee, are of special interest. A crucial primary source for issues concerning women members of the party and their activities is the nonparty, *Socialist Woman*,

1907-1913; this periodical changed its name in 1909 to the *Progressive Woman* in an effort to attract more subscribers, and eventually assumed the name the *Coming Nation*. The *Socialist Woman* published biographies of the prominent women in the Socialist party. The *International Socialist Review*, publishing from 1900-1917, is another nonofficial socialist journal that frequently carried articles pertinent to socialism and feminism. Newspapers in various locales can be perused in tracing regional issues or local party leaders, such as the *New York Call*, which began publication in 1910, and the *Milwaukee Leader*, which began to publish in 1911. Another most significant primary source is the *proceedings* of the various national meetings in this period, the National Conventions of 1901, 1904, 1908, 1912, 1917, and 1919, and of the National Congress of 1910, which included, in 1910 and 1912, the "Report" of the Woman's National Committee. Also see *Rapports pour le Première Conférence Internationale des Femmes Socialistes tenue à Stuttgart le samedi 17 août à 9 heures du matin dans la salle de la Liderhalle* (1907), and the program of the *Second International Conference of Socialist Women*, which is bound with the *Report* of the Socialist party delegation to the International Socialist Congress, 1910, both of which were of interest to the American women socialists. Copies of these programs are found at the International Institute of Social History in Amsterdam. The most important party publications for the topic are those leaflets, mentioned above, which were issued by the Woman's National Committee in the years 1910-1913.

The party platforms, most easily reviewed in the *Socialist Handbook*, which was revised and reissued for each congressional election, should be perused for the changing party platform planks and an overview of current activities. Manuscript collections of correspondence were, for the most part, not extant for this essay or were of peripheral interest. The articles in the socialist press written by the women activists were useful as were their statements in party *Proceedings* to trace their ideas over time, in lieu of their lost papers and correspondence. Manuscript collections of male party leaders can be helpful for indicating the informal milieu of the party in which these women worked. See, for example, the Social Democratic party Papers (Socialist party) of Milwaukee which are located at the Milwaukee County Historical Society and which include the papers of Victor Berger, and the Morris Hillquit Papers at the State Historical Society of Wisconsin, which are also available on microfilm.

The few secondary articles useful for this essay include Mari Jo Buhle, "Women and the Socialist Party," *Radical America* 4 (February 1970): 36-55, her dissertation, "Feminism and Socialism in the United States, 1820-1920,"(unpublished Ph. D. dissertation, University of Wisconsin, 1974), and her article, *"Socialist Woman, Progressive Woman, Coming Nation,"* in Joseph R. Conlin, ed., *The American Radical Press, 1880-1960* vol. 2

(Westport, Conn.: Greenwood Press, 1974), pp. 442-49; Bruce Dancis, "Socialism and Women in the United States, 1900-1917," *Socialist Revolution* 6
(January-March 1976): 81-144; Sally M. Miller, "From Sweatshop Worker
to Labor Leader: Theresa Malkiel, A Case Study," *American Jewish History*
68 (December 1978): 189-205; Bernard J. Brommel, "Kate Richards
O'Hare: A Midwestern Pacifist's Fight for Free Speech," *North Dakota
Quarterly* 44 (Winter 1976): 5-19. A number of papers have been read in re-
cent years and, while they are not as readily available, they suggest the di-
rection of the field, and, therefore, are of interest: they include Blanche
Weisen Cook, "Toward the New Woman: The Contributions of Crystal
Eastman and Emma Goldman," paper read to the convention of the Organ-
ization of American Historians, April 14, 1973, and Mari Jo Buhle, "The
Politics of Sex and Class in American Socialism: the Careers of Lena
Morrow Lewis and Margaret Sanger," paper read at the same session; Sally
M. Miller, "Women in the Socialist Party of America: Ideological Schizo-
phrenia," paper read to the Canadian Association for American Studies,
October 11, 1974; Sharon Z. Alter, "American Women Dissenters in World
War I: Jane Addams, Emma Goldman, and Kate Richards O'Hare," paper
read to the Third Berkshire Conference on the History of Women, June 9-
11, 1976.

May Wood Simons is one of those women whose life records have been
retained in part because her husband's papers were collected. The Wisconsin State Historical Society is the repository of the Algie and May Simons
Papers, which include letters between the couple (excluding those they together decided to destroy in the 1940s) and also a diary kept by May Wood
Simons during the early years of the twentieth century. The collection is essentially a repository of the papers of A. M. Simons, however. May Wood
Simons's fullest expression of her view on the Woman Question in addition
to the appendix here, is found in "Woman and the Social Question," (Chicago:
Charles Kerr and Co., 1899). She published many articles in the socialist
press from the beginning of the century until the eve of the First World War.
She often wrote for journals her husband edited, such as the *International
Socialist Review, Chicago Daily Socialist*, and the *Coming Nation*. Some of
the variety of topics she wrote on include the economic interpretation of
history, a revised system of public education, the changing American home,
art and socialism, and suffrage and socialism. For the life of May Wood Simons
as reflected in a biography of her husband, see Kent and Gretchen Kreuter,
An American Dissenter: The Life of A. M. Simons (Lexington: University of
Kentucky Press, 1969).

Lena Morrow Lewis, unlike most of her sister socialists, has had some of
her papers collected in repositories. Anyone interested in her career should
review the Lena Morrow Lewis Papers at the Tamiment Institute of New
York University. Lewis wrote many articles over the years in various party

organs, and articles may be found in issues of the *Chicago Daily Socialist*, the *Los Angeles Socialist*, the *Seattle Socialist*, the *Oakland World*, and the *New York Call*. Glimpses of her youthful organizational work for the Woman's Christian Temperance Union in Illinois may be found in the records of the Illinois chapter of the W.C.T.U. which are located in Springfield, Illinois. A contemporary sketch of Lewis is available in the *Socialist Woman* 1 (September 1907):2.

For the essay which surveys socialist agitators in the southwest, the author used a variety of hard-to-find, scattered, primary sources, including the few manuscript collections, interviews with survivors and their descendants, and especially local socialist newspapers. Useful were the Freda Hogan Ameringer Papers, located in Oklahoma City, and the Ida Hayman Callery Papers, located in Santa Barbara, California, each of which are privately held. The author also examined the Phil and Ida Callery Papers, Pittsburg State College, Pittsburg, Kansas, and the Walter Dietz Papers, Louisiana State University, Baton Rouge. Interviews were conducted with Gertrude Branstetter Stone, Hattie Hayman Graham, and Freda Hogan Ameringer. Correspondence was received from Gertrude Branstetter Stone and Theresa Taft (daughters of Winnie E. Branstetter).

Local papers reviewed either in their entirety for the 1901–1917 period or for individual issues of interest, include the *Appeal to Reason, Pawhuska* (Oklahoma) *People's Tribune, Cestos* (Oklahoma) *Reporter, Stillwater Common People, Oklahoma City Social Democrat, Industrial Democrat,* and *Pioneer,* (Oklahoma) *Voice, Joplin Free Press,* (Oklahoma) *Tenant Farmer, Cornish* (Oklahoma) *New State Socialist,* Snyder (Oklahoma) *Otter Valley Socialist, Texarkana* (Arkansas) *Socialist, Dallas Laborer, Alva* (Oklahoma) *Constructive Socialist, Gibson* (Missouri) *Justice, Tuttle* (Oklahoma) *Vagrant Socialist, Wichita Social Ethics, Winfield* (Kansas) *Southwestern Advocate, Pittsburg Worker's Chronicle, People's College News, St. Louis Labor, Carl Junction* (Missouri) *Socialist News,* Butte *Montana Socialist, Coming Nation* (Girard), *Santa Barbara People's Party, Los Angeles Socialist, San Diego International, Abbeville* (Louisiana) *Red Flag, Maryville Southern Clarion,* and (New Orleans) *Woman['s] Era.*

In addition to the perusal of the Socialist party papers at Duke University, the author utilized the *Proceedings* of the Socialist State Convention of Oklahoma and *Minutes* of the State Executive Committee, located in the Oklahoma Historical Society in Oklahoma City, and he also examined the Oklahoma Socialist Party Papers in the Bureau of Government Research Collection at the University of Oklahoma.

Secondary sources used by the author include Garin Burbank, *When Farmers Voted Red: The Gospel of Socialism in the Oklahoma Countryside* (Westport, Conn.: Greenwood Press Inc., 1976); James R. Green, *Grass-Roots Socialism: Radical Movements in the Southwest, 1895-1943* (Baton

Rouge: Louisiana State University Press, 1978); James R. Green, "The 'Sales-men-Soldiers' of the *Appeal* 'Army': A Profile of Rank-and-File Socialist Agitators," in Bruce M. Stave, ed., *Socialism and the Cities* (Port Washington, New York: Kennikat Press, 1975), pp. 13-40; Neil K. Basen, "Kate Richards O'Hare: The 'First Lady' of American Socialism, 1901-1917," *Labor History* 21 (Spring 1980): 165-99.

The essay on the socialists' campaigns for woman suffrage in Wisconsin and New York is based on primary sources from each state. Manuscript sources include the unpublished autobiography of Meta Burger, the collected papers of Morris Hillquit, Ada L. James, Emil Seidel, A. M. Simons, and Seymour Stedman at the State Historical Society of Wisconsin. At the same repository, relevant records consulted by the author included the *Minutes* of the Social Democratic party of Wisconisn and the Papers of the Wisconsin Woman Suffrage Association. Useful collections at the Milwaukee County Historical Society include the Papers of Victor L. Berger, Daniel W. Hoan, Emil Seidel, and John M. Work, as well as records of the Social Democratic party. Campaign manuals, *Proceedings* of the National Congress of the Socialist party of 1910, Wisconsin *Assembly* and *State Journals* as well as the Wisconsin *Blue Book* for the period were used. Other primary sources included newpapers, such as *Advance* (New York), the *New York Call*, the *Chicago Daily Socialist*, the *Socialist Woman*, and the *Milwaukee Journal* and the *Milwaukee Leader*.

Contemporary articles containing information used by the author included Theresa Malkiel, "Where Do We Stand on the Woman Question?," *International Socialist Review* 10 (1909): 158-63, Jesse E. Molle, "The National Convention and the Woman's Movement," *International Socialist Review* 9 (1908): 687-91, and in the same journal, Algie M. Simons, "Report on the Stuttgart International Socialist Convention," 8 (1907): 129-43. Also used were Mary Oppenheimer, "The Suffrage Movement and the Socialist Party," *New Review* 3 (1915): 358-61, and in the same journal, Vida Scudder, "Women and Socialism," 3 (1915): 454-70.

Secondary sources which proved helpful for this topic include Frederick I. Olson, "The Milwaukee Socialists, 1897-1941," (unpublished Ph. D. dissertation, Harvard University, 1952); Sally M. Miller, "Milwaukee: Of Ethnicity and Labor," in Stave, *Socialism and the Cities*, pp. 41-71, and her "Americans and the Second International," *Proceedings* of the American Philosophical Society 120 (1976): 372-87; Joseph P. Mahoney, "Woman Suffrage and the Urban Masses," *New Jersey History* 87 (1969): 151-72; Sharon Hartman Strom, "Leadership and Tactics in the American Suffrage Movement: A New Perspective from Massachusetts," *Journal of American History* 62 (September 1975): 296-315; and Arthur Goren, "A Portrait of Ethnic Politics: The Socialists and the 1908 and 1910 Congressional Elections on the East Side," *American Jewish Historical Quarterly* 50 (1961):

202-38. Books consulted included Irving Howe, *World of Our Fathers* (New York: Harcourt Brace Jovanovich, 1976) and Moses Rischin, *The Promised City: New York Jews, 1870-1914* (Cambridge, Mass.: Harvard University Press, 1972), and also Marvin Wachman, "History of the Social Democratic Party of Milwaukee, 1897-1910," *Illinois Studies in the Social Sciences*, 7, No. 1 (Urbana: University of Illinois Press, 1945).

The essay on the Reading, Pennsylvania, socialist movement is based essentially on party records and interviews with survivors of the movement. The essential manuscript collection is the Darlington Hoopes Papers at Pennsylvania State University (available on microfilm), containing the *Minutes* of Local Berks County, the Central Branch, and the Northeast Branch of the party. The Benjamin Fryer Scrap Books, also of importance, are located at the Historical Society of Berks County. Interviews were conducted with Mark L. Brown, Darlington Hoopes, Raymond E. Kiebach, and Catherine E. Tomlinson, and written communications were received from Austin E. Adams, Eugene Haag, Hazelette Hoopes, and Frank Zeidler. Newspapers used in this study of the Reading local include the *Reading Labor Advocate* and the *Reading Eagle*. Monographs of particular relevance were William T. Parsons, *The Pennsylvania Dutch: A Persistent Minority* (Boston: Twayne Publishers, 1976) and Henry G. Stetler, *The Socialist Movement in Reading, Pennsylvania, 1896-1936* (Storrs: published by the author, 1974). Other pertinent secondary sources were Kenneth E. Hendrickson, Jr., "The Socialists of Reading, Pennsylvania, and World War I—A Question of Loyalty," *Pennsylvania History* 36 (October 1969): 430-50, and by the same author in ibid., "The Socialist Administration in Reading, Pennsylvania, Part 1, 1927-1931," 39 (October 1972): 417-42, and "Triumph and Disaster: The Reading Socialists in Power and Decline, 1932-1939- Part 2," 40 (October 1973): 381-411; and the earlier version of this paper, "Women and American Socialism: The Reading Experience," *The Pennsylvania Magazine of History and Biography* 99 (January 1975): 72-91, and William Pratt's dissertation, "The Reading Socialist Experience: A Study of Working Class Politics," (Ph.D. Dissertation, Emory University, 1969). A useful article for its insights is Julie Roy Jeffrey, "Women in the Southern Farmer's Alliance: A Reconsideration of the Role and Status of Women in the Late Nineteenth Century South," *Feminist Studies* 3 (Fall 1975): 72-91.

For autobiographical writings of women who were sometime socialists, see Bertha Washburn Howe, *An American Century: The Recollections of Bertha W. Howe, 1866-1966*, recorded and edited by Oakley C. Johnson (New York: Humanities Press, 1966); Helen Keller, *Helen Keller: Her Socialist Years: Writings and Speeches*, Philip S. Foner, ed., (New York: International Press, 1967); Elizabeth Gurley Flynn, *The Rebel Girl: An Auto-biography, My First Life (1906-1926)*, (New York: International Publishers, 1973); Dorothy Day, *The Long Loneliness: The Autobiography of Dorothy*

Day (New York: Harper and Row, 1952); Mary White Ovington, *The Walls Came Tumbling Down* (New York: Harcourt, Brace, and Co., 1947); *Crystal Eastman on Women and Revolution*, Blanche Weisen Cook, ed. (New York: Oxford University Press, 1978); and *Kate Richards O'Hare: Selected Writings and Speeches*, Philip S. Foner and Sally M. Miller, eds. (forthcoming).

For secondary readings on women socialists, see Dorothy Rose Blumberg, "Florence Kelley: Revolutionary Reformer," *Monthly Review* 11 (November 1959): 234-42; Josephine Clara Goldmark, *Impatient Crusader: Florence Kelley's Life Story* (Urbana: University of Illinois Press, 1953); D.O. Carrigan, "Forgotten Yankee Marxist [Martha Moore Avery]," *New England Quarterly* 42 (March 1969): 23-43; Judith Nies, *Seven Women: Portraits From the American Radical Tradition* (New York: Penguin Books, 1977); Robert E. Snyder, "Women, Wobblies, and Worker's Rights: The 1912 Textile Strike in Little Falls, New York," *New York History* 55 (January 1979): 29-57; Rosalyn F. Baxandall, "Elizabeth Gurley Flynn: The Early Years," *Radical America* 8 (January-February 1975): 97-115; and Hugh Lovin, "The Banishment of Kate Richards O'Hare," *Idaho Yesterdays* 22 (Spring 1978): 20-25.

Readings of general interest which portray women in political roles include Eleanor Flexner, *Century of Struggle: The Woman's Rights Movement in the United States* (New York: Atheneum Publishers, 1968); Aileen Kraditor, *The Ideas of the Woman Suffrage Movement, 1890-1920* (New York: Columbia University Press, 1965); David Morgan, *Suffragists and Democrats: The Politics of Woman Suffrage in America* (East Lansing, Michigan: Michigan State University Press, 1972); Alan P. Grimes, *The Puritan Ethic and Woman Suffrage* (New York: Oxford University Press, 1967); Anne F. and Andrew M. Scott, *One Half the People: The Fight for Woman Suffrage* (Philadelphia: J. B. Lippincott and Co., 1975); and Stanley J. Lemons, *The Woman Citizen* (Urbana: University of Illinois Press, 1973). Other titles of interest are Miriam Schneir, ed., *Feminism: The Essential Historical Writings* (New York: Vintage Books, 1972); William Chafe, *The American Woman, 1920-1970* (New York: Oxford University Press, 1972); William O'Neill, *Everyone Was Brave: The Rise and Fall of Feminism in America* (Chicago: Quadrangle Books, 1969); Rita MacKelly and Mary Boutelier, *The Making of Political Women: A Study of Socialization and Role Conflict* (Chicago: Nelson-Hall, 1978); and Richard J. Evans, *The Feminists: Women's Emancipation Movements in Europe, America and Australasia, 1840-1920* (London and New York: Barnes and Noble Books, 1977).

Relevant works on the general subject of American socialism in the early twentieth century which may be consulted include David A. Shannon, *The*

Socialist Party of America: A History (New York: Macmillan, 1952); Donald Egbert and Stow Persons, eds., *Socialism and American Life*, vol. 2 (Princeton: Princeton University Press, 1952); Ray Ginger, *Eugene V. Debs, A Biography* (New York: Macmillan, 1962); Ira Kipnis, *The American Socialist Movement, 1897-1912* (New York: Columbia University Press, 1952); Sally M. Miller, *Victor Berger and the Promise of Constructive Socialism* (Westport, Conn.: Greenwood Press, 1973); James Weinstein, *The Decline of Socialism in America, 1912-1925* (New York: Monthly Review Press, 1967); Frank A. Warren, *An Alternative Vision: The Socialist Party in the 1930's* (Bloomington: University of Indiana Press, 1974); John Laslett, *Labor and the Left: A Study of Socialist and Radical Influences in the American Labor Movement, 1881-1924* (New York: Basic Books, 1970); John M. Laslett and Seymour Martin Lipset, *Failure of a Dream? Essays in the History of American Socialism* (Garden City: Doubleday, 1974); Norma F. Pratt, *Morris Hillquit: A Political History of an American Jewish Socialist* (Westport, Conn.: Greenwood Press, 1979); Philip S. Foner, *American Socialism and Black Americans* (Westport, Conn.: Greenwood Press, 1977).

For a further perspective of the overall issue of women and socialism, the following few titles might be consulted: Sheila Rowbotham, *Women, Resistance and Revolution: A History of Women and Revolution in the Modern World* (New York: Vintage Books, 1972) and her *Hidden From History: Rediscovering Women in History From the Seventeenth Century to the Present* (New York: Vintage Books, 1976); Marilyn J. Boxer and Jean H. Quataert, eds., *Socialist Women: European Socialist Feminism in the Nineteenth and Early Twentieth Centuries* (New York: Elsevier, 1978); Evelyn Reed, *Problems of Women's Liberation: A Marxist Approach* (New York: Pathfinder Press, Inc., 1971); Hal Draper, "Marx and Engels on Women's Liberation," *International Socialism* (July/August 1970); Rodelle Weintraub, ed., *Fabian Feminists: Bernard Shaw and Women* (University Park, Pennsylvania: The Pennsylvania State University Press, 1977); Richard Stites, *The Women's Liberation Movement in Russia: Feminism, Nihilism, and Bolshevism, 1860-1930* (Princeton: Princeton University Press, 1978); and Robert Shaffer, "Women and the Communist Party, USA, 1930-1940," *Socialist Review* 45 (May-June 1979): 73-118.

INDEX

THE CONTRIBUTORS

NEIL K. BASEN is completing a doctorate in American History at the University of Iowa, and is currently a project assistant at the University of Wisconsin-Madison. He has contributed review essays to the International Labor and Working Class History *Newsletter* and to *In These Times*, and is the author of an article on Kate Richards O'Hare in *Labor History*. He has read several papers to historical conferences.

JOHN D. BUENKER holds a Ph.D. from Georgetown University and is Professor of History at the University of Wisconsin-Parkside and Director of its Center for Multicultural Studies. He is the author or *Urban Liberalism and Progressive Reform*, co-author of *Progressivism*, and co-editor of *Immigration and Ethnicity: A Guide to Information Sources*. He has published articles in the *Journal of American History*, the *New York Historical Society Quarterly*, *Mid-America*, the *Pennsylvania Magazine*, the *Journal of the Illinois State Historical Society*, and many other journals. He has been a Guggenheim Fellow, an American Philosophical Society Fellow, and a Wisconsin Alumni Research Foundation Fellow.

MARI JO BUHLE holds a Ph.D. from the University of Wisconsin and is Assistant Professor of history and American civilization at Brown University. She specializes in U.S. women's history and has taught in the women's studies program at Sarah Lawrence College. She is co-author of "Women in American Society: An Historical Contribution," which first appeared in

Radical America. Her most recent publication is *The Concise History of Woman Suffrage,* which she edited with Paul Buhle. She is currently writing a history of women and American socialism, 1870-1920.

KENT AND GRETCHEN KREUTER received their Ph. D. degrees from the University of Wisconsin, and together published *An American Dissenter: The Life of Algie Martin Simons.* Kent Kreuter is Professor of History at Hamline University, St. Paul, Minnesota, and Gretchen Kreuter is Assistant Professor of History and coordinator of women's studies at St. Olaf College, Northfield, Minnesota. They have each contributed book reviews and articles to scholarly journals and to the *Saturday Review.*

SALLY M. MILLER, who holds a Ph. D. from the University of Toronto, is Professor of History at the University of the Pacific, and was the 1978-1979 Visiting Professor of labor history at the University of Warwick. She is the author of *Victor Berger and the Promise of Constructive Socialism* and *The Radical Immigrant, 1820-1920.* She has published articles in *Science and Society,* the *Journal of Negro History,* and in Bruce M. Stave's *Socialism and the Cities,* and other journals. She has received University of the Pacific Faculty Awards, American Philosophical Society grants, an American Council of Learned Societies grant, and has been selected as "An Outstanding Educator of America." She is presently editing the writings of Kate Richards O'Hare with Philip S. Foner.

WILLIAM C. PRATT holds a Ph.D. from Emory University, and chairs the Department of History of the University of Nebraska at Omaha. He has contributed articles to *The Nation,* the *Pacific Northwest Quarterly,* the *Journal of Southern History, The Pennsylvania Magazine of History and Biography,* and to Thomas G. Paterson's *Cold War Critics* and Bruce M. Stave's *Socialism and the Cities.*

L. GLEN SERETAN received a Ph.D. from the University of Toronto, and has served as lecturer at that university and is now teaching at the University of Western Ontario. He is the author of *The Life and Career of Daniel DeLeon, 1852-1914: An Interpretation,* and has published articles in *Labor History,* the *American Jewish Historical Quarterly,* and the *Wisconsin Magazine of History,* as well as presented papers to history conferences in the United States and Canada.